MAGIC
WEAPONS

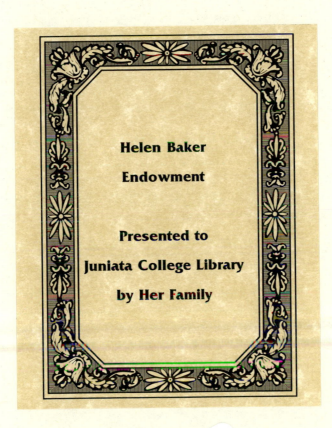

MAGIC WEAPONS

Aboriginal Writers
Remaking Community
after Residential School

Sam McKegney

Foreword by
Basil H. Johnston

University of Manitoba Press

University of Manitoba Press
Winnipeg, Manitoba R3T 2N2
www.umanitoba.ca/uofmpress
Printed in Canada by Friesens.

Cover and text design: Grandesign Ltd.

Library and Archives Canada Cataloguing in Publication

McKegney, Sam, 1976-
    Magic weapons : Aboriginal writers remaking community after residential school / Sam McKegney.

Includes bibliographical references and index.
ISBN 978-0-88755-702-6

1. Canadian literature (English)—Indian authors—History and criticism. 2. Canadian literature (English)—Inuit authors—History and criticism. 3. Indians of North America—Canada—Residential schools. 4. Inuit—Canada—Residential schools. 5. Indians of North America—Canada—Ethnic identity. 6. Inuit—Canada—Ethnic identity. I. Title.

E96.2.M325 2007   C810.9'897   C2007-904064-0

The University of Manitoba Press gratefully acknowledges the financial support for its publication program provided by the Government of Canada through the Book Publishing Industry Development Program (BPIDP), the Canada Council for the Arts, the Manitoba Arts Council, and the Manitoba Department of Culture, Heritage and Tourism.

CONTENTS

FOREWORD

Until I read *Magic Weapons* I didn't realize that those of us who had attended residential school and then written about some of our experiences could cause such an uproar in the academic world so as to open the floodgates of the sea of deep thoughts and let loose a torrent of words.

Reminded me of my father, Rufus's, astonishment when I told him of my newfound knowledge that I had gained upon joining the ranks of scholars at the Royal Ontario Museum in Toronto in 1970. I told him that I had learned that our Anishinaubae words fell into two categories, animate and inanimate; and that our verbs had a tense called "dubitative" that English didn't have. Dad stood, as if dazed, for some moments before remarking, "Gee Whitakers! I didn't know that we were that smart!"

Like my father, I'm taken aback to learn that our words had such impact as to incite debates in the academic world. I didn't know that we, myself included, meant to heal, empower, and help people find their identities. If the works of Highway, Thrasher, Joe, and myself bring about these results, well and good.

But I didn't have such lofty aims when I wrote *Indian School Days*. Mine were much more modest. It was simply to amuse the readers of *The Ontario Indian*, a magazine of the Union of Ontario Indians that ceased publication in the mid-1980s.

After graduation from residential school in 1950, I and ten other former inmates of the school went to Wawa to work in the mines. There we formed a sort of community, often reliving some of our experiences while we were locked up in the Spanish school. For five summers I worked in Helen Mine, consorting with my old schoolmates; as always, we rehashed old memories.

Upon my graduation from Loyola College, Montreal, Quebec, I went to Toronto. In the late 1950s there may have been fifteen former Spanish residential school students working in Toronto. We found each other and kept in touch, drawn together by our common background and heritage and training in residential school.

At home in Cape Croker, there were more than thirty people who had gone to residential school: my father, mother, uncles, and many others, who said not a word about their years at Spanish to us, their children. Eugene (Keeshig), Hector (Lavalley), Charlie (Akiwenzie), and I talked about residential school, but not to our children.

When I started writing some of the stories that originated in Spanish and its residential school, former students came to me or called me to tell me more stories. "Write a book! Why don't you write a book?" they said.

And that is how *Indian School Days* came into being. First, it was intended to amuse readers, to recount and to relive some of the few cheerful moments in an otherwise dismal existence, a memorial to the disposition of my people, the Anishinaubaek, to find or to create levity even in the darkest moments. And this is how I would like my book to be seen.

Had I known what I now know, perhaps I might have written an entirely different text. But I didn't know what I know now, and not knowing would have trivialized the residential school experience. But it's not likely that I would have changed the purpose I had in mind in setting pen on paper to write about my schoolmates and friends.

When word got out that I was writing about Garnier Residential School, I've reason to believe that there were a few uneasy Jesuits. One day Father Felix, then pastor of St. Mary's Catholic Church on the reserve, remarked with a smirk, "Heard you're writing about Spanish. Please don't exaggerate as writers are in the habit of doing!"

"You needn't worry, Father!" I replied. "My account is a model of restraint!"

Even afterwards, I heard from Father Wm. Maurice that none of the stories were documented or dated, and from Miss Alice Strain that they were all lies.

In 1959 the former students of the Spanish Residential School held a reunion. Many did not come, too bitter to come to the scene of their degradation and humiliation. After two days of speeches, religious exercises, eating, and reliving horrors and capers, we went home. That so many came may be seen as customary among Indians; they like to visit and to revisit old times.

I think it was around 1995 that I heard rumours of a lawsuit being launched against the Jesuits and the federal government by former students of the Spanish Residential School. I heard that a lawyer from Meaford, Ontario, had been retained to represent the plaintiffs.

I wasn't interested. I wanted to get on with life. Besides, I didn't want my wife, Lucie, to know that she had married damaged goods and that I had not trusted enough in her love to confide in her what had been done to me at school.

One Saturday afternoon I left the house to drive around the community and take in the sights of home, my roots. Around the band administration building were cars. Must be important, I thought, for so many people to give up going to town on a glorious Saturday afternoon; there must be something special going on.

As a rule I avoid public meetings. But something drew me to stop and drew me to the building.

Inside was a large crowd. As I stepped into the dim interior, the gentleman standing at the head of the table asked what I was doing at the meeting meant only for residential school survivors.

"He's one of them, one of us," the people sitting around the table spoke before I could explain.

I gave my name, then sat down as invited.

The gentleman conducting the meeting, which was primarily an information session, was John Tamming, a lawyer from Meaford, Ontario, who had been retained first by Renee Buswa and his wife of Whitefish Falls, Ontario, back in 1996. When the lawsuit was converted into a class action lawsuit, Mr. Tamming was retained to represent hundreds of complainants from the Spanish Residential School.

I was, as it were, roped into the class action lawsuit.

As one of the parties in the action against the Jesuits and the federal government, I had to make an affidavit declaring that the violations inflicted upon me during my incarceration in residential school actually occurred.

In preparation for the interview with Mr. Tamming, I girded myself to tell the story that I'd never told anyone before, without breaking down. But I broke down. I wept.

Why did I weep? Shame! Guilt! I don't know. Did I feel relief? I don't know. Did I feel better? I don't know.

For years I had laboured under the conviction that I was the only one to be debauched in Spanish Residential School. But during the course of the meetings of our negotiating team, of which I was now a member, I realized that the sexual degradation of students was far more widespread than I had imagined.

My cynicism, which had been set off by Howard Skye back in 1968 and nurtured by my reading of history in the succeeding years, was exemplified by the question that I now asked about our keepers at residential school: "Is there anyone who wasn't?"

During the negotiating meetings, not only did I learn that I was not the only one who had been befouled and desecrated, but that we had all been damaged in some way. Even those who had not been ravished suffered wounds, scars, and blemishes to heart, mind, and spirit that would never fully heal.

As part of any settlement, the federal government suggested that all claimants undergo psychological assessment and treatment. Wilmer Nadjiwon of Cape Croker would have none of the government's proposal, snapping, "I don't want no twenty-two-year-old kid fresh out of university waving a degree in psychology rooting into my psyche!" I think that all of us were of like mind.

From my readings of newspapers and the reports in the bulletins sent to us by the Aboriginal Healing Foundation, we were all taken to be robots or automatons, quite incapable of realizing what a state we were in and not having sense enough to work our way out of the muck and slime that we had been pitched into, there to remain wallowing in self-pity, calling out for someone to throw a rope or to offer a hand to pull us out of the morass.

Some of us, lucky ones if you will, managed to claw our way out of this quagmire and to go on with life. We may not have done so saying, "This is what happened to poor me. I must overcome the hurts and the bruises and the indignities and the violations that were heaped upon me. I must go on." Nothing rational like that was in our thoughts. Rather, it was from the heart and spirit that the will to get up and to go on came.

Those who suffered most damage were the little four-, five-, and six-year-old boys and girls, cast into these prison-like institutions when they were just out of babyhood. Little outcasts they were, cast out of their communities, homes, families; motherless, fatherless, unwanted, unloved. They had nothing. What they needed was love. All they received was the assurance that Jesus loved them. But in their lives there was no love such as a child's spirit and heart yearn for, no hand to hold their little hands, no voice to say "I love you," no arms to enfold them in love and care when they had need of caress when they felt alone and unloved.

For such, there was no childhood. They were snatched from their homes and cast into a grown-up world, living in an institution, doing what adults told them to do. They learned nothing of the outside world and its ways, learned nothing of the ways of families and the make-believe world of children. That part of their lives that should have been theirs was stolen from them.

When later, by ten to twelve years, they were released into the world, they knew nothing that they ought to have known. It was an alien world that did not readily accept them. Their communities had forgotten them; they did not belong; their families had forgotten them; they didn't know their fathers, mothers, brothers, sisters; they had no identity. They were broken in heart, mind, and spirit, unready for the world outside an institution.

I may have been lucky by not having been committed to residential school in Spanish until I was ten years old. How I was damaged I cannot say. If I've healed I cannot say. But I do bruise.

Within six weeks of being committed to Spanish, I was sodomized by two fifteen-year-old boys. Soon after, immediately following a mass that I served, I was fellated by Father J. Barker. Over the next three and a half years he asked for me to assist him at mass whenever he was in the school. At the end of mass he always pleasured himself with my penis. From 1940 to 1943, I worked in the chicken coop. There I was subjected to Brother Manseau's loathsome kisses. I was also invited to touch a lay teacher's penis.

From the Halloween night in 1939 when I was first sodomized, I went about guilt-ridden, dishonoured, a worthless being. Terror, terror at night, terror of dying and going to hell, dogged me for years.

On reflection today, I believe that I escaped crippling damage by putting into application a lesson that I learned from the boys on the playgrounds of the residential school itself. "When knocked down, get up!" Some of my fellow outcasts took huge delight in teasing me, making fun of the way I skated, my awkwardness, my reading, anything to provoke me, for I was easily provoked into a fight. I fought. When I was clubbed to the ground and felt the world was against me, I was provoked into getting back to my feet and resuming the fight with, "Come on! Get up! You scared, you!"

From those fist fights I learned that one doesn't stay down when one is belted if one wants to retain his pride. There was another lesson that I learned, a lesson that took three and a half years and many black eyes, bloodied noses, and loosened teeth to drill into me: the unpleasant realization that I couldn't punch a hole in a doughnut. I got up, put my fists down.

What one loses when one is sodomized, fellated, and victimized, as I have been, is one's sense of integrity and worth, which is all that the very young have. No one would believe me, no priest or layman. I told no one. I kept the sordidness to myself. No one would ever know.

But the feeling of worthlessness lingered, following me wherever I went; to Loyola College in Montreal, to Toronto; luck accompanied me as well. It conducted me to find lodgings in the residence of Mr. and Mrs. R.W. Wadds, an investment dealer with McLeod, Young, Weir, now Scotia McLeod. Mr. Wadds was later a president of a bank in Florida and one in Boston. For free room and board, I babysat young Richard, then about nine, whenever the Wadds went to a club for the well-to-do. I was also expected to wash pots and pans.

In the third year of my lodging with the family, Mr. Wadds suggested that I go out. It wasn't healthy for a young man to stay indoors, cloistered like a monk. He told me to go to the Young People's club at Holy Rosary Parish on St. Clair Avenue.

There I went the following Tuesday. As I looked about in the parish hall, I felt self-conscious, the only person with darker complexion, black hair, oriental eyes, high cheekbones, and a peculiar accent. I didn't belong, but I stayed.

In late 1956 a very attractive young woman came to the club. I gazed longingly at her, wishing that I were fair of feature and gallant. But I wasn't; I could only gaze longingly at the young woman.

Six months later I screwed up enough courage to ask the young woman of my dreams for a dance. She didn't rebuff my request of "May I have this dance?" as I'd fully expected.

Before the year was out, Lucie said, "I love you."

I was exultant. The declaration of Lucie's love was many things, among them instilling in me a sense of worth in my being. I would try to be worthwhile for her sake, and for mine. We married in 1959.

I loved her in mind but I didn't know how. I didn't know how to express it or show it. She it was who taught me how, but it took me thirty years to learn and to earn her approbation. "You're getting better ... finally learning how."

I'd heard a great deal about love, in sermons and songs and poetry, but hadn't seen love in its most prosaic expressions and acts.

With Lucie's love began the restoration of my sense of worth.

I didn't know it then, but my service with Native organizations in and around Toronto contributed to the recovery of my sense of worth, as well.

The Indians, long neglected, were growing restless. In 1968 three events changed the course of my life and forced me to look into my heritage, into myself, as it were.

One block away from where we were living on Ellerslie Avenue in North York was Churchill Avenue Public School. I was invited to take in an exhibit mounted by the grade five youngsters after they had studied Indians in-depth over a five-week period. One of the students I spoke with asked me, "Is that all there is to Indians, Sir?" Our heritage was represented in the books that he and his colleagues had studied as consisting of wigwams, snowshoes, loincloths, bow and arrows, dried and smoked meat, and no more. People knew so little about us.

I was invited to take part as a seminar leader in a grand conference of scholars and Indians at Glendon College in Toronto. In the very first session a participant asked, "Just tell us about your heritage!" I knew my ancestral language, some stories, but that was about the extent of my knowledge. I didn't know much, and, not knowing enough, didn't know where to start. I floundered and beat around the bush for the entire weekend. It was a humiliating experience.

As coordinator of the Indian Hall of Fame at the Canadian National Exhibition, I met Howard Skye, lacrosse-stick maker from Oshweken, Ontario, a Six Nations community. After he heard me tell an audience that what aroused "the Iroquois" to the point that they torched Fort Ste. Marie and dispatched some missionaries into early sainthood was economics, trade, as I heard and read in history books, Howard asked, "Do you want to hear our side of that story?"

I said yes, and Howard took me aside. He told me that the missionaries had built a school there and were teaching the local Indians there how to read, write, count, and many other good things. We sent our children up there too, to learn new things. The next spring, when our people went to bring their children back, some of the boys and girls complained that the teachers molested them and that some of the older girls were pregnant. So our ancestors put the mission out of business. Howard's story is completely different from the official, documented version. I've also heard that the missionaries torched their own institution.

Thus began my re-education. Since then I've had many fine teachers, among them Sam Ozawamik, Alex McKay, Ron Wakegijig, Fred Green, Tom Medicine, Ernie McGregor, Wm. Meawassige, Tm. Toulouse, Flora Tabobandung, Marie Seymour, Bea McCue, Jane Rivers, Dr. Cecil King, John Angus, and hundreds of others. All the Native people who spoke the language touched my spirit, heart, and mind.

It was love, Lucie's love, that restored my sense of worth. As well, it was the regard of my people who still cling to their language that lent strength to the conviction that made me feel worthwhile, rendered so by the worth of my heritage. It is language that has enabled me to gain some understanding of my people's institutions, beliefs, values, perceptions, outlooks, attitudes, their literature and history.

Though I have tried, and succeeded in doing so to a certain degree, to put behind me the years of pain, shame, guilt, and terror from hellfire, I can still bruise.

Six years ago I was crossing the hall of the Georgian Bay Friendship Centre where a young woman going in the opposite direction stopped for a moment to say, "I'm from the Enatig Healing Centre. If you ever want be healed, you can come to us."

"You can go to hell! I don't want to be healed," I snapped, outraged by her presumption.

A psychologist was conducting a seminar on the effects of residential schools on former students in the Saugeen Band Administration Centre. Out of curiosity I went to Saugeen to learn what new insights "psychology" had unearthed in its in-depth studies of former students of residential schools. On the graphs on printouts that he had distributed, we were slotted neatly into categories. I told him that such studies were gibberish.

Then there are self-proclaimed advocates. We've got one here on our reserve. She assumes that those of us who attended residential school are incapable of looking after ourselves or of understanding the issues in our suit against the Jesuits and the federal government. One evening a year and a half ago, she barged into a meeting called for the former students of the Spanish Residential School.

"What's your interest in this meeting?" I demanded.

"I'm an advocate," she screeched while her jaws snapped up and down on her ever-present bubblegum.

"Did you ask her to represent you?' I asked my colleagues.

Several of my colleagues shook their heads and said, "No."

"Then you have no business in our meetings," I told the self-appointed advocate.

It hurts to be exploited, as I sometimes believe we are being exploited by our own people, or by those who claim to be our own people.

It hurts to think that we would all be suspected of visiting upon our wives and children what had been inflicted upon us.

But I don't dwell upon the hurts; it's a waste of time. Besides, doing so is self-destructive, as has been seen in so many ruined lives among former residential school students.

What kept me from running aground was my wife Lucie, who knew how to love and raise a family; my circle of friends, mostly former students of the Spanish Residential School; the Native people whom I met over the years in the course of my career; and the richness of my heritage. And I've tried to live by three lessons that I learned from my heritage: to live in harmony with the past and the present, to be as fair as I could be, and to aspire to the highest degree of accuracy.

When I returned home that Saturday afternoon in 1998 from my excursion around the reserve, during which time I was delayed by several hours attending the Spanish Residential School orientation meeting, my wife Lucie asked me, "Where were you?"

It was then and only then that I told her what happened to me in Spanish. I cried. Later, much later, she remarked, "Now, that explains a lot of things."

I didn't realize until I read *Magic Weapons* that what Thrasher, Highway, Joe, and I had written about our confinement to an institution had a much wider and longer lasting influence in the country than we could have anticipated when we set down to write of our experiences. For bringing this out, *Magic Weapons* needs to be read.

– Basil H. Johnston
2007

ACKNOWLEDGEMENTS AND PERMISSIONS

I was humbled and thrilled when Basil Johnston, whose Indian School Days helped inspire the project in the first place, agreed to read and offer commentary on my manuscript. I was positively floored when he offered to write its foreword. Meegwetch, Basil, for your wisdom and your willingness to share it with others through written and spoken words.

In the seven years since I first conceived of this project, I have been fortunate to work with many exceptional teachers, writers, and scholars, foremost among them in terms of my own intellectual and ethical growth, Glenn Willmott and Bonita Lawrence. Passing under Glenn's rigorous critical eye, my writing and research have become stronger and I a better scholar. Passing under Bonita's, my ethical commitments have been drawn to the fore, and I have become a more conscious Indigenous rights activist. I think warmly on all I've learned from each of you, and hope one day I can mentor new scholars in a manner similarly generous. Thank you also to Daniel Heath Justice, who has not only offered inspired critical readings of my work over the past few years, but embodies the type of political engagement to which I aspire as a scholar.

Magic Weapons has benefited from the careful critical attention of many readers at various stages, although its limitations remain my own. Sincere thanks to Sylvia Söderlind and Kathy Brock for their insightful and coherent commentary. To Laura Murray, who offered many useful observations, thanks in particular for helping me recognize how atrocious my original title was, and to Richard Harrison, for helping me bring to life the new title by massaging it into its current form. Others who have offered strong feedback include Warren Cariou, Kristina Fagan, Joanne Episkenew, and Perry Millar; my thanks to you all. And to the staff at University of Manitoba Press, and in particular Pat Sanders, David Carr, and Cheryl Miki, thank you for seeing the book's potential and for making it better.

Furthermore, I'd like to thank retired lawyer William Stilwell for graciously providing me access to Anthony Thrasher's original prison writings, to editor Charis Wahl for kindly discussing with me the generic development of Tomson Highway's Kiss of the Fur Queen over e-mail, and to my friends Kateri Akiwenzie-Damm and Niigonwedom James Sincair for ongoing inspiration, advice, and the occasional couch to sleep on.

To my parents, Ian and Bubbles, thank you for the boundless love and support that placed in such stark relief the fundamental betrayal of familial connection at the heart of this study. To my partner, Sher, who has shared the agonies and joys of this enterprise and who doesn't seem to realize how much inspiration I glean from her strength, I am grateful. Of our daughters, Caitlyn and Kyara, who remind me daily of the majesty of parenthood, allowing me to work when I must and forcing me to play when I need to, I am in awe.

Portions of chapters 3, 4, and 5 have been published in modified forms in English Studies in Canada, The American Indian Culture and Research Journal, and Studies in American Indian Literatures, respectively.

I gratefully acknowledge the assistance of the Government of Canada for four years of Social Sciences and Humanities Research Council funding, which made possible the research for and initial composition of the manuscript that would become this book. I am also grateful to Queen's University for providing the environment in which much of the original research for this project was conducted and to Mount Royal College for providing some release time for its completion.

The author and publisher wish to thank the following for permission to reprint material:

"Boarding School" and "Nitotem" by Louise Bernice Halfe, from the collection *Bear Bones & Feathers*, published by Coteau Books, Regina, Canada. Used by permission of the publisher.

"Indian Residential Schools," "I Lost My Talk," and "Hated Structure" by Rita Joe, from *Song of Rita Joe: Autobiography of a Mi'Kmaq Poet*. Published by University of Nebraska Press, Lincoln NE. Used by permission of the publisher.

"Cycle (of the Black Lizard)" by Gregory Scofield, from *Native Canadiana: Songs from the Urban Rez*. Used by permission of the author.

MAGIC
WEAPONS

INTRODUCTION

"Our poets ... are the only ones today who can provide this bridge, this reflective statement of what it means and has meant to live in a present which is continually overwhelmed by the fantasies of others of the meaning of past events."
Vine Deloria, Jr.,
"Foreword" to *New and Old Voices of Wah'Kon-Tah*

"And today, we are talking about the imagination of tribal stories, and the power of tribal stories to heal. Stories that enlighten and relieve and relive. Stories that create as they're being told. And stories that overturn the burdens of our human existence."
Gerald Vizenor,
"Trickster Discourse"

A survivor of horrific residential school abuse stands alone and tormented beside the highway in the opening of Teetl'it Gwich'in author Robert Arthur Alexie's *Porcupines and China Dolls*.[1] Lifting his head "to the heavens as if to ask a question," he is greeted by "something he didn't expect: the hate, the rage, the anger and the sorrow" (2). "After a lifetime," he wrenches from his anguish the question—"*Why?*"—to which the sky offers nothing but the realization that "he'd always been alone. He'd always be alone" (2).

Battered by despair and loneliness shaped into action by fury, "this time, he knew he'd do it":

> All in one smooth motion he got down on one knee, put the barrel in his mouth, then pushed the trigger. He watched the hammer fall and closed his eyes. He tensed, waiting for the explosion. After a million years, he heard it: metal on metal. It was the loudest sound he'd ever heard. It shook his whole body and deafened him.
>
> He took a deep breath, dropped the gun, then exhaled. He heard it: the peace and the silence.
>
> He waited for his ultimate journey into hell. (2)

In 1991 Grand Chief of the Assembly of First Nations Phil Fontaine said the "motive for disclosure" of residential school experiences and abuses is "to stop our people from killing themselves."[2] The suicide rates of Aboriginal people in Canada have been among the highest in the world for several decades. The precise statistics, while appalling and significant, are not the main point; that they refer to Aboriginal lives teeming with complexities of human experience, to mothers, fathers, daughters, sons, to friends and classmates and lovers—this is essential. And while influenced by myriad historical and contemporary factors, the epidemic of Aboriginal suicide remains intimately bound to over a century of residential school policy and practice in Canada, something Fontaine acknowledges astutely.[3]

In fact, a perverse irony in the connection between the suicide rates and the residential school experience is that Aboriginal suicide participates in one of the ostensible goals of the residential school system: it speeds the disappearance of Aboriginal people from the geographical space of Canada without forcing Euro-Christian Canadians to feel violent or culpable. It allows the non-Native majority to witness the death of Indigenous impediments to 'progress' without seeing themselves holding the trigger.

Now, painting Euro-Christian Canada monolithically as bent on the destruction of Native individuals and cultures is an oversimplification. Not all non-Native Canadians disregard their responsibility for oppressive history and therefore their implicatedness in the social problems plaguing Native communities. Even the moniker "Euro-Christian Canada" seems out of place, given the various levels of theological commitment among non-Native Canadians then and now and the various Christian denominations involved in the administration of residential school policy. Not all clergy, teachers, principals, and administrators endorsed the systemic goal of decimating Indigenous cultures, just as not all of them abused the children in their care physically, psychologically, or sexually. And, as difficult as it is to acknowledge, even some of those who did wound Indigenous children in the service of their cultural annihilation weren't insincere in their belief that this was in the children's best interests.

These are the troubling complexities of a system administered by various religious and political bodies to distinct First Nations in disparate parts of an enormous land mass over the course of a century fraught with ideological, social, and political change. Seldom do things fit readily into pre-ordained categories—whether these categories belong to the colonial story of civilized Christianity bringing light and truth to pagan savagery or to the post-colonial story of hegemonic Eurocentrism being inflicted violently upon passive Indigeneity. We must be wary of all unqualified generalizations, as we must be wary of polarizing binary thinking. Heroes aren't always heroic, abusers don't just abuse, and victims are never victims only. However, the suicide analogy, properly contextualized, reminds us that the residential school system was designed to sever students' connections to Indigenous languages, spiritual systems, and knowledges—and thereby to 'kill' that which was deemed 'Indian' in the child—and that this culturally genocidal objective provoked adverse effects throughout Indian country (including high suicide rates). An adequate understanding of residential school history must recognize that these institutions actively sought the decimation of Aboriginal cultures, leading to problematic social, spiritual, and familial conditions in contemporary Aboriginal communities—but not in an entirely programmatic and solely negative way.

Fontaine's early effort to intervene in this chronology of violence, like that of many courageous survivors, took the form of "disclosure." To disclose is to open up to view what has been hidden, to give voice to what has been silenced. By speaking the traumatic past, Fontaine and others sought to drag into public view the violent and oppressive aspects of residential schooling that had previously been obscured by official history. The desire of Fontaine and others to disclose the "truth" of residential school history led to numerous historical studies of the system throughout the 1990s.[4]

In often exhaustive treatises, historians and other researchers probed government archives, church diocese records, and survivor testimonies, establishing that, in the words of historian John Milloy in *A National Crime*, "the residential school experience was, beyond question, intolerable."[5] For Milloy, this

> inescapable reality was determined by the system's fundamental logic that called for the disruption of Aboriginal families and by the government's and churches' failure to parent the children in accordance with the standards of the day or to be vigilant guardians. As a result, all too often, 'wards of the Department' were overworked, underfed, badly clothed, housed in unsanitary quarters, beaten with whips, rods and fists, chained and shackled, bound hand and foot, locked in closets, basements and bathrooms, and had their heads shaved or hair closely cropped. (154–155)

Due to the diligence of Fontaine, Milloy, and many others, the reality of residential school oppression and abuse is now firmly established in historical and political spheres, no longer an alternative counter-narrative to official history but, rather, the contemporary orthodoxy.

Bringing to public light the often violent reality of residential school existence is, however, but one aspect of progressive reactions to the residential school legacy. Narrow historicization won't reverse the system's corrosive social and political effects unless harnessed to a clear vision for the future and mobilized in the service of Indigenous empowerment. Perceived over the past two decades as *the* principal vehicle for engaging the residential school issue, historicization (alone) dangerously orients our thinking away from the present and future, binding us in a reactive manner to the power dynamics of the past. And, with compensatory and restructuring funds finally being freed from government coffers by virtue of the Reconciliation and Compensation Agreement (November 2005), imaginative visions for plausible futures of First Nations are essential. This is where the understudied resource of Native literature becomes so valuable.

Unlike strictly historical discussions, Indigenous residential school survival narratives cannot be so readily confined to the past. Although they depict historical disparities in power and often traumatic personal events, they render these imaginatively, affording the Indigenous author interpretive autonomy and discursive agency while transcending the structural imperatives of proof and evidence embedded in historical paradigms. They invoke residential school history as a creative element in provocative visions of growth, healing, and change. The residential school experience does not generate the survival narrative beyond the creative agency of the Indigenous author, which immediately locates the survivor outside standard fallback positions of victimhood implied by much historical and psychoanalytic discourse. These writers are not defined solely by their experiences of institutionalization, nor are they confined by the system's acculturative mandate or bound to neuroses spawning from neglect and abuse. In fact, they expose the failure of residential school social engineering by *defining themselves* in their writing, by "touch[ing] [themselves] into being with words."[6]

MAGIC WEAPONS

The past is not wholly behind us—nor is it "holy" behind us—just as the future is not unaffected by what we do today. This book takes as its focus the understudied resource of *literary* engagements with residential school history, composed by residential school survivors, in order to gauge their impact on the future of the First Nations, Métis, and Inuit in the geographical space of Canada. My purpose is twofold: first, to examine how the residential school system has influenced Native literature; and, second, to examine how looking at Native literature alters our understandings of residential school history and the residential school legacy. I confine my study predominantly to Indigenous life-writings with a residential school component, although I include a chapter on Tomson Highway's 1998 novel, *Kiss of the Fur Queen*,[7] which is based loosely on the author's own residential school experiences, and I touch on narratives by nonattendees throughout. In each case, I examine not only the author's depiction of residential school, but also how she or he re-envisages identity, culture, spirituality, and politics in the aftermath of institutionalization.

These interweaving strands signal the ethical horizon of the study. Although residential schools sought to decimate Aboriginal cultures (and thereby handicap Aboriginal political persistence), survival narratives document the perseverance of certain raw materials of cultures against the relentless undertow of genocide; they reinvigorate what survived, recreate what didn't, and re-imagine the place of the creative Indigenous individual in relation to her or his community (or, better, communities). They articulate—and so proclaim—the beauty and power of writing as an Indigenous individual in a post-residential school Canada, and they re-imagine the relations between Aboriginal communities and the Canadian state.

At a crucial impasse in *Kiss of the Fur Queen*, a dying father imparts to his two sons the spiritually significant Cree hero myth of the Son of Ayash. Adopting the voice of the hero's mother, the dying man exclaims, "'My son,' … 'The world has become too evil. With these magic weapons, make a new world'" (227). The world that exists for First Nations people in the wake of residential schooling is in many ways "too evil." But they are not without the creative weaponry to change it, nor must the changes be restricted by visions for the future determined from without. In *Kiss of the Fur Queen*, the "magic weapons" with which the sibling protagonists conquer the corrosive aftermath of residential school abuse are unlikely skills in classical piano and ballet, learned in Euro-Canadian environments but adapted to Cree spiritual knowledge actively garnered in adulthood. Building from their personal strengths and talents (emerging in relation to, but not totally caused by, the particular circumstances of their institutionalization), Highway's protagonists disseminate their artistry through the public vehicle of drama. They employ their magic weapons not simply to heal themselves but to provoke positive change in others—to "make a new world" through art.

So it is with all the authors dealt with in these pages. Having little control over what has happened to them in the past, they exercise the weaponry they've attained and developed in the service of positive change for their tribal communities and a pan-tribal readership across the continent. This they endeavour with skill, imagination, and courage. My job in these pages is to trace out the trajectories of these imaginative acts, link them to other discourses on the histories they relate, and interpret their actual and potential influence on the audiences and communities in which they are intended to circulate.

I Lost My Talk

I lost my talk
The talk you took away
When I was a little girl
At Shubenacadie school.

You snatched it away;
I speak like you
I think like you
I create like you
The scrambled ballad, about my word.

Two ways I talk
Both ways I say,
Your way is more powerful.

So gently I offer my hand and ask,
Let me find my talk
So I can teach you about me.

From *Song of Rita Joe: Autobiography of a Mi'kmaq Poet* (1996)
by Rita Joe (Mi'kmaq)
Survivor: Shubenacadie Residential School,
Shubenacadie, Nova Scotia

CHAPTER 1

Acculturation through Education: The Inherent Limits of 'Assimilationist' Policy

"After all this, the white man had concluded that the only way to save Indians was to destroy them, that the last great Indian war should be waged against children."
David Wallace Adams,
Eucation for Extinction

"The night of the sword and the bullet was followed by the morning of the chalk and blackboard. The physical violence of the battlefield was followed by the psychological violence of the classroom."
Ngugi wa Thiong'o,
Decolonizing the Mind

The residential school haunts Native literature in Canada: as subject matter, as setting, as repressed (communal or individual) memory, as source of anger, shame, pain, and violence, and as unspoken backdrop to conditions of authorship. But it is nearly always *there*—even when it isn't. Residential schooling has so marked the social, political, and karmic contexts out of which First Nations writers write and at which they aim their creative work that it persists as subtext to even those modern First Nations works that deign not to speak of it explicitly. It maintains a shadow presence, an unspoken antagonism that threatens community through its very silence. Haisla/Heiltsuk author Eden Robinson examines this danger through a metaphor of nautical navigation: "The [logs] you can see aren't as dangerous as the ones submerged just below the surface, the deadheads, which can puncture your keel."[1] That which is unseen, as that which is unspoken, poses the greatest threat because the sailor cannot read and react to it; she or he is literally at its mercy.

The residential school legacy enacts just such an unspoken threat throughout Robinson's debut novel, *Monkey Beach* (2000), which interrogates how experiences of victimization by an earlier generation of attendees insinuate themselves into the lives of Haisla youth in the post-residential school period. Although neither Robinson's narrator, Lisa-Marie, nor her friends have experienced residential schooling themselves, they remain vulnerable to the cyclical extension of violence seemingly initiated through residential school abuse.[2] Yet, even though residential school transgressions appear to be at the core of the novel's contamination by violence, they persist far more as an absence than a presence. In a book of 374 pages, residential school is discussed explicitly only a handful of times, and mainly in vague or speculative terms. Beyond the anguished cries of Lisa-Marie's alcoholic aunt Trudy, who exclaims "'there were tons of priests in the residential schools, tons of fucking matrons and helpers that 'helped' themselves to little kids just like you'" (255), and the arguments of her Uncle Mick against "'a religion that thought the best way to make us white was to fucking torture children—'" (110), the reality of residential school abuse remains, for Lisa-Marie, cryptic and elusive; the "torture" to which Uncle Mick refers remains a communally repressed memory (all the more threatening due to its clandestine nature). Silence becomes a shadow that hangs over Lisa-Marie's story, supplying the dark cover under which unspeakable acts occur, while residential schooling remains a hidden weapon, a deadhead lying beneath the water's surface.[3]

Many Indigenous authors engage creatively with the corrosive impact of the residential school legacy, from Louise Halfe's poetic depictions of traumatic institutional experiences and their aftermath in *Bear Bones & Feathers* (1994)[4] to Inuit writer Alice French's analysis of how residential schooling has had an adverse impact on her adult life in *The Restless Nomad* (1992)[5] to Robert Arthur Alexie's depiction of pervasive dysfunction in a post-residential school Teetl'it Gwich'in community in *Porcupines and China Dolls* (2002). Employing a multitude of genres, narrative techniques, and perspectives, Aboriginal writers repeatedly mobilize narrative and poetry in creative efforts to intervene in the adverse aspects of this legacy. Maria Campbell's groundbreaking autobiography, *Halfbreed* (1973),[6] offers one of the earliest discussions of the residential school experience in Aboriginal literature. Despite attending residential school for only a single year at the age of eight, and describing the experience in a mere two paragraphs in the autobiography, Campbell predicts many of the elements that have become key to literary resistance, reclamation, and empowerment in survival narratives by Native writers. Campbell's entire discussion of residential schooling reads:

> The year I was seven Grannie Dubuque brought a different kind of gift for her special granddaughter. At dinner, after her arrival, she announced a surprise. She had made arrangements for me to go to a residential school in Beauval. It sounded exciting, but looking at Dad's shocked face, Mom's happy one, and Cheechum's stony expression—a sure sign of anger—I was confused. Dad went out after dinner and did not return until the next day. Meanwhile Momma and Grannie planned my wardrobe. I remember only the ugly black stockings, woolly and very itchy, and the little red tam I had to wear and how much I hated it.
>
> I can recall little from that part of my life besides feeling lonely and frightened when I was left with the Sister at the school. The place smelled unpleasantly of soap and old women, and I could hear my footsteps echoing through the building. We prayed endlessly, but I cannot recall ever doing much reading or school-work as Momma said I would—just the prayers and my job, which was cleaning the dorms and hallways. I do recall most vividly a punishment I once received. We weren't allowed to speak Cree, only French and English, and for disobeying this, I was pushed into a small closet with no windows or light, and locked in for what seemed like hours. I was almost paralyzed with fright when they came to let me out. I remember the last day of school, and the sense of freedom I felt when Dad came for me. He promised that I would never have to go back, as a school was being built at home. (44)

The confusion experienced by the young child over conflicting emotions of excitement in anticipation of monumental change and fear of familial separation and the unknown;[7] the loneliness and sterility of buildings smelling "unpleasantly of soap and old women," in which the echo of the child's footsteps bespeaks an emptiness both physical and symbolic;[8] the omnipresence of prayer and forced labour at the expense of the instruction and learning the child had been told to expect;[9] the viciousness of physical and mental punishments that remain "vividly" in the child's mind long after her or his emancipation from institutionalization;[10] the attacks on Indigenous languages that would torment

Indigenous voice for generations;[11] the glorious "sense of freedom" for the former student upon graduation, removal, or escape;[12] all these emerge throughout literary engagements with the residential school legacy, but not in stereotyped, deterministic, or repetitive ways.

In the same year *Halfbreed* was published, two important autobiographies emerged, focusing at length on the residential school experience: Jane Willis's *Geneish: An Indian Girlhood* and Alice French's *My Name is Masak*.[13] Their dedications announce their divergent trajectories (despite a common focus on cultural identity alluded to in the issue of naming embedded in both titles).[14] French's dedication reads:

> Listen, listen my children. And I'll tell you a story of where I
> was born and where I grew up.
> About your ancestors and the land
> we live on.
> About the animals and the birds.
> So you can see. (i)

French's emphasis on landscape and connection with nature (as configured by "the animals," "the birds," and "the land") constructs the text itself as antidote to the sterility of residential school isolation and enforced familial disconnection. Positioning the reader as child in search of parental insight—through "Listen, listen my children"—the dedication suggests that the autobiography will remove the myopic lenses of Eurocentric tutelage in order to facilitate personal vision (so that the reader "can see"). Combining *the natural* with stories about "ancestors" told through parent-child dialogue, French alludes to *the unnatural* intervention of residential school in traditional Inuit familial existence.

French's dedication, and the narrative by which it is followed, is thus quite different from Willis's, which questions the solidity of parent-child bonds even in light of residential school as an unwarranted imposition. "*To my mother,*" writes Willis, "*whose lack of faith made the story possible, and to my husband, whose faith made the book possible*" (i). As Deena Rymhs argues, Willis's story documents a personal struggle against restrictive and imposed identities—be they imposed by residential school assimilation strategies *or* by power dynamics peculiar to a particular family.[15] Refusing to be defined either by her mother, represented in the dedication as lacking faith (presumably in her daughter), or by the instructors at St. Philip's Indian and Eskimo Anglican Residential School, the autobiographical self developed in *Geneish* emerges, in Rymhs's words, as "fiercely individualistic" (143). Willis's family, who frowned upon her marriage to a non-Cree man, is thus shown to conceive of relationships in a restrictive and racialized manner that is eerily reminiscent of the racist pedagogy she received in residential school. Reconnection with family (in a traditional environment) is not presented as an ideal in *Geneish* (which values breaking "dependency" in all its guises), while, in *My Name Is Masak*, traditional familial relationships and their resurrection are foregrounded as integral to growth and healing.

Since the creative contributions of Willis and French in the early seventies, several Aboriginal writers have included sections on residential school experiences in their autobiographies. Anthony Apakark Thrasher entitles Part One of *Thrasher ... Skid Row Eskimo* (1976) "You never went to Hell on venials,"[16] humorously acknowledging the rigid codes of behaviour demanded in the Roman Catholic residential school he attended while celebrating potential transgressions by noting the sins one can 'get away with.' Discussion of residential school experiences takes up just less than one third of *Skid Row Eskimo*, but it remains crucial in its prefiguring of the carceral space in which the narrative was composed: prison. A chapter concerning Thrasher's residential school experience, entitled "Playing with Girls is a Sin," has been anthologized in Terry Goldie's and Daniel David Moses's *An Anthology of Canadian Native Literature in English.*[17] Rita Joe's 1996 autobiography[18] similarly includes an important section on her residential school experiences, but one that takes up less than ten percent of the text as a whole. Her discussions are powerful and evocative, melding poetry and prose, but they do not dominate Joe's narrative, which is far more focused on perseverance and forgiveness than on disclosure and recompense. More recently, Earl Maquinna George has included a brief discussion of his residential school experiences in *Living on the Edge* (2003).[19] George's depiction is intriguing, given his refusal to judge residential schooling as either beneficial or debilitating. A second-generation attendee of the Ahousaht Residential School, George concludes his discussion by saying, "You can see that the residential school played a strong role in my personal history" (20), but he stops short of evaluating that role as conducive to his growth or oppressive and limiting. The most significant autobiographical account of residential school published in the 1980s came from Ojibway writer Basil Johnston, whose *Indian School Days* (1988) offers counterbalance to accounts focusing on disclosure of abuses and the malevolent actions of overseers by concentrating narrative attention on the dynamic, precocious, and resistant actions of young students. Written with humour and poignancy, *Indian School Days* refuses to overshadow or neglect the spirit of the boys at St. Peter Clavers by constructing them solely as victims of residential school social engineering. In fact, Johnston champions the sense of community created among the students as fertile consolation to the loss of traditional communities caused by residential school intervention.

Several fictional accounts of residential school experiences have also emerged over the past fifteen years to supplement the autobiographical record. For example, Salish author Shirley Sterling's children's novel, *My Name Is Seepeetza* (1992)[20]—emulating through its title French's *My Name Is Masak*—tells the story of twelve-year-old Martha Stone through the conceit of a year's worth of secret journal entries written at Kalamak Indian Residential School, or "KIRS" (pronounced "curse"). Like Johnston, Sterling highlights the subversive power retained by students even in the most oppressive and rigidly dictatorial of circumstances by recognizing Stone's ongoing imaginative and authorial freedom through the written word (well hidden, of course). Sterling celebrates the capacity for residential school students to maintain beliefs, memories, and stories—the very cultural vehicles residential school sought to extinguish—through the vehicle of story (even if only partially). Tomson Highway's much anticipated first novel, *Kiss of the Fur Queen*, came out in 1998, telling the story of Champion and Ooneemeetoo Okimasis, brothers who seek to reconnect with their Cree spirituality through art in efforts to heal themselves from the trauma of residential school sexual abuse and to recreate the world for a suffering Aboriginal population. The novel, replete with references to Christian and Cree theologies, is built from the foundation of Highway's own residential school experiences, along with those of his brother, René, to whom the novel is dedicated, but reimagined in a magical ornamented style "as is the Cree way of telling stories, of making myth" (*Kiss* 38). Robert Arthur Alexie's debut novel, *Porcupines and China Dolls*, published in 2002, has been referred to by Dogrib author Richard Van Camp as "one of the most important books I will ever read in this lifetime" and as "hard but good medicine" capable of "initiat[ing] more healing than any of us will ever know."[21] Like *My Name Is Seepeetza* and *Kiss of the Fur Queen*, *Porcupines and China Dolls* builds from its author's experience of residential schooling and its aftermath; however, Alexie, Sterling, and Highway choose to present their work as fiction, straining against the limitations of historical representational validity implied by autobiography.

16

These creative works—along with Mohawk author Beth Brant's short story, "A Long Story" (1990),[22] Maria Campbell's transcription, "Jacob" (1995),[23] Métis writer Gregory Scofield's poem, "Cycle (of the Black Lizard)" (1996),[24] Thomas King's novel, *Truth & Bright Water* (1999),[25] and the list goes on—offer profound complications to the historical record as it stands, commenting not only on how residential schooling is remembered but also on how its legacy ought to be reacted to, its transgressions addressed, and its survivors (and their communities) empowered. Residential schooling was not an isolated imposition, a self-contained experiment wholly meaningful in itself. It did not initiate the conscious corrosion of Indigenous language and culture by Euro-Christian Canada, nor did it embody the sum of colonial assimilative violence. The evangelical impulse, as well as its secular manifestation in cultural progressivist thought and scientific racism, was alive and well long before the walls of these institutions were raised and it has survived their dissolution. Residential school merely formed a chapter—albeit a particularly brutal, oppressive, and encompassing one—in the ongoing genocide, cultural and otherwise, of Indigenous peoples in this country.[26] In J.R. Miller's formulation in *Shingwauk's Vision*, residential schools were "merely one important cog in a machine of cultural oppression and coercive change."[27]

What renders residential schools particularly significant to studies dedicated to the disentangling of colonial duplicities and the empowerment of Native communities is that the technologies of quasi-assimilative acculturation became codified within identifiable institutions, leaving a large paper trail—at times sanitized and/or cryptic—within church diocese, government archives, and the records of the Ministry of Indian Affairs. By "quasi-assimilative acculturation," I mean to acknowledge that the assimilative endeavour undertaken under the ideological umbrella of racial superiority and cultural progressivism strategically ensured the impossibility of complete identification between missionary and Native student, regardless of the degree of the student's adoption of Euro-Christian accoutrements—students would always be, in Harold Cardinal's terminology, "brown white men"[28]—and that such an endeavour was always marked more by the suffocation of the primary culture than assimilative acquisition of the secondary one. Ironically—and, to a certain degree, triumphantly—despite institutional efforts to undermine the efficacy of oral modes of transmission and cultural expression, an enormous body of oral testimony has emerged within the past fifteen years, complicating the written records and bespeaking the trauma inherent to culturally oppressive modes of pedagogy. The Royal Commission on Aboriginal Peoples (1996), as well as countless interviews, conferences, and healing circles conducted by such Native and non-Native scholars and activists as Celia Haig-Brown (1988), Isabelle Knockwood (Mi'kmaq) (1992), J.R. Miller (1996), Judith Ennamorato (Mohawk) (1998), Constance Deiter (Cree) (1999), and Cherlyn Billy (Stuctwesemc Bonaparte) (2001) have enabled Native survivors to enter the discourse of recognition and retribution, speaking their experiences, their anger, their criticisms, their endorsements, and their judgments of this system that deigned to claim as its own their young minds, bodies, and souls. Furthermore, literary narratives by residential school survivors and others affected by its legacy—the body of writing I've just outlined that *Magic Weapons* takes as its focal point—have provided a profoundly understudied, yet valuable, discursive addition. All these records—archival, testimonial, and literary—make residential schools the most textually analyzable of Euro-Canadian colonial transgressions and therefore enormously important to the understanding of Euro-Canadian colonialism entire.

JESUIT GENESIS

The initial forays into residential schooling by Jesuit missionaries in New France in the seventeenth century were unsurprisingly envisaged and enacted on a proselytizing rather than pedagogical premise, in which both education and custodial acquisition were wielded in the service of religious conversion. Children were selected as the optimal audience for the Jesuits' evangelical sermonizing because they were deemed less culturally entrenched, and the boarding school or "seminary" was selected as the optimal venue for such sermonizing because it blocked the supposedly corrosive influence of parental figures. Child and youth education, then, became a necessary companion to religious instruction, insofar as certain concepts, pieces of knowledge, and modes of understanding were required to render Roman Catholicism comprehensible to the young audience, while at the same time acting as a sales pitch to Native parents unwilling to relinquish their children yet interested in affording them the technological advances available only through the Europeans.

However, such eagerness to acquire new technologies and knowledges, unaugmented by any material necessity for economic change, was not enough to convince Native parents to traverse the ideological gulf between missionary and tribal societies and offer forth their children on any grand scale, leaving the Jesuits' experiment an unmitigated failure—understanding, of course, that in the area of coercive proselytization concepts of "success" and "failure" must be understood as floating, ideologically entrenched, and problematic. As Father Paul Le Jeune recognized in a 1633 letter detailing an altercation between a French boy and a Native boy, such ideological differences included disparate ways of conceptualizing familial relations:

> One of them was looking very attentively at a little French boy who was beating a drum. As the Indian approached close to see him better, the little boy struck him a blow with one of his drumsticks and made his head bleed badly. Immediately all the people of his nation who were looking at the drummer took offense upon seeing this blow given. They went and found the French interpreter and said to him: "One of your people has wounded one of ours. You know our custom well; give us presents for this wound." As there is no government among the Indians, when one among them kills or wounds another, he is (assuming he escapes immediate retaliation) released from all punishment by giving a few presents to the friends of the deceased or wounded one. Our interpreter said: "You know our custom: When any of our number does wrong, he is punished. This child has wounded one of your people, and so he shall be whipped at once in your presence." The little boy was brought in, and when they saw that we were really in earnest, that we were stripping this little boy, pounder of Indians and of drums, and that our switches were ready, they immediately asked that he be pardoned, arguing that he was only a child, that he had no mind, that he did not know what he was doing. As our people were going to punish him nevertheless, one of the Indians stripped himself entirely, threw his robe over the child, and cried out to the man who was going to do the whipping: "Strike me if you will, but you will not strike him"; and thus the little one escaped. All the Indian nations of these parts—and those of Brazil, we are told—cannot punish a child, nor allow one to be chastised. How much trouble this will give us in carrying out our plans of teaching the young![29]

The nature of childhood and the role of adult intervention in the growth and development of children could scarcely have been conceived more differently between the Jesuits and the Algonquin, Huron, and Montagnais First Nations with whom they were principally engaged. While these First Nations placed great value on the individuality and integrity of children, allowing them autonomy in their own learning processes, the Jesuits viewed the imposition of structure and discipline as integral to proper development. Le Jeune astutely interprets this divergence of childrearing practices as bearing on the effectiveness of educating Native youth in a Euro-Christian manner that would refuse to 'spare the rod' and thereby 'spoil the child.' While much within Euro-Christian ideology developed over the intervening centuries before residential schools were again deemed practicable by evangelical bodies, the violent disciplinary impulse evident in Le Jeune's account made its way unscathed into the churches' vision of Native education, wherein "discipline was curriculum and punishment was pedagogy."[30]

Placed strategically distant from parental and community figures, whose natural duty would have been to protect the children, and largely beyond the surveillance of the Department of Indian Affairs, which acted legally in those parents' stead but oversaw individual institutions far too seldom and then usually with advanced warning, and staffed predominantly by underqualified individuals often convinced of their own racial superiority to the wards placed under their authority, it is entirely unsurprising that modern residential schools fostered atmospheres of abuse. From punishments seeking to extract retribution from students' bodies and to provoke a potentially deterring fear of physical anguish, like "push[ing] sewing needles through [the] tongue[s]" of "language offenders,"[31] or whipping with switches the naked legs of runaways, to those targeting students' psyches through the wielding of shame, like "being made to lick milk from a saucer on all fours, like a cat, in front of a room full of children; being made to wear soiled panties over heads because they did not wipe themselves properly; having their heads shaved because they ran away; being made to eat the food they had vomited; being forced to wear a worn sock pinned to their collar all day,"[32] residential school discipline all too frequently moved beyond the socially sanctioned corporal punishment of its time into flagrant abuse. And while the extent of the abuse and its effects has yet to be fully understood, acknowledged, and addressed by those administrative bodies who failed to protect Native children—although the official apologies of the government and the churches in the 1990s and the recent Reconciliation and Compensation Agreement were certainly a start—we must be careful to avoid what Chrisjohn and Young refer to in *The Circle Game* as a "methodological individualism,"[33] which encourages us to view such transgressions as incidents of power exchange between individuals, a perpetrator and a victim. Rather, such transgressions can be fully understood only through the lens of systemic conditions that rendered them possible. By focusing too narrowly on the abuses of individual perverts and sadists, suggest Chrisjohn and Young, we ignore the culpability of the institutional bodies that created the schools and their capacity for violence.[34] Similarly, Celia Haig-Brown argues that "the sensationalism [of media attention to stories of abuse] tends to isolate the abuse from a context in which First Nations' languages, spiritual beliefs, and entire cultural competencies were negated."[35] It is crucial to recognize that residential schools were not the site of a possible assimilative violence, they were assimilative violence itself. Residential schools were a colonial technology strategically and violently employed. As Chrisjohn and Young eloquently argue in *The Circle Game*, "We cannot understand the full horror of Indian residential schools until we understand that *their very existence*, in however benign a form, constituted an abomination" (emphasis original, 41).

Modern residential schools were created when the missionary call for a forum in which to indoctrinate Native youth found an enthusiastic endorsement from the inaugural Canadian government, eager to rid itself of the financial burden of the Indian Affairs department—to whom the dream of complete absorption of the Indigenous population into the body politic seemed a fiscally responsible endeavour—and a counter-echo from the economically (and physically) devastated Native population, eager to provide for its children the opportunity to learn new ways of adapting to the radically altered economic, social, political, and even geographical landscapes. J.R. Miller has been most strident in his insistence on recognizing the interplay among these "three distinct interest groups"—the churches, the government, and the First Nations—who "participated in the creation, and contended over the maintenance and eventual closure of these schools,"[36] arguing that collapsing the church and government into a single body and/or ignoring Native influence creates a false or at least oversimplified picture of the system itself. While Miller is right to insist on the reinsertion of Indigenous voices and agency into this history, acknowledging that the omission of such voices re-enacts a form of colonial oppression, John Milloy's assertion that "the residential school system was conceived, designed, and managed by non-Aboriginal people"[37] suggests the need to recognize the varying degrees of impact each of Miller's three interest groups had on the actual operation of the institutions. Native factions that endorsed European-style schooling for their children did so as a strategy for coping with the changes brought about by Euro-Canadian presence on the continent and explicitly called for day schooling located on reserves, a desire ratified by treaties. So although Euro-Canadian education was solicited by many Native individuals and tribes, residential schools that would remove children from their communities were a significant contradiction of Native desires rather than acquiescence to them.

The residential schools that emerged out of this matrix of agendas were different in many ways from those of the Jesuits in New France, but, as with the disciplinary impulse, the primacy of religious conversion and tutelage endured, altered by a shift in ideology. Miller explains:

> In the post-Confederation period, ...when the evangelical mission was reconceptualized within an educational setting, it underwent profound changes. A major reason for the modification was that Christian thinking in Canada, as in the United States and Great Britain as well, had become suffused with racist preconceptions, partially as a result of 'scientific racism' and partly as a consequence of the domination of the world by countries that were primarily Caucasian. ... In this highly charged atmosphere of scientifically racist Christian attitudes, it was increasingly likely that missionaries would assume that the most effective and lasting way of converting the Aboriginal population to Christianity was simultaneously to reconstruct them as pseudo-Caucasians.[38]

As the seeming contradiction—between racist thinking, which would judge individuals according to characteristics perceived to be endemic to their racial profile, and the concept of cultural reconstruction and progression towards civility in Miller's statement—implies, the ideological positions underlying the creation of modern residential schools were informed by numerous mutually implicated, yet frequently conflicting, discourses, including the political imperatives of a burgeoning settler nation, the crude applications of Darwinian thought to models of racial progression, and the literary output of writers intent on forging a Canadian voice out of the semiotic encapsulation of Natives. Ideas of racial hierarchy and racial identity could never be entirely reconciled with the ideals of cultural progressivism in the residential school system, which remained in its conceptualization and its administration fundamentally confused.

In her article, "Indian Literacy, U.S. Colonialism, and Literary Criticism,"[39] Maureen Konkle argues convincingly within an American context that the discourse of "inherent difference" between Indigenous and settler cultures was produced strategically in the service of land ownership at an historically specific time by non-Native political and judicial figures. Because treaties between the United States and tribal governments necessarily conceded Native political autonomy (identifying Native nations as political entities with which the US government could carry out diplomatic relations, and, as such, *not* different in any absolute way from the settler population), US control over the land could only be ensured by Native "disappearance, which was effected in the production of knowledge about their inferiority and imminent extinction" (154). According to Konkle, this production of knowledge re-envisaged Native nations as fundamentally different in their natural state from European or American nations, according to a rubric of traditionalism, spirituality, and language. After such difference had been established, the same voices identified cultural adaptation and miscegenation as evidence that Natives were no longer culturally distinct and therefore could not claim political autonomy. In her article, Konkle quotes Edward Everett's "Address Delivered at Bloody-Brook, 1835": "'in the Anglo-American settlements, treaties will be entered into, mutual rights acknowledged; the artificial relations of independent and allied states will be established; and as the civilized race rapidly multiplies, the native tribes will recede, sink into the wilderness, and disappear'" (156). For Everett, the fact that among the New England Indians, "'not an individual, of unmixed blood, and speaking the language of his fathers remain[ed]'" (156) suggested the unavoidable disintegration of the 'authentic' American Indian, and, by extension, the Indian nation as a viable political entity. Konkle's argument is that the idea of an initial inherent difference upon which Everett and others based their conceptions of Native political viability was itself a product of their own political ambitions and therefore suspect when imported into modern critical discourse.

In Canada the concepts of "inherent difference" and "imminent extinction" had gained wide currency by the inauguration of residential schooling as federal policy, which occurred at roughly the same time as the signing of each of the numbered treaties between 1871 and 1921. However, while Konkle is careful to focus her discussion on conceptions of cultural difference, the issue of race inevitably complicates the Canadian situation. Since the opening pages of John Richardson's *Wacousta* (1832)[40]—in which not only race but class and military rank are thrown into confusion on the Canadian frontier as the supposed "intruder" to the fort, who seemed "at first [to have] the dusky and dingy hue of a half-naked Indian" (59), turns out to be a lowly servant dressed in "the gay and striking uniform of a British officer" (60)—race has been a problematic signifier within what might be overgeneralized as the non-Native imagination in Canada. Nowhere is this more evident than in the work of Duncan Campbell Scott, whose poetry seems at once to support and undermine his work with the Department of Indian Affairs. While the basic premise behind residential school assimilation, in support of which Scott struggled for decades, derives from a notion of cultural progressivism that seems at odds with racialized conceptions of identity, Scott's 1898 poem, "The Onondaga Madonna," seems to locate savage otherness firmly in the blood:

> She stands full-throated and with careless pose,
> This woman of a weird and waning race,
> The tragic savage lurking in her face,
> Where all her pagan passion burns and glows;
> Her blood is mingled with her ancient foes,
> And thrills with war and wildness in her veins;
> Her rebel lips are dabbled with the stains
> Of feuds and forays and her father's woes.
> And closer in the shawl about her breast,
> The latest promise of her nation's doom,
> Paler than she her baby clings and lies,
> The primal warrior gleaming from his eyes;
> He sulks, and burdened with his infant gloom,
> He draws his heavy brows and will not rest.[41]

Scott initially represents race as physically manifest in the woman's face, where her "tragic savage[ry] lurk[s]" and her "pagan passion burns," suggesting a corporeal conception of inherent difference between speaker/audience and Onondaga art object. However, not only does the woman's face exhibit racial characteristics, but it also displays the scars and "stains" of a cultural and familial history that is written *on* the body rather than emerging *from* the body. In this way, Scott establishes the possibility of difference being constructed culturally and socially rather than being based solely on race. The power of the distinction, however, is undermined as the very history etched upon the woman's face is also to be found in her blood, which "thrills with war and wildness in her veins," conveniently matching in both theme and metre the "feuds and forays" evident upon her lips. Motionless, she neither enacts nor declares a cultural or personal identity; her identity is deduced by the onlooking speaker, who reads it "in her face," in "her rebel lips," and in "her blood," epitomizing the corporeality of her otherness. Ultimately the woman's racial primitivism is too great to afford any possibility of cultural progression or to stave off the imminent extinction of her "weird and waning race," emblematized most powerfully by the baby at her breast, who ought to bear the potential for growth and cultural survival but is "paler than she" and merely the "latest promise of her nation's doom."

The purpose of the above reading is not to imply that Scott's ideological position with respect to racial difference is entirely available within an individual sonnet, but rather to illustrate the complexity (and perplexity) of the thought processes behind the residential school system. The assimilationist objective of residential schooling, although requiring some belief in the capacity for cultural progressivism, does not preclude notions of racial inferiority. Ideology is never completely unambiguous. Clearly, for Scott, notions of inherent racial difference and Native savagery did not mean Native children were incapable of being adequately adorned in the accoutrements of Euro-Canadian society and absorbed into the body politic, even if they would never be *equal* to Caucasian Canadians. "Onondaga Madonna" exemplifies both the tension between cultural and racial conceptions of difference and the 'solution' residential schools sought to apply: its formal and thematic characteristics domesticate the savage otherness of its title character and render her palatable to a non-Native readership with which she can never truly identify. Choosing the Petrarchan sonnet, a rigidly structured and quintessentially European form, to represent his Onondaga maiden, Scott further sanitizes her "pagan passion" through obvious comparisons to the Blessed Virgin Mary and Christ; however, whereas Mary embodies purity and chastity, the Onondaga Madonna is of "mingled" blood and "burn[ing]" "passion," and whereas Christ signals the perpetual life of his people, the "primal warrior" signals his people's demise. In both his poetry and his career in Indian Affairs, Scott sought to recast Indigenous people within what he perceived as a civilized and civilizing framework from which residential school emerges as the most tangible example.[42]

RESIDENTIAL SCHOOLING IN PRACTICE

Regardless of the aforementioned ideological confusion, a rigidly regimented and prescriptive system, legislatively ratified by the Canadian government who would fund the schools and theologically endorsed by the churches who would administer their operation, thus evolved in the early years following Confederation, which sought to recreate identity by altering behaviours. By dictating when students would sleep, eat, work, and pray, what clothes they would wear, and what language they would speak, under the omnipresent threat of Jesuit-style punishment, the government and the churches argued (and perhaps even hoped and believed) they would metamorphose Native children, culturally conditioned to value individual freedom and integrity, into Christian Canadians academically and economically prepared for entry into the capitalist workforce. This was the articulated design of the system. The historic partnership between the federal government and the churches was thus borne out of complementary goals: the churches desired first and foremost to create Christians, but to do so they would first need to make Canadians; the government desired to obliterate Native nationhood and consume the Native populace into Canada at large, while sharing the churches' view that for the 'betterment' of Native people, they must be converted to Christianity.

In *Indian School Days* (1988), Ojibway author Basil Johnston documents in great detail students' daily existence at St. Peter Clavers Indian Residential School on the northern shore of Lake Huron in Spanish, Ontario, where he was a student from 1939 to 1947. Although school conditions varied somewhat over the century in which residential schools operated and among institutions staffed by different religious orders across the country,[43] Johnston's account captures the regimentation endemic to the system, wherein staff and instructors were the students' "constant attendants and superintendents, regulating our time and motions, scheduling our comings and goings, supervising our work and play, keeping surveillance over deeds and words, enforcing the rules and maintaining discipline with the help of two instruments of control and oppression—bells and the black book" (43–44).

From the moment Johnston and his classmates were awoken by the "Clang! Clang! Clang!" (28) of a Jesuit prefect's bell, to the moment after 'lights out' when the silence of the dormitory "was broken by the sobs and whimpers of boys who gave way to misery and sadness, dejection and melancholy, heartache and gloom" (45), the students' day was controlled as rigidly as possible, every moment aligned with an activity whose duration remained subject to the authority of ringing bells and shouting voices, and also the spectre of punishment. From their beds, the children were herded in two lines to the chapel where even their morning prayer was legislated by the clapper in the Jesuit Father's hand: "Down on one knee we dropped in united genuflection, remaining in that position until the clapper clapped a second time in signal for us to rise and to stand once more at attention. Only after one more clap did we slide into our assigned pews" (31).

After returning to the dormitory to make their beds, the students were led to the dining area, where they received the omnipresent tasteless porridge before departing for school or work, depending on which half of the day the individual student had been assigned to offer his labour to the functioning of the school. After a lunch consisting of "just enough food to blunt the sharp edge of hunger for three or four hours, never enough to dispel hunger completely until the next meal" (40), the students experienced a brief period of "relative freedom" (37). However, even this free time was often prescribed by the authorities who would schedule sports, games, or theatre rehearsals to prevent the children being left to their own devices. The students then moved on to the counterpart of their morning activity—either work or school. After a small snack, usually raw vegetables, the students did more chores and then spent one hour in silent study. They ate a meagre supper of stew or soup, bread, and tea, had another hour of semi-free play time, more study time, said prayers, and went to bed. Each moment of the day scripted for them, each day the same, as their autonomy, their individual integrity, and their cultural heritage were assaulted by numbing repetition and oppressive authority.

Taught by the rigidity of the system that they were unfit to govern their own lives, that all important decisions must be made externally, survivors were seldom given the opportunity to develop senses of self-worth and personal integrity so crucial to empowered social interaction as adults. Further infected by institutionalized abuse and the enforced absence of parental nurturing, the wounds caused by lack of personal autonomy often emerged as all the more debilitating in forms of lateral violence and social dysfunction. Furthermore, because the students were seldom instructed in vocations that would provide later employment and were provided with only the most rudimentary educational skills through inferior teaching practices and brevity of instruction, their economic success was imperilled by residential schooling even if their psychological and emotional development had been nurtured more humanely. The majority of residential school students emerged from the assimilative grasp of these institutions with insufficient job skills, academic skills, and life skills.

Perhaps more insidious than such pedagogical failures was the culturally genocidal impulse in service of which the schools functioned.[44] As Sir John A. Macdonald affirmed in 1887, "'The great aim of our legislation has been to do away with the tribal system and assimilate the Indian people in all respects with the inhabitants of the Dominion as speedily as they are fit for the change,'"[45] an objective echoed by Minister of Indian Affairs Duncan Campbell Scott in an oft-quoted declaration from 1920: "'I want to get rid of the Indian problem.... Our objective is to continue until there is not a single Indian in Canada that has not been absorbed into the body politic, and there is no Indian question, and no Indian Department.'"[46] The residential school conspiracy between the government and the churches was explicitly genocidal in its intention to obliterate Native societies by rendering their children 'non-Native.' Despite the manifold failings of the residential school system, the vigour with which the goal of separating children from their cultural, spiritual, and linguistic heritages was pursued ensured that most of the children would experience a profound sense of disconnection from family, culture, and community upon re-entering Aboriginal society. The results of this onslaught are now widely documented: Native children divorced from their traditional Native cultures, while at the same time refused entry into prosperous white Canada because of inferior educational practices and racism, and occupying a liminal space characterized by disillusion, identity crisis, and despair. The legacy of this genocidal atrocity ripples throughout Native Canada, its fingerprints on the domestic violence, poverty, alcoholism, drug abuse, and suicide rates that continue in many Native communities.

Genocidal policy and practice, however, cannot always ensure the destruction of a people, as the history of Native resilience and defiance in this country has shown. Native students internalized only to varying degrees the assimilationist practices imposed upon them in residential school, and many subsequently sought Native spiritual and cultural teachings upon release from the institutions' grasp. Out of the gaping wound inflicted upon Native cultures by residential schools have emerged vibrant revitalization movements, of which many Native authors are a part, which have sought to reclaim and re-imagine the Native cultures these institutions sought to decimate. Rejecting the lack of control afforded them in residential institutions, many survivors have struggled tirelessly to promote Indigenous control over Indigenous education (with manifold successes, including the establishment of Indigenous education programs at numerous institutions of higher learning, the development of culturally sensitive curricula on and off reserves, the implementation of instruction in Indigenous languages, and the establishment of First Nations University in Regina, Saskatchewan).

The purpose of this study is to examine and evaluate how identities that were strategically pressured to deny certain ways of knowing and ways of being by the violence of a specific colonial and state technology have been able to survive, reclaim, and re-imagine themselves—while in full recognition that many who have suffered such oppression have not survived.

Boarding School

In the late fall
ice waited
outside our cabin.

Inside
crackling fire
licked the guts
of the woodstove.
The coal oil lamp
flickered in the
one-room shack.

Two white-skins
talked in tongues.
Father's long face
stretched further
to the floor.
Mother's crimson cheeks
turned like swirling ashes
in the stove-pipe.

Behind
Mother's draping dress
a six-year-old sister.
Her small fist
white against
brown skin.

I sat behind a
thick home-made
wooden table,
trembling.
My stomach couldn't hold
the fresh cinnamon roll.

The air was
wrapped in
raven darkness.

Namôya mâskoc.
It's a mistake.
Father's voice
shook.
Mother swayed.

The white-skins
left.
The cold seeped in the
cracks of the door,
its fingers wrapped
in silence.

The world
was silent.
The family gone.

The family not ever more.

From *Bear Bones & Feathers* (1994)
by Louise Halfe (Plains Cree)
Survivor: Blue Quills Residential School,
St. Paul, Alberta

CHAPTER 2

Reading Residential School: Native Literary Theory and the Survival Narrative

"The role of Indians themselves, in the storytelling of Indian America.... reflects our struggle with the colonial experience of our concomitant histories. If that sounds benign, it is anything but that. On the contrary, how the Indian narrative is told, how it is nourished, who tells it, who nourishes it, and the consequences of its telling are among the most fascinating—and, at the same time, chilling—stories of our time."
Elizabeth Cook-Lynn,
"American Indian Intellectualism and the New Indian Story"

"Everyone laughed at the possibility of it,
but also the truth. Because who would believe
the fantastic and terrible story of all of our survival
those who were never meant
to survive?"
Joy Harjo,
She Had Some Horses

With the denial of Indigenous identities and the imposition of foreign behaviours, desires, thoughts, and attitudes as the system's fundamental objectives (not to mention deprivation, derogation, and physical punishment as its primary tools of implementation), it is unsurprising that residential schools have been called "the foundation of loneliness and hopelessness, alcoholism and suicide"[1] in Native communities. Okanagan author Jeannette Armstrong calls the residential school system "the single most devastating factor in the breakdown of our society. It is at the core of the damage, beyond all other mechanisms cleverly fashioned to subjugate, assimilate, and annihilate."[2] It is difficult to overstate the wounding effects of residential schooling on contemporary Native individuals, families, and communities throughout Canada. In the almost two decades between the emergence of the residential school issue in public discourse and the official apology of the Canadian government in 1998, historical researchers, Native rights activists, and government bodies like the Royal Commission on Aboriginal Peoples have amassed a tremendous body of archival and testimonial evidence that affirms unequivocally a connection between residential schooling and social problems in Native Canada.[3] The fact that residential schools had an adverse impact on Native societies is no longer up for meaningful debate.[4] Yet, the way we discuss, understand, and react against that adverse impact remains vital to Indigenous empowerment and cries out for critical attention. My engagement with these crucial issues begins with two questions. First, why literature? Why not engage the historical record and exploit archival resources to interrogate how the past has begotten a problematic present and thereby arm ourselves with a knowledge base that might potentially aid in altering structures of power? What does literature do that history doesn't? Second, how do we develop and articulate a mode of critical inquiry that is capable of understanding the complexity of residential schooling's historical effects but does not lapse into determinism and thereby fail to recognize the ongoing agency of Aboriginal writers and the potential for positive change?

Recent historical discourse on the residential school legacy has (perhaps more than occasionally) invoked the language of determinism in its effort to establish a causal relationship between the system's implementation and the current status of Natives in Canada, which is entirely understandable, given the utilitarian necessity of 'proof' to the processes of pressuring systemic change and initiating judicial redress. For example, in her article, "Rebuilding Community after the Residential School Experience," Maggie Hodgson argues that "those of our people who have difficulty adjusting, who are in jail, who are alcoholics, who suffer from poor self-esteem, are actually reflecting the effects of the Canadian government's residential school policies."[5] Similarly, Chief Bev Sellars of the Soda Creek First Nation argues that "'all the suicides, the alcoholism, the very low self-esteem of our people, the sexual abuse, the loss of our language and culture, the family breakdown, the dependency on others, the loss of pride, the loss of parental skills, and all the other social problems that have plagued our people can be traced directly back to the schools.'"[6] Both Hodgson and Sellars identify a relationship between residential school and Native social ills in totalizing language that presents potential problems, the first in terms of historical accuracy and the second in terms of efficacy in the struggle. The suggestion that "all" the "social problems" in Native communities are "directly" the result of residential schooling is discursively dangerous because it diminishes the complexity of colonial history, isolating residential school as an autonomous intervention whose effects can be readily divorced from those of broader colonial imposition. The precise assimilative technologies of the residential school indeed contributed in crucial ways to the corrosion of Native communities, but these effects achieve their full resonance and meaning only in relation to a more inclusive history of acculturation and genocide. Conscious infringement on Indigenous identity and tribal affiliation by Euro-Canadian institutions (such as colonial governments, churches, and trading companies) preceded, and has outlasted, the implementation of residential school policy. The realities of dispossession, relocation, missionary intervention, and governmental control have all contributed to the rise of the "social problems" referenced by Sellars and Hodgson; in fact, these ongoing realities have corroded the traditional Indigenous institutions through which communities might have better dealt with specific acculturative technologies like the residential school. To speak of residential schooling as the sole cause of social problems in Native communities is to (perhaps inadvertently) overlook other ongoing oppressions and, perhaps even more dangerously, as Chrisjohn and Young warn, to imply that "since there are no residential schools in the old sense any more, abuses are 'all in the past' and no present systemic changes are necessary."[7]

Furthermore, by locating in the residential school legacy a deterministic causal relationship that binds survivors to negative aftermath, scholars and commentators risk painting survivors entirely as social constructs, with neither free will nor personal control; we risk divesting survivors further of personal agency by declaring them the 'product' of an oppressive system;[8] and we risk crystallizing survivors' disempowerment by ignoring their capacities to intervene in socially destructive behaviours and conditions and to induce positive change.[9]

What is needed is a nuanced understanding of the residential school legacy that obscures neither its debilitating effects nor the continuing capacities of survivors to reclaim traditional heritages, (re)create viable Indigenous identities, and struggle against assimilation in the pursuit of collective healing and empowerment. This chapter represents my attempt to develop an approach to residential school history and its legacy that acknowledges the complex, intricate, and multiple ways in which residential schooling has influenced what Armstrong calls "the breakdown of our society," without suggesting that such breakdown is everywhere and always the same or that it is fated to be perpetually ongoing.

Which brings us back to the initial question of why literature. The life-narratives of residential school survivors are, to my mind, invaluable resources in the struggle against the residential school legacy because they account for the disastrous effects of residential school policy in a manner that is impossible to pass off as somehow predetermined or programmatic. The life-writings at the centre of this study consistently manifest their authors' post-residential school agency through the uniqueness of their artistry and aesthetics—see chapter 3 for analysis of the improbable (and near scandalous) discursive power of Anthony Apakark Thrasher's prison writings from the mid-1970s, chapter 4 for analysis of Rita Joe's uniquely positive authorial stance (which strategically diverges from well-worn frameworks for discussing residential school experiences), and chapter 5 for analysis of Tomson Highway's fictive re-imagining of his own personal experiences through Cree mythology.[10] These survival narratives signify individual engagements with history, both personal and communal, that are active and resolutely non-prescriptive. Thrasher, Joe, and Highway all invoke residential school history in their writings, but each re-imagines and mobilizes that history in a unique way, controlling how it functions within her or his literary creation and using it as a vehicle for change. Although the residential school experience undoubtedly pressures each author to address certain aspects of her or his past through writing, and although its influence on her or his development likely affects, to some degree, the ultimate textual product, *residential school does not create the survival narrative—the Native author creates the survival narrative.* Thus, survival narratives subvert the notion of deterministic or powerless response to residential school experiences while recognizing (and even, as we shall see, fighting against) the system's effects on Native individuals and their communities.

I'll engage the crucial question of 'why literature', whose initial response is above, more fully through the analyses of individual survival narratives that occupy most of this book. For now I'll probe the more practical question of 'how literature.' How can the survival narrative be approached most knowledgeably, sensitively, and effectively by the techniques of modern literary criticism? What critical tools are most expedient and valid? And what are the responsibilities of the critic of Indigenous survival narratives in relation to authors, texts, and communities?

Because multiple bodies are involved in the negotiation of meaning in Native texts and the actualization of those texts' potential social and political impact, astute critical engagement with residential school survival narratives must begin with a clear understanding of the bodies themselves. "Meaning" and "significance," as dealt with in this book, are generated at the site of text through the mutual engagement of author, audience, and community (*all* of which can be conceived fruitfully in the plural). These three positions are unfixed and in motion; they expand, overlap, and interpenetrate. Both author and critic can be part of the variously imagined communities out of which the text arises and toward which it is primarily directed—but they do not have to be. The critic is a particular audience in relation to other audiences, who observes relations of meaning among her or himself, the author, and the community/communities out of which the story is created and toward which it is directed. In critical discourse,[11] the text exists in a dynamic state of meaning in constant negotiation among these invested parties:

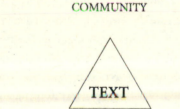

COMMUNITY

TEXT

AUTHOR   CRITIC

LOCATING THE (OUTSIDER) CRITIC, CRITICALLY

In reaction to the violence done to Aboriginal texts by decades of literary criticism dominated by non-Native academics wielding analytical strategies developed outside Native communities and largely beyond the surrounding shores of the continent, much recent criticism of Aboriginal texts has been intensely self-reflexive about the (often privileged) position of the critic, whether non-Native or otherwise.[12] Declaration of ties to particular Native communities or, even more importantly, confession of lack of community ties and non-Native status have become near obligatory elements of contemporary criticism of Native literatures, and rightly so, given the general desire of such criticism to intervene in and destabilize unequal power relations and the basic truth that non-Native members of the academy enjoy positions of privilege, authority, and power.

This development in Native literary criticism has emerged alongside calls for the privileging of Indigenous critical voices, although the latter has yet to be implemented in as widespread a manner. In two of the most significant critical interventions of the last decade or so, *Tribal Secrets: Recovering American Indian Intellectual Traditions* (1995)[13] and *Red on Red: Native American Literary Separatism* (1999),[14] Osage critic Robert Warrior and Muskogee Creek critic Craig S. Womack argue, respectively (in distinct but interpenetrating ways), for the development of analytical strategies in Native literary studies that emerge from Native people and Native communities. Warrior "explores the extent to which, after more than two centuries of impressive literary and critical production, critical interpretation of [Native] writings can proceed primarily from Indian sources" (xvi), and Womack explores the extent to which "Native literature, and the criticism that surrounds it," can be engaged through the lens of "tribally specific concerns" (1).[15] Both critics focus on the work of other Native writers, critics, community members, and activists not solely as a means of addressing the historical denial of Native voices from the critical arena,[16] but also as a reasoned position concerning what generates the most effective interpretations of the literature. Reacting against "an unfortunate prejudice among scholars against American Indian critical, as opposed to fictional, poetic, oral, or autobiographical, writings," Warrior calls for "bibliograph[ies] dominated by ... the criticism of American Indian writers" and critical discourse in which "native writers [are] taken seriously as critics as well as producers of literature and culture" (xv–xvi). Womack similarly seeks out "Native perspectives" by "prioritizing Native voices" within his work and by "allowing Indian people to speak for themselves" (4).

The need for what Cherokee scholar Jace Weaver calls a "Native American literary criticism"—as opposed to "criticism of Native American literature"—that resides "in the hands of Native critics to define and articulate, from the resources [they] choose"[17] is paramount. However, let me rehearse for a moment not the strengths of the insider critic but the limitations of the outsider, of which I am one. In *How Should I Read These?*, non-Native critic Helen Hoy worries about "unfortunate occasions either for absolute, irreducible distance or for presumptuous familiarity,"[18] which emerge for the outsider critic by virtue of cultural naïveté. Lack of cultural immersion leaves most non-Native critics unaware of the symbolic archives, historical and cultural backdrops, generic categories, and even languages relied upon by specific Native authors, all of which conspire to render interpretations by such critics suspect, if not dangerous. Thus the outsider reader with limited understanding of cultural contexts or the nuances of particular cultural productions risks being repelled by their difference or glossing over such difference completely, both of which undermine what Hoy calls that difference's "oppositional potential" (9). She elaborates: "Too-easy identification by the non-Native reader, ignorance of historical or cultural allusion, obliviousness to the presence or properties of Native genres, and the application of irrelevant aesthetic standards are all means of domesticating difference, assimilating Native narratives into the mainstream" (9).

Although I agree with Hoy's insistence on self-reflexivity and acknowledgement of limited cultural understandings, I would argue that lack of cultural initiation and knowledge is actually a secondary reason for privileging the work of Native critics (as well as a bit of a generalization). Knowledge can be obtained. Neither unproblematically, of course, nor completely, and certainly not with the depth of a lifetime of experiential learning through simple academic study, but those non-Native critics willing to put in the time and effort in terms of research, dialogue, social interaction, and community involvement can *approach* valid cultural understandings. Furthermore, because of violent colonial interventions like residential school, not all Native individuals have inherited full understandings of their tribal cultures, let alone those of other tribal cultures. In the aftermath of attempted genocide, requisite cultural knowledge cannot be taken as a given by Aboriginals or non-Aboriginals. For example, Cree author Tomson Highway was denied aspects of his Cree heritage by a series of factors including his father's Christianity, his removal to residential school at the age of six, and his confinement to non-Native foster homes in southern Saskatchewan and Manitoba throughout his adolescence. This denial meant that in early adulthood, Highway's connection to Cree culture was strained. Highway's eventual reclamation, examination, and re-imagining of Cree heritage materials—from trickster figures, to mythological heroes like the Son of Ayash, to the Cree language—must be understood not just as the creative tapping into an internal archive of tribal knowledge, but also as an investigative and imaginative response to the conditions of colonialism. To presume a particular level of cultural knowledge (or other types of knowledge) from Highway or any Indigenous critic is to deny the complexity of personal history and interactions with colonialism and community. As Métis author Kim Anderson writes, "'Native experience'" is complicated "because, unfortunately, part of our experience as Native peoples includes being relocated, dispossessed of our ways of life, adopted into white families, and so on."[19]

The primary reason for privileging the work of Indigenous scholars to the exclusion of others is rather what Womack calls in *Red on Red* the "intrinsic and extrinsic relationship" between Native communities and Native writing[20] and what Weaver calls the "dialogic" nature of Native texts, which "both reflect and shape Native identity and community."[21] Native literature grows out of Native communities and, in turn, affects Native communities. In analyzing, contextualizing, grappling with, and elucidating Native texts, literary criticism seeks to participate in this reciprocal process (most often to serve as catalyst). To borrow from Julie Cruikshank, criticism of Native literature generally seeks to engage in the social lives of stories.[22] Stories influence the extra-textual world, not straightforwardly and not transparently, but stories and critical discourses about stories *do* influence people's lives. And in the field of Native Studies, the stories under analysis, quite frankly, have a more profound impact on certain lives than on others. As much as intellectual empathy and ethical commitment can pervade the work of a scholar with neither biological nor immediate social connection to Aboriginal community, the consequences of that individual's work cannot be experienced by her or him personally with the same intensity as one whose day-to-day lived experience is of being Aboriginal in this country.

I spoke in the opening of this book about the contagion of suicide infecting Aboriginal communities throughout Canada, and I truly hope that in working through the issues that it does, this book might offer some insights into potential pathways that writers have used toward communal and individual empowerment that might alleviate the senses of futility and despair out of which the contagion grows. However, I am not faced with the direct consequences of those words (and the potential arrogance they might betray). Similarly, although I have many Aboriginal friends, colleagues, and students, my engagements with the residential school legacy are largely intellectual and analytical, and I am painfully aware that for many, if not most, Aboriginal people in Canada—not just survivors, but parents, children, and community members—the legacy constitutes ongoing lived experience. I simply do not stand to inherit adverse social and political consequences of my critical work and this, it seems to me, influences the relevance of the work itself. The non-Native critic can learn as much as possible about the cultures she or he studies and can display as much sensitivity and empathy as she or he is able to muster, but, ultimately the non-Native critic's work will be limited in how it can relate to Native communities and how it will be received by them.

Given such a bleak appraisal of the potential of non-Native criticism, the recent efforts of non-Native critics to alter sites of analysis and thereby stifle the oppressive potential of their work is understandable. The following are the most popular among what I'll refer to as "strategies for ethical disengagement" by non-Native scholars.

Strategies for Ethical Disengagement

1) Retreat into Silence: Faced with the conundrum of either misunderstanding (and therefore misrepresenting) Indigeneity or recolonizing the Indigenous literary artist by "submit[ting] him or her to a dominative discourse,"[23] many non-Native former critics of Native literature have simply moved on to other areas of study. A popular site of migration has been white representations of Indigeneity, which can be critiqued in terms of racism, colonial myths, and semiotic imprisonment without the fear of appropriating Native voice.

2) Focus Inward: Intense self-reflexivity is far from uncommon in the age of postmodern literary analysis, but contemporary analyses of Native literary productions by non-Natives at times take it to a new level in which the actions of the critic become the primary site of inquiry rather than a cautionary apparatus designed to render the primary analysis more fertile. Given the dangers of appropriation and misrepresentation, the analytical process itself presents a safe site where the critic can be assured against doing violence to Native voice because the voice under scrutiny becomes her or his own. An example of this in process—although one that needs to be contextualized as an analysis of collaborative autobiography—would be Kathleen Sands's focus, in *Telling a Good One*, on a "narrative-ethnography methodology, in which the reader is made privy to the [non-Native] collector's self-conscious participation [in the autobiographical project] and doubly self-conscious hindsight."[24] Sands's work is a model

39

of critical self-reflexivity because she makes explicit her own feelings, reactions, and observations throughout the collaborative process so that any infringement on the voice of the Indigenous informant will be well documented. However, in her effort to avoid corrupting the voice of Theodore Rios, the Native subject of the autobiography, Sands, somewhat counterintuitively, gives priority to her own words over those she is attempting to protect; she makes her own involvement in the collaborative process as much the focus of her inquiry as the words of Rios, himself.[25]

3) Deal in the Purviews of Non-Native Critics: Although he is only one among many, Arnold Krupat presents the foremost example of this type of reaction to external critical positioning (particularly in his early work). Krupat's attachment to a social scientific approach to Native literature is undoubtedly informed by a keen awareness of his outsider status as a non-Native critic.[26] He clearly recognizes the perils of cross-cultural analysis, explaining, "The danger the would-be practitioner of ethnocriticism must try to avoid is ... to speak *for* the 'Indian,' 'interpreting' him or her ... in a manner that would submit her or him to a dominative discourse."[27] However, his defence against producing such an exploitative critical discourse is to retreat from Native narratives themselves to deal in the domains of other non-Native scholars—anthropologists, sociologists, historians, philosophers—which is why Krupat's *Ethnocriticism* is, by its author's own admission, "very little concerned with specifically literary texts" (31). In fact, Krupat's ethnocritical literary theory has very little to do with the content of literature at all. It deduces textual meaning predominantly through analyses of material production and cultural collision, a process that implies—much like some of the literature on the legacy of residential school discussed earlier in this chapter—a deterministic relationship that obscures the possibility of enduring Indigenous agency. It suggests that the work of Native authors is determined by forces outside themselves, be they cultural, economic, or political.

4) Present Only Tentative, Qualified, and Provisional Critical Statements: From the all too frequent "Please let me know if I'm saying this wrong, because I don't speak Anishinabe" prefaces at Native Studies conferences, to the two-paragraph qualifications at either the beginning or the end of

articles, tracing the author's complex subject position and her or his capacity to make only a particular type of reticent truth claim regarding these
distant literatures, many non-Native critics flirt with this technique. Renate
Eigenbrod, for example, is careful to "problematize [her] subjectivity, the
situatedness of [her] knowledge, and the *context* of [her] subject position
in order to underscore partiality and de-emphasize assumptions about the
expert."[28] At every turn, Eigenbrod acknowledges deficiencies in her own
relationship to the literatures she studies and teaches, encouraging skepticism among her readers about all interpretive claims found within the
pages of her book, *Travelling Knowledges.* Similarly, Hoy strives in her work
"to keep to the forefront the assumptions, needs, and ignorance that [she]
bring[s] to [her] readings, the culture-specific positioning from which
[she] engage[s] with the writing." "[B]y making explicit various sources
of [her] responses," Hoy endeavours to "render the readings more clearly
local, partial, and accountable, relinquishing the authority that clings to
detached pronouncements."[29] Both Hoy and Eigenbrod take action against
the power imbalance between Indigenous community and non-Native
academy by forsaking access to positions of "authority" and thereby calling
into question the validity of their own readings. Politically this is astute, ad-
mirable, and probably ethical, but it does lead to questions about the point
of reading work that professes to be problematic throughout.[30]

Alternative Strategies for Ethical Engagement

Because you're reading this book, you can guess that I've not chosen silence as
a viable option. While I recognize that clearing the way for Native scholars is
crucial to restoring balance to a discursive environment in which the "'mental
means of production' in regards to analyzing Indian cultures have been owned,
almost exclusively, by non-Indians,"[31] I fail to see how diverting my own attention toward simulations of Nativeness by non-Natives is the best way to acknowledge and respect Indigenous creative agency. In fact, I think the two issues
embedded in the preceding sentence, both involving Native voice, can be use-
fully separated and then re-imagined. On the one hand, all scholars of Native
literatures should facilitate the development of young Native scholars through
involvement in graduate courses, symposia, conferences, edited collections, and
journal special issues, thereby contributing to conditions of possibility for the
inevitable and necessary predominance of Natives in the critical field.[32] On the

other, we need to continue to respect and examine Indigenous creative work as a front line to Native empowerment and agency. If we indeed desire to expand the field—something desperately needed, particularly in Canada—scholars need to welcome new insights, new critical strategies, and new critical minds (particularly those emerging from Native communities), while not ceasing to engage with Native artistic creation. The two need not be mutually exclusive. Respecting and privileging Native voices in the critical arena as well as enabling Native scholarly growth and achievement do not, I contend, preclude non-Native scholars studying Native literatures. In fact, I see the alternative of avoiding Native literary works and focusing even more attention on the cultural creations of the dominant society as contrary to the goal of respecting Native voice and forwarding the social and political objectives embedded in text; it again takes focus away, willingly failing to heed the creative voices of those who feel the impact of Canadian colonial oppression.

Option number two, focusing inward, while to a certain extent necessary, has always seemed to me slightly masturbatory. The idea that the best way to ensure that Native voice is not stifled or misunderstood is to study another voice altogether is counterintuitive. It's kind of like the backhanded paternalism of saying, "You might get hurt in the ring, so please stay on the sidelines while I shadow box myself." In the effort to protect the oppressed, one disregards her or his decision-making authority. Yes, scholars need to be aware of their own limitations, and yes, they must be self-reflexive about process and interaction, but no, they don't need to make themselves the star of the study, especially to the ongoing neglect of Indigenous voices.

To play with my earlier analogy a bit, the third option, with its attention outside, is somewhat like saying, "You may get hurt on the field, so please stay on the sidelines and watch the rest of us play." The Native writer and the ideas embedded in her or his text are rendered secondary while context and theory are charged to the fore. The non-Native critic examines the work of other non-Native scholars, critics, and theorists in order to explain away the textual product without having to engage much at all with the *ideas* of the text. "Unwilling to speak *for* the Indian," writes Krupat, "and unable to speak as an Indian …, the danger *I* run as an ethnocritic is the danger of leaving the Indian silent entirely in my discourse" (emphasis original).[33] Krupat identifies a mighty risk, and one that seems far more threatening to Indigenous empowerment than the alternative of engaging Native literature directly, despite the possibility of misinterpretation.

Non-Native critics like Krupat must indeed be ever conscious of the limitations of their experiential knowledge and of the mediated manner in which they often access Indigenous cultures, spiritualities, and histories; however, this awareness cannot lead them to avoid Native voices without compromising the critical and political validity of their work. As Matt Herman argues in relation to Krupat, "Form [is not] solely responsible for literary production. People produce texts, maybe not exactly in the way they choose to do it or with the exact message they intend to broadcast, but people make texts, and it seems to me that any inquiry into textual production ought to pass through the producer."[34] Although, clearly, contextual information from a variety of sources and discourses is crucial to a knowledgeable, sensitive, and productive engagement with any literature, such information must never *replace* the literary analysis, particularly among literatures that have been heretofore marginalized. Knowledge of cultural collision, traditional spirituality, colonial history, and modes of textual production inform the meaning and potential effects of specific Native texts, but they do not produce that meaning and those effects alone, beyond the creative agency of the Native author. The priority in Native literary studies, it seems to me, must be Native voice as evidenced by the writing of the Native author. The function of literary criticism, in the Indigenous context as elsewhere, is to engage in the understanding and elucidation of specific literary texts, not bury those texts beneath mountains of anthropological and historical data.

The final strategy for disengagement, qualification, is, in many ways, the most necessary for the non-Native critic. Recognizing the limits of the outsider's historical and cultural knowledge, as well as the ethical limits generated by lack of day-to-day community involvement, the non-Native critic must acknowledge the inherent tenuousness of her or his critical claims in order to avoid presumptive arrogance and what Hoy and Eigenbrod recognize as the erroneous "authority" of the external expert. However, this process, when taken to an extreme, can lead to critical irrelevance and, worse, critical licence. By qualifying her or his statements with admissions of lack of cultural knowledge, the critic can perceive her or himself freed from attempting to gain that knowledge, which inevitably will lead to weak(er) criticism. The wise person may well recognize that she or he knows nothing, but the wiser person takes this as incentive to learn. Furthermore, remaining cognizant of limitations must not prevent the outsider critic from making the interpretive claims that are the earmarks of engaged scholarship. Critical dialogue, argument, and dissent are positive because they enable the refinement of thinking and the growth of the field. Critical interventions, even when they are flawed, can forward others' thinking by inciting reactions in which might be developed new avenues of investigation and new methods of inquiry. If an interpretation is flawed, then why is it so, and how can another critic in dialogue remedy its errors?

According to Womack, critics of Native literatures need to "interrogate each other's work as much as celebrate it…. The backslapping that has characterized our discipline has not gotten us very far."[35] Warrior agrees, arguing that "the tendency to find in the work of other American Indian writers something worthy … of unmitigated praise … stands in the way of sincere disagreement and engagement."[36] In *American Indian Literary Nationalism*, Warrior declares that "dissent, disagreement, and the questioning of orthodoxies and received wisdom must be valued."[37] Although non-Native critics can never and should never claim 'big A' *Authority* in their discussion of Native texts, the need for endless qualification is mitigated by the dialogic nature of critical discourse. All critical claims unleashed upon the critical arena are offered up for debate, and those that are inept, or worse, communally damaging, must be countered with astute, powerful, and ethical responses. I apologize for any weaknesses that might emerge in my analysis throughout *Magic Weapons*, but I don't apologize for analyzing. And I expect and desire other critics (especially those with connections to the communities for whom the issues of the book are lived concerns) to engage with some of the things I've said and to disagree with them where necessary. This is how the critical field will grow; this is how I will get better as a critic and produce more empowering and communally generative work in the future.

In short, I reject the reigning strategies for ethical disengagement in order to seek out strategies of ethical engagement. To respect the creative work of Native writers, the intellectual work of Native critics, and the activist work of Native community members, one must engage—listen, learn, dialogue, and debate. The critical posture I endeavour to occupy as a non-Native critic of Native literatures, therefore, is that of the ally. Weaver states:

> We need simpatico and knowledgeable Amer-European critical allies…. We *want* non-Natives to read, engage, and study Native literature. The survival of Native authors, if not Native people in general, depends on it. But we do not need modern literary colonizers. We only ask that non-Natives who study and write about Native peoples do so with respect and a sense of responsibility to Native community.[38]

An ally, in my understanding, acknowledges the limits of her or his knowledge, but doesn't cower beneath those limits or use them as a crutch. She or he recognizes the responsibility to gain knowledge about the cultures and communities whose artistic creations she or he analyzes before entering the critical fray and offering public interpretations. She or he privileges the work of Native scholars, writers, and community members—not as a political gesture, but in sincere attempts to produce the most effective criticism—yet, she or he doesn't accept their work uncritically; healthy skepticism and critical debate are signs of engagement and respect, not dismissal. Further, she or he appreciates that multilayered and ultimately valid understandings of cultures and communities can never emerge solely from book research, and that the ongoing vitality and lived experience of Indigenous communities must serve to augment and correct what Jana Sequoya calls "the alienated forms of archive material."[39] Most importantly, the non-Native ally must recognize and act out of a sense of responsibility to Indigenous communities in general and specifically to those whose creative work is being analyzed.

In the context of *Magic Weapons*, my role as a non-Native ally is to participate through analysis, contextualization, and elucidation in the political, social, and creative objectives of the texts with which I engage. This means privileging Native voice, in terms of authorial and critical perspectives, while respecting the integrity of Native voice by engaging with, analyzing, and perchance critiquing those perspectives. Emerging in the wake of a context of institutionalized assimilation in which the autonomy and agency of the Native individual were suffocated by the fist of authoritarian control, residential school survival narratives court the re-imagining of individual and cultural identities beyond the reach of colonial power; they endeavour to actualize Indigenous empowerment and rejuvenate spiritual, cultural, and political structures placed under erasure by governmental intervention. To truly value these efforts, the non-Native ally must respect the creative integrity of the Native author, not by uncritically agreeing with everything she or he says, but by analyzing closely the significance of her or his representations. This means, in the words of Kimberly Blaeser, being "alert for critical methods and voices that seem to arise out of the literature itself" rather than simply applying "already established critical language ... and categories of meaning."[40] Lastly, in light of the intended cultural and political decimation of Indigenous nations that lay at the heart of residential school policy, my allied critical stance to survival narratives holds as the furthest horizon of its utility the objectives of economically, socially, and culturally flourishing Indigenous communities and, ultimately, of political self-determination.[41]

IDENTITY AND IDENTI-TEASE: ANALYZING THE ABORIGINAL AUTHOR

Having clarified my role as critic, I'd like to discuss and refine the far more crucial role of the Native author as it is understood in *Magic Weapons*. As a framework for doing so, I offer the following simplified yet utilitarian model of how the residential school survivor emerges as a literary voice—fully acknowledging that it must be adapted to the specifics of any given narrative situation. The three stages correspond to periods of the authors' lives before, during, and after residential school.

1) "Communal/Tribal Identity"
- already complicated in varying degrees by colonial contact
- characterized by connection to Native family and/or tribal community

2a) "Institutionalized Identity"
- emerging from violent assimilative technologies of residential school
- characterized by denial, and at times loss, of connection to family, community, tradition, and language

2b) "Spectral Identity"
- what the individual might have been without the imposition of residential school
- characterized by potentiality

3) "Imaginative Literary Identity"
- interacting in complex ways with previous three
- characterized by creative self-definition

Each of these sections requires elaboration to render it useful in the formation of a viable criticism of post-residential school literature. The term "communal/tribal" is invoked in stage one as a reminder that, prior to removal to residential schools, these children were part of modern Native communities by whom they were influenced, nurtured, and taught. The term is appropriate, given the centrality, in most Native cultures, of community in the development and understanding of individual identity. This is not, however, meant to imply that before residential school, the identities of the authors in this study were subject solely to unadulterated tribal influences or to a mythically pure type of pre-modern community. Rather, I mean to suggest that each eventual writer had not, at this point, been subject to the specific assimilative technologies of the residential school and that her or his identity was therefore primarily the product of tribal, communal, and familial influences, although that is not the same as saying that prior to residential school, each had an 'authentically Native' identity that residential school inevitably altered or tainted.

Any criticism concerned with questions of Native identity must acknowledge the complexity and variance of influence among individuals and among tribes across the continent with diverse cultural, spiritual, and political practices, for whom colonialism came at different times and in different manifestations. For instance, Rita Joe's Mi'kmaq ancestors in what would become Nova Scotia had had to contend with European settlers for nearly half a millennium prior to her entry into Shubenacadie Indian Residential School in 1944 and, as such, had developed many diverse ways of resisting oppression while also assimilating many practical and cultural implements from those with whom they lived in such close quarters. Joe's experience of residential school was thus understandably different from those of Anthony Thrasher (Inuit) or Tomson Highway (Cree), who had previously lived nomadically and largely beyond non-Native contact in Canada's far North. Even Thrasher and Highway, however, were raised in Christian homes. A sophisticated criticism of the literature of residential school survivors, therefore, must analyze both the individual's pre-residential school experiences and the experiences of her or his cultural community; it must understand each Indigenous Nation's worldview, traditions, and knowledges, and the history of its interactions with colonial powers, in order to comprehend with proficiency the ways in which the potential writer might have interpreted and internalized her or his sense of personal and cultural identity prior to residential school. In other words, such a criticism must seek out and attempt to understand interwoven strands of context.

Stage two is meant to recognize the way residential school derails what might be termed the 'natural' course of identity growth. Residential schools were designed and conducted to alter—and, by altering, obliterate—Native identity, and although they were not everywhere and always as successful as their brutal regimen intended, in the words of Chrisjohn and Young, "even those who managed to escape the more sensational abuses ... could not have emerged unscathed."[42] Through prescribed behaviours, denial of familial contact, Jesuit-styled punishment, and propagandist pedagogy, those planning and running the schools sought to intervene in the growth of young Native individuals in order to make them *identify* with non-Native Canada. Emboldened by scientific racism and the cultural narcissism of the 'white man's burden,' residential schools strove to deny students access to Native cultures and to thereby encourage their denial of Native identities, making them 'civilized' Christians and, in Cree author Harold Cardinal's term, "little brown white men." The residential school experience was, therefore, often characterized by denial and loss. Constance Deiter, for instance, acknowledges that "some survivors and their communities have lost the skills needed to be healthy individuals. The loss of nurturing parents; loss of parenting skills; loss of identity; low self-esteem; the inability to think independently; the lack of unity within families and communities; the loss of language, culture, and respect for self; and finally, the loss of spiritual values have left communities in chaos."[43] The term "loss," as cadence in Deiter's remarks, enunciates the thievery of a system that not only stole children from their families, but also stole from those children enabling cultural systems. Children were *denied* their families, *denied* their languages, *denied* their songs, dances, and ceremonies, and, as a result, many lost the ability to parent, lost the ability to speak their languages, lost touch with their spiritual systems.

We must caution ourselves, however, against collapsing denial into loss and thereby affording residential schools more perverse success than they achieved. Active separation of a child from the world into which she or he was born could not invariably ensure the suffocation of that world within her or his psyche or future; many means of expression and cultural understanding survived their intended genocide, driven underground and muted. As Celia Haig-Brown argues, despite every effort to render cultural amputation complete, "people resisted and found strength within that resistance. Aspects of their family cultures persisted, enough to build on, enough to feed the renewal process which continues."[44] Again, the reminder must be to recognize and interrogate the complexity of individual experiences, guarding against generalizations without ignoring the overarching unity of political purpose surrounding the interpretive endeavour. The struggle of the critic of residential school literature is to recognize the plurality and specificity of individual circumstances and experiences without reifying the individualism of survivors as divorced from political units of family, community, and culture; it is to acknowledge the unique nature of each life story and history without framing the communally expressive act of writing as what Julia Watson and Sidonie Smith call "a cult of individuality and … loneliness."[45]

As section 2b in my model, I include the by-product of residential school denial: the youth and youthful identity the child cannot claim due to her or his institutionalization. What I have called a "spectral identity" refers to what the child might have been if not for the anomalous intervention of the state. Conceived as a denied potentiality, the spectral identity can only be speculative, but as we shall see, this does not remove its psychic importance for the institutionalized child or her or his adult self, particularly when the latter ruminates on personal development in an exercise like autobiography. As the writer comes to analyze her or his life, the spectral identity can act as a vague beacon toward which she or he can aspire in the process of healing or a corollary by which to understand the institutionalized self. The spectral identity is most evident in the work of Anthony Thrasher, discussed in chapter 3, who periodically includes among his prison writings an ongoing dream narrative about a traditional Inuit life he can no longer claim (due not only to residential school but also to the industrialization of the Arctic and his incarceration). Thrasher's use of the dream narrative, as I will argue more fully below, provokes audience awareness of Inuit losses at the hands of colonial intervention and produces an imaginative construct in relation to which Thrasher, the imprisoned artist, can re-imagine himself.

My use of "imaginative literary identity" in section 3 seeks immediately to impart some qualifications on my use of autobiography in this project. The individual looking back upon her or his life in order to set it down in words is *not* the "literary identity," but, rather, the "literary identity" is *created* in that articulation process. My interest lies in how the textual product—and the act of writing—influences the writer's identity as well as the communal identification of those at whom the text is principally aimed. In his work on post-colonial identity,[46] Homi K. Bhabha argues that for those whose lives have been problematized or placed under erasure by the oppressive violence of colonial encounter, the concept of an *identity*, singular and self-contained, becomes less important and counter-discursively utilitarian than the act of *identifying*. For Bhabha, "the question of identification is never the affirmation of a pre-given identity, never a *self*-fulfilling prophesy—it is always the production of an image of identity and the transformation of the subject in assuming that image."[47] This proposition has received profound gestures of corroboration from among the elite of Native North American letters. Kiowa author N. Scott Momaday famously asserts that "in a certain sense we are all made of words; that our most essential being consists in language. It is the element in which we think and dream and act, in which we live our daily lives. There is no way in which we can exist apart from the morality of a verbal dimension."[48] Thomas King declares, as cadence to his recent Massey Lecture series, "The truth about stories is that that's all we are."[49] Gerald Vizenor further claims,

> I touch myself into being with my own dreams and with my imagination. I am what I say I am, and I emphasize I am a state of being, and I gather all those words that feed and nurture my imagination about my being.[50]

The question for these authors, and for this project, is not 'who is the writer,' but rather 'how is she or he created in the writing.'

Created identity must not, however, remain solely an imaginative construct. A politically responsible criticism of post-residential school literature must locate materially and historically the goals and significance of creative 'identification'; it must trace out the literature's extra-textual effects. By analyzing the material textual products in relation to publication, critical history, and audience reception, I intend to uncover how the life-writings at the centre of this study strategically provoke personal, social, and political change in the service of Indigenous empowerment. In this way I wish to distinguish *Magic Weapons* from psychological studies focusing on the cathartic effects of writing for authors who have suffered trauma. Although, in some cases, the authors whose works I study may have experienced healing through writing—Tomson Highway makes this very point, suggesting, "If I couldn't have written [*Kiss of the Fur Queen*], I would have killed myself"[51]— by the time their manuscripts reached publication, that specific healing process had ended, or, at least, had shifted from cathartic writing to discussing the book, giving readings, and perhaps working on other projects. Furthermore, the final textual form of each work is so vastly different from its initial (perhaps purgative) articulation as to leave only traces of such a healing process. As a result, this project focuses primarily on the ultimate textual product itself—on the *content* of the literature—analyzing how it affects both its author and the wider community.

Autobiography is essentially a creative engagement with personal experience and identity, and reserves for the author the capacity to conceive and narratively construct a self beyond external limitations, and herein lies the genre's social relevance and political potential. For Bhabha, the recognition that "identity is never an a priori, nor a finished product"[52] opens up for writers strategies of "subversion. … that [seek] not to unveil the fullness of Man but to manipulate his representation. It is a form of power that is exercised at the very limits of identity and authority, in the mocking spirit of mask and image."[53] The power of autobiography thus lies not in its ability to express a given identity, but rather to present an identity in rhetorically and politically effective ways.

My focus on narrative manipulation and artistry, however, does not negate the function of autobiography as a record of actual or perceived personal growth. Clearly, autobiography remains indebted to the 'real' for its generic status, and the idea of a representable 'real' permeates its use. It is just such an examination of individual history and personal development that affords the residential school survivor the keen understanding of colonial duplicities and oppressive cultural relations required to create an imaginative literary identity that will be politically effective, which, in turn, perhaps makes that representation more personally relevant or 'true.' Because the imaginative literary identity bespeaks the author's knowledge of, and insight into, the political and cultural dynamics that have influenced her or his development and continue to influence the narrative situation, it suggests a great deal about the author, even as she or he manipulates its articulation for effect. An understanding of the 'real' thus forms the foundation of socially and politically potent autobiographical representations, even as they depart strategically from the 'real.' "For the colonial subject," argue Watson and Smith, "the process of coming to writing is an articulation *through* interrogation, a charting of the conditions that have historically placed her identity under erasure" (emphasis original).[54]

The act of speaking that history is itself an act of defiance, of denying one's own non-being. As Lee Maracle diagnoses,

> The result of being colonized is the internalization of the need to remain invisible. The colonizers erase you, not easily, but with shame and brutality. Eventually you want to stay that way. Being a writer is getting up there and writing yourself onto everyone's blackboard.[55]

Autobiography, for residential school survivors, is reciprocal. It is borne out of a specific reality, and it, in turn, affects that reality. It documents the attempted suffocation of a particular identity, but, *through such documentation*, revitalizes and so recreates, performs, and displays that identity anew, while establishing spaces of introspection in which readers can conduct similar examinations of their own experiences.

POSITIONING COMMUNITY AT THE FOREFRONT
OF PROGRESSIVE CRITICISM

The critic's primary access to the author is through text. Sure, the critic can attempt to contact authors to gain further insights, but, as exemplified by Thomas King and Gerald Vizenor,[56] many Native authors tend to frustrate attempts to clarify authorial "intent" in interviews. In a tricksterish manner, authors can adopt performative poses, choosing when and how audiences obtain access to their interiority and the interiority of their texts. What's more, authors aren't the best critics of their own work; intended authorial meaning doesn't always match textual product or audience reception. And, most importantly, meaning is actualized through the engagement of audience—as is what I've referred to above as "imaginative literary identity"—making the reading community partners in meaning creation and rendering the published text to which audiences have access the essential site of analysis.

As illustrated in my earlier model of literary relationships, the text is the vehicle that connects critic, author, and community, with community serving as conduit to extra-textual significance, to the political and social consequences that make literary analysis worthwhile. The community provides an anchor of ethical responsibility for both author and critic and a source of analytical methods and materials that can facilitate the interpretive process. However, the term "community," in the singular and untheorized, fails to present adequately either the complex way in which community functions in residential school survival narratives or the matrix of overlapping, plural, and interpenetrating communal jurisdictions throughout Native North America. What is needed is a nuanced historical and creative understanding of Indigenous communities and their contemporary contamination by legacies of colonial imposition, a nuanced understanding found in the work of Jace Weaver.

While Weaver's *That the People Might Live: Native American Literatures and Native American Community* (1997)[57] "is about Native community," it takes "as both its lens and its focus Native American literature," arguing that in "communities deeply fractured by the continuing impact of invasion and colonialism" (viii), Native writings "both reflect and shape Native identity and community" (41). Weaver demonstrates how Native writers are not only the product of Native communities—which can be neither static nor singular—but that they, in turn, develop, alter, influence, and recreate those very communities through imaginative discourse and the material creations of textual production, a relationship that affords Native writers and Native literature remarkable discursive and political power. Weaver terms this narrative commitment to community "communitism," a neologism "formed by a combination of the words 'community' and 'activism'" (xiii). He explains,

> In communities that have too often been fractured and rendered dysfunctional by the effects of more than 500 years of colonialism, to promote communitist values means to participate in the healing of the grief and sense of exile felt by Native communities and the pained individuals in them.(xiii)

The methodological manifestation of such values in literary criticism involves, for Weaver, biographical discussion of the community (or communities) out of which a particular Native author writes, analysis of her or his literary configurations of community and their political and/or communal function, and, finally, recognition of what impact the ultimate textual product has on the community (or communities) at which it is directed. After all, as Weaver argues, "how a given work is received, consumed, appropriated by Native community is part of the work itself. It helps complete the process. Communitism is, as the word itself implies, communal" (45).

Like Womack's tribal-specific criticism, Weaver's communitism attempts "to break down oppositions between the world of literature and the very real struggles of … Indian communities, arguing for both an intrinsic and extrinsic relationship between the two."[58] And like David L. Moore, Weaver explores how land-based, urban, and pan-tribal communities "reside as … audience in [Native] texts, as a tacit chorus for the communal values reflected in those texts, and as a beneficiary of the writers' political performances related to those communal values."[59] Communitism examines, again along with Moore, how the "political linkage between text and context establishes a particular dimension of ethical commitment between performance and performer," and how "the communal and political dimensions" of Native literature "call for and call into being a readership to participate imaginatively in the performance."[60]

The communities toward which specific Native texts are oriented, however, are not predetermined by tribal affiliation or other factors, but are identified— "call[ed] into being"—within the texts themselves. *Indian School Days*, for instance, is not necessarily directed toward the Ojibway community, despite the fact that its author, Basil Johnston, has devoted a large percentage of his prolific literary output to discussions of Ojibway history, spirituality, and culture. This particular text by Johnston celebrates the inter-tribal community forged among Native students at a Roman Catholic residential school in Spanish, Ontario, in reaction to, and defiance of, their being denied access to their particular tribal communities. Although written by a decidedly Ojibway author, *Indian School Days* is oriented primarily to the concerns of a pan-tribal readership struggling with the legacy of institutionalized acculturation and invasive control.

Similarly, Cherokee-Greek writer Thomas King, who was raised by his non-Native mother and grew up in a largely non-Native community before going to a Catholic boarding school at fourteen,[61] writes out of life experience based, in his own words, more on "'a pan-Indian existence and more urban and rural existence than a reservation one.'"[62] While King invokes Cherokee spirituality and history in his works, as in the Trail of Tears references from *Green Grass, Running Water*[63] and the figure of Rebecca Neugin from *Truth & Bright Water*,[64] he generally situates such references outside a uniquely Cherokee setting, most often among the prairie Blackfoot, around whom King spent a good deal of his early adult life while teaching in Lethbridge, Alberta. In fact, King uses Cherokee cultural material in relation to myriad tribal materials from across the continent and around the world, all of which complicate, interrogate, and enhance the creation of meaning in King's texts, and all of which enable the texts to perform their social and political acts. The result, according to Weaver, is a literary oeuvre that seeks to analyze and articulate what it means, has meant, and will mean to live as part of the pan-Native community, helping to shape that community through artistic expression, rather than a reification of the author's tribal background through an intense refocusing of authorial energy on a tribal community of which King's personal history prevented him from feeling wholly a part.[65]

Evident throughout *That the People Might Live* is Weaver's sense of the manifold relationship between Natives—writers and otherwise—and their communities. His recognition of "exile" as a category of Native communal identification suggests that the battle to reinvigorate Native communities is fought from without as well as from within. In the shadow of assimilationist violence and colonial duplicity, Native community survives as an essential critical category even in the absence of particular physical communities, especially for "urban Natives separated from their tribal lands and often from their cultures and religions as well" (viii). Weaver's communitism creates the critical space for literary examination of colonially created cultural alienation that still posits an "Indigenous" communal identity as a value. Such a position enables critical engagement with questions of Native identity and Native culture that acknowledges and interrogates colonial interventions like residential school that have sought to sever individuals' ties to their communities, and also acknowledges the ongoing importance of those communities themselves.

In a particularly Vizenorian passage, Weaver argues that "criticism not focused on and rooted in Native community only serves the myths of conquest and dominance that seek to subdue and conquer, render tame, our stories" (165). Firmly situating its primary analysis within the discursive realm, while diligently attending to the political and social realities affecting and affected by discourse, communitism reveals how Native communities, both in historical and contemporary contexts, are forged through the stories groups tell about themselves. Traditional stories, for Weaver, "are communal. They belong to the People and define the People—the community—as a whole" (42). Modern Native stories reconstitute this dialogic and creative process within a socio-political climate that has more than occasionally rendered community problematic.[66] Native authors redefine and refine what it means to be part of Native communities in their writings, and, in the process, they engage in the empowerment of communities and the individuals within them, even of those in exile. As Weaver boldly declares, "Stories can heal" (161). Communitism is, therefore, extremely helpful for the analysis of residential school survival narratives, which attempt to rekindle, through literary creation, authors' communal affiliations, be they pan-tribal, tribal-specific, or otherwise; it offers critical tools with which to analyze how writers articulate for themselves—and, by extension, their readers and communities—what it means to live and write as Native individuals and members of living, evolving communities.

A communitist reading of the residential school survival narrative thus does not assert that the text's narrative content is necessarily determined by the personal history of the author, but, rather, analyzes how the author engages often traumatic history through literary artistry in such a way as to aid in the empowerment of her or his community (or communities) in a movement toward positive change. The focus on community therefore serves several functions. First, it mitigates the individualistic undertow of standard western autobiography. This is particularly important, given the isolation and loneliness to which survival narratives often bear witness and the efforts of residential school policy to replace communal cultures with an ideology of capitalist individualism. Second, it forces from the critic recognition of culture and history. To adequately deduce the existence of communities imagined in text, the critic must gain an understanding of the historical conditions that may have influenced those communities and their cultural inner workings. Third, the acknowledged presence of community as a value in Native texts binds culture to politics, forcing extratextual relevance on critical environments that all too frequently forsake "specific Political (with a big P) topics within Native literature.... to focus on small-p politics—that is, on power relations."[67] As Kristina Fagan adeptly notes in her article, "Tewatatha:wi," "'culture' can be a politically soft and shifty term," and "persistently focusing on culture over politics can be a way of disengaging from important parts of Aboriginal peoples and their literatures" (14).

Focus on community connects culture to politics irrevocably because culture becomes a lived series of acts within actual political units of community, whether those units involve individual Indigenous nations, reserve communities, urban communities alienated from traditional land bases, or pan-tribal communities like that represented by the Assembly of First Nations. By centring understanding and effect in community, communitist scholars heed Fagan's call to attend critically "to whether [Native literature] exerts a force for change outside the text itself" (15). They do what Native American writer Devon A. Mihesuah suggests scholars of "indigenous history and culture should be doing. And that is using our knowledge, resources, and talent for writing to better the lives of Indigenous people."[68]

Thus, uniquely, I believe, in relation to the study of residential school memory, *Magic Weapons* reorients the impetus for literary discussion from "healing"—which is primarily individual or vicarious—to "activism"—which is inherently and insistently communal. The book seeks to keep at the centre of its analyses and the horizon of its ethical commitment the survival, enrichment, and eventual self-determination of Indigenous communities (variously construed and internally defined). Cherokee author, academic, and activist Daniel Heath Justice argues in "Conjuring Marks" that "to be a thoughtful participant in the decolonization of Indigenous peoples is to necessarily enter into an ethical relationship that requires respect, attentiveness, intellectual rigor, and no small amount of moral courage" (9). *Magic Weapons* aspires to such participation.

Hated Structure

If you are on Highway 104
In a Shubenacadie town
There is a hill
Where a structure stands
A reminder to many senses
To respond like demented ones.

I for one looked in the window
And there on the floor
Was a deluge of misery
Of a building I held in awe
Since the day
I walked in the ornamented door.

There was grime everywhere
As in buildings left alone or unused.
Maybe to the related tales of long ago
Where the children lived in laughter, or abuse.

I had no wish to enter
Nor to walk the halls.
I had no wish to feel the floors
Where I felt fear
A beating heart of episodes
I care not to recall.
The structure stands as if to say:
I was just a base for theory
To bend the will of children
I remind
Until I fall.

From *Song of Rita Joe: Autobiography of a Mi'kmaq Poet* (1996)
by Rita Joe (Mi'kmaq)
Survivor: Shubenacadie Residential School,
Shubenacadie, Nova Scotia

CHAPTER 3

"We have been silent too long": Linguistic Play in Anthony Apakark Thrasher's Prison Writings

"Now ... the unemployed man, the starving native do not lay claim to the truth; they do not say that they represent the truth, for they are the truth."
Frantz Fanon,
The Wretched of the Earth

"George Washington never told a lie?
Neither do I. So here is the truth we all do lie
in every truth even just a little."
Anthony Apakark Thrasher,
Unpublished Manuscript

Few residential school survival narratives have found their way to publication *as literature*. Segments of hundreds of (largely anonymous) survivor accounts exist within historical studies and government publications like the *Report of the Royal Commission on Aboriginal Peoples*, but these are mainly invoked as testimonial evidence and discussed in distinctly non-literary terms. (Such presentation is unsurprising, of course, given that the veracity of such accounts depends on their perceived transparency, on the orator's reluctance to ornament, to mould, to play.) In a few instances, however, Indigenous survivors have recorded their residential school experiences within book-length memoirs, which cannot be fully understood without recourse to a literary framework.

Such life-writings emerge, for the most part, from an extremely small sector of Native Canada. A cursory glance at the careers of some of the authors studied within these pages—Tomson Highway, Basil Johnston, Rita Joe—reveals their distinguished status among the elite of Native letters: all have multiple publications; all are educators, lecturers, and activists as well as writers; all are considered pillars of their tribal communities and of the Native arts community in general; all have received honorary doctorates from Canadian academic institutions and two of the three are members of the Order of Canada (Johnston is a member of the Order of Ontario). Highway, Johnston, and Joe are among the extraordinary success stories to emerge from the assimilationist machinery of the residential school system. As a result, their life-writings both dramatize, and serve as evidence for, the capacity of the individual to overcome institutionalized trauma. They also relate how tribal languages, customs, and spirituality can participate in the healing of wounded identities, which can ultimately be reasserted as viable, healthy, and ongoing through the magic of art. In short, these texts inspire hope with messages of possibility.[1]

However, these narratives remain haunted by the absence of other stories. They exist in the shadow of a far greater number of tales of perpetual disillusion, unhealed pain, and ongoing fragmentation of Indigenous identity, tales that have remained either untold or hidden from the literary community within obscure sociological, political, and academic archives. As Highway, Johnston, and Joe are only too aware, their survival narratives carry with them, as obligatory subtext, the understanding that others have not similarly survived, that many former residential school students have never been able to achieve a stable Indigenous identity, much less write about it.[2] As Cree writer and editor Greg Young-Ing has noted in his article, "Aboriginal Peoples' Estrangement":

> [The residential school system] was hardly a training ground or a vehicle for promoting Aboriginal literature. One impact of the residential school system was to effectively stifle the Aboriginal Voice by denying generations of children access to their cultural knowledge while instilling in them negative perceptions of their cultural identities. Even if exceptional children were able to miraculously overcome these impositions, as well as the other racial, social and economic barriers, they were not given adequate skills enabling them to write.[3]

Young-Ing continues by quoting Stoh:lo writer Lee Maracle's assertion that residential schools produced "'languageless generations' [by forbidding] 'them to speak their own language and imped[ing] their mastery of English, creating an entire population, with few exceptions, who were unfamiliar with language in general.'"[4] Furthermore, residential school denied its students access to those resources that might otherwise have assisted their struggle to overcome trauma incurred within the residential school setting (including, of course, appallingly common sexual and physical abuse, but also the trauma of familial separation and denial of nurturing and affection). Residential school policy endeavoured to drive a wedge between youth and elders, children and parents, students and their cultural heritages, creating a situation in which communal and cultural networks for healing were seldom accessible to students after their release from institutionalization. Within this context, it is entirely unsurprising that Highway, Johnston, and Joe are the exception rather than the rule for post-residential school literary accomplishment.

I begin my analysis of individual residential school narratives with Inuit writer Anthony Apakark Thrasher's 1976 autobiography, *Thrasher ... Skid Row Eskimo*, because his is one of the 'other stories.'[5] Written predominantly in a Calgary prison while Thrasher awaited trial for the killing of an elderly man—he was eventually convicted of manslaughter—*Skid Row Eskimo* chronicles its author's descent into alcoholism, poverty, violence, and despair on the streets of southern Alberta cities. It publicly airs the thoughts, feelings, and experiences of a man who was not successful in navigating his post-residential school existence in the economically devastated North or in the alien and unforgiving South. Unlike the choreographer in Alootook Ipellie's "Walking Both Sides of an Invisible Border,"[6] Thrasher could never "invent" the "distinctive dance steps" necessary to thrive in both Inuit and non-Native worlds. As a result, rather than mapping a path from institutionalized oppression to intellectual and spiritual emancipation, Thrasher's writing remains mired in un-freedom, powerfully symbolized by the cage from which he writes.

The trajectory of Thrasher's autobiography is, therefore, in many ways antithetical to the *Bildungsroman* structures of other survival narratives studied in *Magic Weapons*. As Thrasher's editors note in their "Foreword," "This book ends with the author ... on his way to a hospital for the criminally insane. [And although] Thrasher has since been released from that institution[,] ... he is not better and the bad things go on happening."[7] The informed reader today also knows that Thrasher's alcoholism persisted after this release and that he was subsequently reincarcerated and convicted of a 1979 Edmonton rape.[8] He died on the streets of that same city ten years later. Unlike other residential school survival narratives, Thrasher's does not inspire hope with a positive message. In fact, according to

Thrasher's editors, "to hold out hope is to cheat on him" (viii). *Skid Row Eskimo* serves as a double warning: first, as its author intended, it is a cautionary tale for Inuit youth who might read of Thrasher's life and "know what to watch out for, so they [won't] end up like me, in a white man's cage" (132); second, it warns the critic of residential school literature against generalizations regarding the political, social, and literary function of survival narratives. For example, the common assumption that trauma writing is inherently cathartic and that by writing one's experiences of oppression, she or he can achieve psychological and emotional healing must be re-evaluated in light of Thrasher's pointed failure to get "better." That is not to say the composition of this narrative served no redemptive function for its author, but, rather, that such effect must be understood in complex dialogue with his eventual recidivism and the perpetuation of destructive and self-destructive aspects of his life. Similarly, the assumption that Indigenous literary autobiography, by documenting state-sponsored oppression and even violence, inevitably implies political effects must be weighed in relation to *Skid Row Eskimo*'s poor publication record—having been out of print since the 1970s—and its mediocre distribution among northern peoples.[9]

Furthermore, *Skid Row Eskimo* illustrates that the conditions of possibility for Indigenous life-writing—both of composition and reception—should never be assumed homologous or coherent. More so than any of the other texts studied in this book, Thrasher's is the product of an extremely complex network of enabling and restricting forces. Thrasher had to negotiate the demands of his lawyer, who intended to use the manuscript in Thrasher's defence; his editors, who wanted the narrative to conform to certain standards of autobiography; and an intended Inuit audience far removed from the site of its composition. Multiple voices were involved in the book's creation, and multiple audiences were intended for its consumption. These pressures were further influenced by Thrasher's incarceration, a condition in which, as Dylan Rodriquez states, "the writer ... is never simply *free to write*" (emphasis original).[10]

Despite writing from a position of relative powerlessness, Thrasher is able to forcefully reject certain forms of colonial domination. In a narrative beset on all sides by carceral spaces, from Aklavik Indian Residential School to the BC penitentiary, Thrasher occupies provisional subject positions (however qualified, circumscribed, or fleeting) capable of momentarily destabilizing power relations and creating the possibility for agency and change. Some of the didactic context from the original manuscript demonstrates that Thrasher positions his struggle for self-determination *within* the cracks and crevices of colonial ideology rather than *against* the overwhelming power of colonial rule. Thrasher never presumes an inviolate stance against the assimilative forces of state and church; however, nor does he accept that the integrity of his cultural affiliation and political agency is completely divested by those bodies. Thrasher certainly self-identifies as a victim of historical circumstance and colonial power, but the resilience of his agency throughout victimhood suggests the incompleteness of colonial systems and inadequacy of unproblematized post-colonial binaries.

However, Thrasher's arguments in this vein are provocative rather than conclusive. They require a good deal of critical manoeuvring to adequately unearth. Highlighting the resilience and adaptability of Inuit traditional culture in the face of hegemonic Christianity, Thrasher's suggestive critique culminates in the juxtaposition of a traditional oral tale concerning the sacred importance of caring for orphans with the violent and parentless residential school setting. While Thrasher, in his typically playful way, admonishes the Roman Catholic Church for its exclusivity—severing the bonds among family and community members to create a supposedly 'saved' in-group of thereby orphaned children—he champions the inclusiveness of Inuit culture, symbolized by its integration of orphans as family members while recognizing and nurturing their individual autonomy.

Here Thrasher's critique becomes unexpectedly complicated. Although he holds aloft Inuit notions of familial responsibility, inclusiveness, and care as values toward which to aspire, he covertly admits in his narrative to abandoning no less than four women he has impregnated and their born or unborn children, thereby troubling the moral legitimacy of his argument. However, I believe that Thrasher's failure to live up to the values he puts forth, rather than vitiating his argument, actually adds to it a new level of meaning. Thrasher's inability or unwillingness to parent reflects the plausible consequences of the violation, by residential schooling, of Inuit familial bonds. This chapter delineates this intricate relationship between text and context, while linking it to the latent political potential of Thrasher's narrative.

THE INUIT EXPERIENCE OF COLONIALISM

The Inuit occupy a distinctive place among Indigenous peoples in the colonial history of Canada.[11] Because their resettlement was not required for repopulation by Euro-descendants, who tended to cluster along what would become Canada's southern border, the Inuit were able to avoid many aspects of assimilationist policy until relatively recently. The federal government had little desire to access

Inuit land prior to construction of the Distant Early Warning (DEW) Line after World War II and the discovery of northern mineral deposits in the 1950s. For this reason, Ottawa employed what Olive Patricia Dickason has termed an "ad hoc approach"[12] to administering Inuit affairs until the mid-twentieth century, leaving the Inuit out of the *Indian Act*,[13] treaty negotiations, and early residential school policy. Considering the Arctic to be an agricultural impossibility and an implausible site for industrial development, the federal government initially avoided encouraging resettlement to permanent communities for the traditionally nomadic Inuit, fearing, quite correctly, that in such conditions the Inuit would have little means of self-support. This affected the extension of residential school policy to the Inuit, for whom the standard program of the Bible and plough, literacy and labour, appeared even less practicable than it had for other Indigenous peoples. John Milloy has noted that even such fervent proponents of the residential school system as Duncan Campbell Scott recognized that, in relation to the Inuit, "such schools defied logic because no thought was being given to 'what sort of education [was] to be imparted and how this education [could] be useful to pupils in after life' when that life, in such an isolated region, would be almost exclusively a traditional one."[14] As a result, traditional modes of existence persisted for the Inuit far longer than for the more aggressively dispossessed and assimilated Indigenous tribes to the South, with subsistence hunting and fishing merely augmented in the years prior to 1950 by trapping for furs. And, as Robin McGrath notes, while trading with Europeans and Euro-Canadians in the nineteenth and early twentieth centuries "disrupted traditional life by fostering a dependence on manufactured goods and by encouraging trapping for fur rather than hunting for food, fuel and clothing, ... it was still in the best interest of the traders to see that the Inuit maintained a nomadic way of life."[15] So it was of the Canadian government.

The non-existence of a defined federal policy did not, however, amount to a complete reprieve for the Inuit from colonial imposition. Despite the climate and the difficulty of proselytizing non-sedentary peoples, missionaries were making inroads into northern communities in the late nineteenth and early twentieth centuries. In 1912 the Roman Catholic Church established a mission at Chesterfield Inlet, NWT, and, as Thasher's editors note in their foreword, "the year [Thrasher] was born, 1937, was the year the Anglican and Roman Catholic Missions were founded in Tuktoyaktuk."[16] In the vast Arctic, "proselytizing required extended travel, by dog sled in the winter and by boat in the summer,"[17] but, by the 1930s, neither Christianity nor literacy was uncommon among Inuit peoples.[18]

Significantly, adaptations to colonialism undertaken *by* the Inuit to this point, including engagement in the fur trade, sporadic religious conversion, and acquisition of literacy, did not necessarily forfeit the integrity of their social and cultural existence.[19] While this is an easier point to make regarding literacy and trapping than Christian conversion, the Inuit still lived off the land, still conducted ceremonies with the help of their medicine men and women, still told stories according to their oral traditions (adapted by some to written literature), and still maintained the agency to determine which aspects of Euro-Canadian culture and religion they would adopt, uncompelled by federal legislation or economic necessity.

In the course of Thrasher's short life, all this would change. Myriad factors conspired to provoke an aggressive about-face in federal policy and to chase the Inuit from their land between 1940 and 1960. First, the collapse of the fur trade economically devastated virtually the entire Inuit population. Thrasher discusses the speed and totality of the market's breakdown during his youth and adolescence:

> I remembered as a small boy ... seeing trappers in the spring coming into Aklivik with big smiles on their faces, their sleds heaped high with furs. ... They were making a good living from trapping, then. The prices were good, the furs plentiful. But as the years passed, I saw their smiles turning to frowns. Fur prices were falling. By 1957, it was no longer possible to live by trapping alone. Half of the population of Aklivik was relying on government handouts. It was either that, or join the white construction gangs, or starve.[20]

The loss of the fur trade, exacerbated by lack of game available for subsistence-hunting, provoked a mass exodus of Inuit into urban communities throughout the North.

Second, in the wake of the Second World War, the Canadian and American governments began the construction of the DEW Line, which, although providing some jobs to economically devastated Inuit, disrupted migratory patterns of game and produced enormous amounts of waste into the fragile Arctic ecosystem, resulting in the further decimation of Inuit food sources.

Third, the discovery of mineral deposits below the Arctic tundra led to exploratory drilling, more waste, more disruption of habitat, and more desire among government and southern business interests to remove the Inuit from their land, which would thereby become more readily accessible to economic exploitation. In a brilliant analogy, Thrasher writes, "We, the Eskimo people are like the sun spots which sometimes appear on the lens of an astronomer. We are in the way, we blur the picture the white man has of the future of the North" (154). In his manuscript he goes further: "If the Arctic coast was made of solid mineral of economical value the Eskimo people would be pushed right into the ocean to get what is under his foot."[21]

The government's desire to exploit the rich resources beneath Inuit land, coupled with the more altruistic goal of addressing the loss of the Inuit economy, led to a more hands-on approach to Inuit affairs in the 1950s. The government wanted the Inuit off the land and into communities—and, in many cases, they were off it anyway because they could no longer glean from it the means of subsistence—yet they wanted to avoid financially supporting the entire Inuit population through welfare. Again, residential schooling seemed a viable (fiscally responsible) option. It could provide the students with skills that might ease their transition to a non-land-based northern economy, and, because it was being introduced over seventy years after residential schooling in the South, it could avoid many of the pitfalls—at least in theory—of the southern institutions that were already moving toward closure. In *A National Crime*, John Milloy writes that the residential school policy applied to the Inuit in 1955 "seemed to strive … to be more than just a replication of the Indian Affairs system" (247); however, he acknowledges that,

> in the operation of the system, no effective balance was struck between cultural preservation, the rather ill-defined idea of modernization, of producing 'better Indians and Eskimos,' and assimilation. … The rhetoric of cultural sensitivity and preservation was not in the end matched by the reality of the system, itself, nor could it ever have been given the wider policy and developmental context in which the system functioned and that it served. (251)

Although gesturing toward respect of Indigenous cultures, the northern residential schools remained largely a church initiative in which English-language instruction and compulsory Christian conversion overshadowed such minimal pedagogical advances as including some Inuit artwork in textbooks and teaching Inuit carving.

THE EXPERIENCE OF ANTHONY THRASHER

At times, Anthony Thrasher's life illustrates with alarming clarity the climate of change affecting the North during these years. He was a residential school student, an early Christian, and among the first Inuit to be transported to the South for technical training by the federal government. As his editors argue, it is easy to see how his life "paralleled the process of urbanisation of the North" (x), and how "in the prime of his life he became a symbol of something new" (viii). However, as they correctly conclude, "in the end none of it was that simple" (viii). Thrasher's life-narrative functions as much at odds as in concert with some paradigmatic storyline about the Inuit experience of northern development and assimilation in this century. The complexity of Thrasher's life story cautions against generalization.

Thrasher was born in Paulatuk, NWT, on July 21, 1937, among the youngest of twenty-one siblings. During his early years, the family lived semi-nomadically, with Anthony's father, Billy Thrasher, hunting, fishing, and trapping for food, clothing, and trade while also working for the Roman Catholic Church, to which he was a convert. According to Thrasher's editors, "his father ... was helpmate to the first missionary Fathers [in Tuktoyaktuk]" (x); Thrasher adds that his father "worked for the church for over twenty years" (54). Billy Thrasher was a relentlessly religious man who demanded prayer and obedience from his children, but he was also a great storyteller of traditional Inuit tales, some of which pepper his son's narrative. Thrasher's early life was thus subject to a variety of traditional and non-traditional influences, from orature to Christian dogma, from subsistence hunting to alcoholism. Thrasher's mother died of alcohol poisoning when he was still in infancy, and his father and stepmother drank heavily throughout his childhood.

At the age of six, Thrasher was sent, by parental authority rather than legislative coercion (as would have been the case in the contemporary South), to the Roman Catholic residential school in Aklavik. The Aklavik school was not a product of the 1955 federal government initiative and, as such, lacked any semblance of "cultural sensitivity" or localized curriculum supposedly infused into the later residential school model. Rather, the Aklavik school belonged to the earlier mode of residential schooling prevalent in the South, presenting somewhat of a northern anomaly. Because the Inuit existed outside the domain of Indian Affairs, the handful of northern residential schools in existence prior to 1950—including the Roman Catholic and Anglican schools at Aklavik, Shingle Point School, and Fort George on the eastern coast of James Bay[22]—were financed initially by the Department of the Interior and then, after government restructuring, by the Northern Affairs Branch of the Department of Mines and Resources, neither of which had a defined residential school policy. These schools were instituted at the behest of missionary bodies and were funded, administered, and overseen in a random fashion by governing bodies with scant experience of either education or Native issues. Without guidance from the federal bodies that officially ran the schools (at least on paper), clerical staff and teachers emulated more southerly residential institutions, allowing religion to dominate pedagogy, corporal punishment to dominate discipline, and frugality to dominate the feeding and clothing of students. Unsurprisingly, Milloy describes these early northern schools as "dreadful monuments" and as "cautionary tales to be read and their mistakes avoided."[23]

Thrasher's experience of residential school, like almost everything else, was mixed. He didn't excel at his studies, but he gained some recognition among both classmates and teachers for his ability to trap for extra food during outdoor activities and for his exceptional physical labour. By his own admission, he "was not too bright, but ... was a physical powerhouse for work" (26). Thrasher raised his status within the student body fairly early by beating up three boys from the local Anglican residential school in a brawl. He suffered, however, from familial separation and, in particular, forced segregation from his sisters at the adjacent girls' school, with whom he could have no contact. Also, although certain nuns did provide a nurturing influence, like Sister Alice Rae, whom Thrasher claims to have "loved as much as [his] real mother" (13), he suffered physical and psychological abuse from some of his instructor-guardians. In one particularly troubling example, Sister Gilbert whipped Thrasher and three other boys with a "three-foot watch chain made of silver" for supposedly "sinning with some girls in the basement of the school" (37). The incident left a profound effect on young Thrasher, who refers to it on three different occasions throughout his autobiography. He says at one point: "My back was bleeding but something else burned more. Shame. It was branded in my brain. The silver chain has never left my mind. Even to this day you can see the scars on my back. When I touch my back I feel the pain in my mind" (38).

At the age of thirteen, Thrasher was discharged from Aklavik Residential School to help look after his family after his father experienced a debilitating stroke. He returned to Tuktoyaktuk and began hunting, fishing, and trapping to support his younger siblings, stepmother, and partially paralyzed father. However, when Thrasher was sixteen, his parents, who had begun drinking more and more heavily after his father's stroke, drove him from home "for good" under the threat of violence. Thrasher recalls "walk[ing] to Aklivik, nearly a hundred miles away. It took me three days, and I cried all the way. ... I'd sooner have taken a whipping with a silver chain than be turned away by my dad" (60–61). Completely alone and relatively autonomous for the first time, Thrasher worked various jobs, from rein-deer herder to construction worker on the DEW Line, before being convinced by a "government man" to fly to Edmonton and take a "six-week course in how to drive machines" (68).

Thrasher left the Arctic for the first time at the age of nineteen, one of the first to take part in a government initiative to make the Inuit more employable in the North. With neither baggage nor money, he and over thirty young Inuit men were abandoned by their federal hosts in a rough section of downtown Edmonton, where they were left for the weekend to adjust to an alienating cityscape among the homeless, the addicts, and the prostitutes. Although he was no stranger to alcohol, it was here under the conditions of exile that Thrasher and his companions began drinking with alarming ferocity. Thrasher began "drinking *before* as well as *after* school" (original emphasis, 78), and, as for his "formal education," he claims, "I don't remember too much of it. I was too busy getting sick and drunk" (78). After six weeks of heavy drinking, health problems related to climate change, and fre-quent hiring of prostitutes, Thrasher and the others were flown back to the Arctic, where they discovered they would actually be paid less at the jobs the government had arranged for them than they had made before taking the course.[24] Besides his newly acquired mechanical skills, Thrasher also brought to the North a debili-tating dependence on alcohol that made holding employment difficult. He claims in his manuscript to have been imprisoned over thirty times in northern towns on "drunk charges" over the next few years. Unable to hold a job or a relationship, Thrasher again migrated south to try his fortunes in urban centres.

Back on the streets of Edmonton's skid row, Thrasher's narrative takes a turn to the macabre. Detailing horrific beatings by thugs and policemen, muggings, agonizing bouts with detox, and trips to the drunk tank, Thrasher's skid row writ-ings chronicle an ongoing enslavement to alcohol addiction augmented by street life's attendant violence. The author's downward spiral culminates—if a life af-fected by something as incoherent as alcoholism can be said straightforwardly to 'culminate'—in the beating death of an elderly man named Charles Ratkovitch on November 6, 1969. As Dale S. Blake, the only other scholar at this point to deal intimately with Thrasher's work, notes, "When Thrasher was arrested later that day for drinking in a public place[,] [p]olice found that he carried two wal-lets, one of them Ratkovitch's, and that he also had in his possession the keys to Ratkovitch's apartment."[25] Thrasher claims never to have met Ratkovitch, and only to remember having "stopped a fight. Two women and two men were beating up an old man."[26] Two days later he was charged with non-capital murder.

Remanded to Spy Hill Penitentiary, "a squat little place in a valley in the rolling hills west of Calgary" (112), where he stayed six months before being convicted of manslaughter,[27] Thrasher "spent most … days and nights in [his] cell, putting [his] thoughts down on paper" (132). Sober by necessity, he began to record his life story, along with some traditional tales, anecdotes about friends and relatives, and extended arguments about the state of Inuit social and political culture and ongoing imperialism in the North:

> It was something to do to pass the time, and it was also a way of edu-
> cating myself. And I thought that maybe some day my writing would be
> read by Eskimo children and they would know what to watch out for, so
> they wouldn't end up like me, in a white man's cage. When I began to write,
> I didn't even know about putting periods after sentences and beginning
> new ones with capital letters. I learned all that and much more by myself
> in Spy Hill. (132)

In the shadow of a woefully inadequate residential school education, Thrasher actually "learned" to be a writer in prison. Thrasher writes in his manuscript that some of those in "jails during the 1960 and 1970 [got] a better education than we did [in residential school] in the 1940s" (251).

When Thrasher's court-appointed attorney, William Stilwell, "discovered that his client was taking this initiative, he encouraged him to preserve the writings."[28] Stilwell had his client send him periodic writing instalments, which he had typed up word-for-word in what would eventually become the completed manuscript. The lawyer's interest in Thrasher's manuscript was not simply aesthetic or historical. Advocating a thoroughness of memory far more acute than simple nostalgic reminiscence—actually telling his client, "'Recall everything you can, Tony'" (132)—Stilwell clearly envisaged an audience for the writings beyond Thrasher and himself. The lawyer would eventually quote from the manuscript during Thrasher's trial in an effort to embed the specific circumstances of the case in a larger narrative of colonial intrusion and violence. As Chris Cunneen has argued in a parallel Australian context, "When theft of the land, dispossession and discriminatory legislation are considered, the answers to the questions of 'Who is the criminal?' and 'What is justice?' take on a different meaning."[29] Stilwell endeavoured, through the manuscript, to contextualize the prospect of Thrasher's criminality within a broader life-history and a cultural/political history (much like

I am attempting to do in this chapter), showing how Indigenous people seldom confront the structures of Canadian criminal law as neutral and how understanding the circumstances of a given criminal act without recourse to its historical backdrop can never be sufficient.[30]

Irrespective of Stilwell's evocative intent, the eventual use of the manuscript during the trial complicates Thrasher's narrative position immensely. The fact that, as Thrasher was well aware, his writings would participate in the struggle toward his release from prison undoubtedly influenced his writing process. In his article "Against the Discipline of 'Prison Writing': Toward a Theoretical Conception of Contemporary Radical Prison Praxis," Dylan Rodriquez reminds us that writing from a carceral space involves a complex mode of "cultural production that is both *enabled* and *coerced* by state captivity, a dynamic condition that pre-empts and punishes some forms of writing while encouraging and even forcing others" (original emphasis).[31] In Thrasher's case, the conditions that make possible his autobiography include not only the time, isolation, and sobriety forced upon him, but also the utilitarian potential of writing for a judicial audience. The daunting prospect of writing to authority, of attempting to influence through words an adjudicating body that could quite literally "punish" his narrative inclusion of certain ideas and incidents, clearly must have "encouraged" Thrasher to write in certain ways, to avoid certain topics, and to self-identify in a particular manner. To reiterate Rodriquez's earlier point, "The writer in prison is never simply *free to write*" (409).

We must caution ourselves, however, against assuming that the imposition of judicial expectation functions in a programmatic way. The carceral conditions do not create the text; the writer creates the text, and the carceral conditions merely apply pressure to the writer to mould her or his writing in this way or that. This is why Rodriquez terms the situation "dynamic" rather than simply restrictive or oppressive; the author can write against or in accordance with carceral pressures, or both (vacillating back and forth), or in an infinite array of positions in between. Throughout his manuscript, Thrasher is clearly cognizant of an audience of non-Native figures of authority, whom he warns not to "[jump] to conclusions on many things I have written and you don't fully understand" (411) and tells not to "be afraid to ask me questions. I like answering things I know" (163). At one point he even acknowledges that something he has said "may be damaging to me. It may even endanger my chance of freedom" (191).[32] His awareness of this particular audience, however, does not necessarily determine what he will write.

In a striking example of nonconformity, Thrasher recounts a story he heard as a small boy about an Inuk man held captive by the RCMP in the eastern Arctic. Collapsing his own narrative voice with that of the prisoner in the story—stating, "I'll put myself in this Eskimo's place. I can think like one"[33]—Thrasher describes the man's inability to understand his incarceration or the unkind treatment he receives at the hands of his captors; he speaks of his fear, his discomfort, and his desire for escape. Thrasher continues: "So I see my chance for freedom a rifle and some shells. With no sound I load the gun to kill my tormentors. I shoot the boss police in the side he looks at me, still alive. He said why, why did you do this. Then he falls dead maybe. I don't like to do this but I want to be free" (426–27). Achieving only a fleeting liberty through the agency of violence, the Inuk man is again captured by "red coats" and led off "in irons and chains like a dog" (427). Taken to Herschel Island, he awaits a terrible retribution:

> A man with a big beard comes to see me with a book. Why? Now they drag me up to a high place. A rope goes around my neck. Some people laughing. Hang the savage the dirty greasy savage. All at once I drop I hear my neck break. My tongue comes out trying for air. My head spins a while. Then peace at last. I have suffered too much anyways in my life. Now I am happy and free for ever. Free from cold and hunger. Free from my tormentors and chains, irons. Now all I have left my soul my spirit. This no one can take away from me. (427–28)

Given that Thrasher is writing in prison to an audience including the judiciary from whom he hopes to secure his freedom, his narrative identification with an imprisoned Inuk who kills his RCMP captors seems a strange and potentially counterproductive manoeuvre. *Of course* it is illogical for a prisoner composing autobiography to narrate in the first person this tale he had "heard" as a child. *Of course* it is strategically unsound for one on trial for murder to publicly sympathize with the killer of two officers of His Majesty King George.[34] But, by doing so, Thrasher introduces an element of play into his writing that qualifies the absoluteness of judicial authority, suggesting that through writing he can self-identify as powerful too, even if only for a moment and even if that power is supposedly another's.

I introduce this passage to illustrate how Thrasher avoids accommodating his writing to the expectations of authority in a straightforward manner. He strains against the pressure of power's gaze as much as he adheres to it. Although the judicial audience was extremely important to Thrasher, particularly in terms of legal expediency, it was not his only intended audience. Any sincere attempt to engage with Thrasher's autobiographical writings must recognize that they were composed for a few different—but not necessarily mutually exclusive—audiences, among whom they were intended to produce a range of effects. It was written not only for the judiciary, but for a non-Native readership ignorant of both Inuit and skid row existence, an Inuit readership robbed of its traditions through colonialism, a Native readership eager to understand the similarities and differences of Inuit colonial experiences, a broad readership unaware of the realities of prison life, and other audiences as well.

Journalist Gerard Deagle covered Thrasher's trial for the *Calgary Herald*. Sitting in a Calgary courtroom in the early months of 1970, he heard startling testimony about the life of the accused, as well as excerpts from the manuscript quoted by Stilwell. As Blake reports, Deagle's "interest [was] piqued by Thrasher's writing,"[35] and he became intent on working with Thrasher to bring the Inuk's life story to public light. According to *Skid Row Eskimo*'s jacket sleeve, Thrasher's manuscript "was turned over to Deagle and fellow-journalist Alan Mettrick, who spent hundreds of hours working on it, and taping more of Thrasher's recollections." Between Thrasher's sentencing in April 1970 and the book's publication in 1976, Deagle and Mettrick edited the 512-page stream-of-consciousness manuscript, containing vexing grammar, unpredictable capital use, erratic spelling, period-only punctuation, and no paragraph breaks, into a 164-page collaborative autobiography of nineteen chapters. Deagle and Mettrick reconfigured Thrasher's sprawling narrative chronologically and divided it into four sections (and hence his life into four periods): infancy through residential schooling, early adulthood in the North, exile on Edmonton's skid row, and the prison years. The last of these sections details the period after Thrasher's initial imprisonment and, of necessity, isn't taken from the manuscript at all, but rather from taped interviews conducted by Deagle and Mettrick and possibly later prison writings.[36] The published text, therefore, can be generically positioned somewhere between the as-told-to autobiographies analyzed by Arnold Krupat in the 1980s and later written autobiographies discussed by David Brumble and others. Thrasher indeed *wrote* the overwhelming majority of *Skid Row Eskimo*, but what he wrote was so heavily edited for both style and content as to warrant, in the eyes of the publisher, Griffin House, the accreditation of 'collaborative' status to both Deagle and Mettrick on the book's title page. Furthermore, much of the book's final section, taken from interviews, was literally *told to* Deagle and Mettrick who copied it down, edited it, and largely determined its place in the text. *Skid Row Eskimo* thus emerges out of an intricate and multifaceted production process through what Brumble has described in his brief analysis of the text as a "quite heavy … editorial hand."[37]

Since Krupat's work in the early 1980s, critics have generally considered delineating the precise nature of collaborative relationships between Native narrators and their non-Native collector/editor/translators to be of great importance to—if not *the* crucial aspect of—progressive literary analysis of Indigenous autobiography. Recognizing the impossibility of neutral editorial and publishing processes for the work of those whose cultures possess very limited control over the means of literary production,[38] Krupat argues that "by persisting in ignoring their mode of production, [critics] do more immediate and immediately discoverable violence to Native texts than to the standard, canonic texts of the Western tradition."[39] Krupat's instigations resonated loudly throughout the 1980s and early 1990s in a critical climate dominated by the interrelated and highly political issues of Aboriginal voice and cultural authenticity. Because the relationship between "white" editor and "Indian" author was inevitably power-laden, how could the literary critic be sure that the textual artefact adequately—or, gasp, 'authentically'—portrayed Native voice? The danger literary critics faced in glossing over the complexities of Native autobiographies' material production, then, was to further stifle Native narrative voice, which had already, perhaps, been imposed upon through the editing process. In response to this difficulty, it became somewhat of a critical imperative during this period to interrogate the methodologies of individual editors in order to gain better access to the original words of Native narrators and thereby less mediated contact with Aboriginal voices. As Kathleen Sands notes, critics began to focus on "the collector/editor [as] the key to unlocking these cross-cultural autobiographical texts because [they] assume[d] he or she possesse[d] the exclusive power to control the narrative presentation."[40]

In the case of *Skid Row Eskimo*, it becomes extremely difficult to determine with any precision the relationship between 'editors' and 'author,' to locate where Thrasher's voice ends and where those of Deagle and Mettrick begin. In their introduction, Thrasher's editors provide only a single sentence to clarify their function in producing the published text: "Our role was to collate what was essentially a loose-leaf diary into narrative form, authenticate that narrative as thoroughly as possible and expand it" (x). Their unwillingness to describe the processes of collation, authentication, and expansion leaves the reader entirely unsure of what they have added to Thrasher's words and what they have suppressed, with significant implications to the meaning of the text.

It would be extremely easy for me, given my good fortune in acquiring Thrasher's original manuscript from Mr. Stilwell, to make *Skid Row Eskimo*'s shadowy editing process the focus of this chapter. By cross-referencing the published text with the manuscript, I could identify omissions, additions, changes, and reorganization, and discuss them all in terms of the editors' 'manipulation' of Thrasher's words. Locating the power wielded by Deagle and Mettrick within a colonial context, I might then have labelled such interventions the 're-victimization' of the narrator. Focusing on the editors' subjection of Thrasher's original manuscript to the laws of the Queen's English and the tyranny of Western generic expectations, I might have claimed that this metaphorical 'imprisoning' of Thrasher's tribal diction emulates the federal government's incarceration of his body, and that both, in a way, re-enact the colonial imposition of residential school. Such an approach, however, would not only be intellectually irresponsible, but also critically untenable (and not simply because the extremity of physical imprisonment cannot so easily be reconciled with actions wrought in textuality and narrative).

The hyperbolic extension of post-colonialist critique to cross-cultural editing processes sketched above is, to my mind, wrong-headed for two reasons. The first is that it takes the focus away from the persisting (and resisting) agency of Indigenous narrators within even the most heavily edited texts. By focusing too narrowly on how non-Native America—in this case, non-Native Canada—controls the ultimate presentation of Native textual products, critics risk muting Native voice, or, by Krupat's own admission, "leav[ing] the Indian silent entirely in [their] discourse"[41]— risks that seem a regression rather than a progression in the decolonization of Indigenous writing. The irony is that in seeking to account for non-Native editorial processes and thereby to gain less mediated access to Native sources, critics like Krupat at times divert attention away from the very source to which they desire greater access. For the result all too frequently can be a discussion among non-Native critics about how non-Native editors and their non-Native publishing houses ultimately influence—or, worse, create—the 'meaning' of Native texts. By ignoring the agency Native narrators maintain throughout the editing process and opting, as Sands argues, to see them as "powerless victims of institutional collectors and inscribers," critics "simply perpetuate the colonial process."[42]

Sands continues that although "it may ease our collective guilt about the texts we study and the careers we have based on Native cultures to read and write about collector/editors as colonial agents, ... it does not advance the discipline. It's a ready-made paradigm that requires little more than picking out the right incidents and examples to prove an already obvious point."[43] The fact remains that without the editing of Deagle and Mettrick, Thrasher's narrative would never have reached publication. And, as he articulates clearly in his manuscript, Thrasher wanted his work read. In 1976 there was virtually no market for Inuit autobiography beyond isolated pockets of academic 'experts' interested predominantly in such texts' anthropological significance. Thrasher's account of Edmonton's skid row, detox, and prison did not, of course, fit the 'documenting dying cultures' anthropological paradigm, rendering it of little interest to the diminutive academic audience of the day, more inclined to appreciate Inuit works like *I, Nuligak*, which focus entirely on northern existence.[44]

And Deagle and Mettrick were journalists, not ethnographers. The journalistic medium strives, in its (generally) concise reportage, toward a perceived 'objective factuality' quite distinct from the cultural relativism that distinguishes modern ethnography. Journalists endeavour to lay bare the 'facts' of a given incident or issue without drawing undue attention to themselves, while modern ethnographers strive to detail self-consciously their own mediating position as a crucial aspect of their eventual critical products (which, scientific though they may be, are considered neither entirely *objective* nor entirely *factual*). Finally, *Skid Row Eskimo* was published by Griffin House, a small Toronto press that neither published academic material nor had the resources to produce a larger, more inclusive version of Thrasher's life story. So while my critical training leads me to regret the lack of self-reflexivity in Deagle and Mettrick's editing process, there doesn't seem much chance that they could have provided a self-conscious, postmodern, anthropological edition of Thrasher's text, even if they had wanted to.

The second reason I believe a hyperbolic post-colonialist critique of *Skid Row Eskimo* to be limiting has to do with the relationship between text and context, and with the social lives of stories. The proposition that an original manuscript offers greater access to a text's 'meaning'—or, at least, the author's intended 'meaning'—is based on two assumptions: first, that the conditions of possibility for the original composition were conducive to unmediated articulation and, further, that the author got it right the first time; and, second, that the 'meaning' of written texts is inherent rather than produced through engagement with readers. Clearly, the carceral context of Thrasher's writing precludes any notion of entirely unmediated composition; but, even had conditions been different, the idea that his original draft would necessarily be more accurate, or more 'authentic', remains speculative. Compare *Skid Row Eskimo*, for example, to Tomson Highway's *Kiss of the Fur Queen*. Recognized as one of Canada's premier writers, Highway claims a level of artistic control over his works that Thrasher could never dream of, and yet even *Kiss of the Fur Queen* was edited down with Doubleday Canada to a publication about half the size of its original manuscript. Also, much like Thrasher's text, *Kiss of the Fur Queen* was divided into sections upon the suggestion of a non-Native editor.[45] Yet no one claims *Kiss of the Fur Queen* to be a tainted work or, to borrow a phrase from Krupat, the product of a white initiative. The point is that both Highway and Thrasher *decided* that the published versions of their texts were worthy of publication. And although Thrasher's power over the ultimate shape of *Skid Row Eskimo* did not likely approach Highway's power over *Kiss of the Fur Queen*, his agency in signing off on the finished product should not be disregarded.

Furthermore, the published text is the one to which audiences have access, the one that functions in the public and political world. The New Historicist attack on Formalism within the literary critical community at large is heightened in the Aboriginal context, wherein texts so frequently engage in political debates, social movements, identity politics, and processes of cultural revitalization. Native literary theorists like Craig Womack have argued convincingly for the necessity of "break[ing] down oppositions between the world of literature and the very real struggles of American Indian communities, arguing for both an intrinsic and extrinsic relationship between the two."[46] In the words of Jace Weaver, "Native literature both reflects and shapes contemporary Native identity and community,"[47] forming a relational and ethical connection he refers to as "communitism." In other words, as weapons in the battle for what Anishinabe writer Gerald Vizenor calls "survivance," Indigenous texts are not inherently 'meaningful' in isolation; their 'meanings' are produced through interactions with audiences who, in the words of David L. Moore, "participate imaginatively in the performance"[48] to create political or social effects out of words on the page. For Womack, Weaver, and Moore, the existence of Indigenous community both prior to composition (as source) and after composition (as audience) forms an a priori backdrop to sophisticated critical praxis. To engage with Indigenous texts according to this relational commitment, one must account for the text that reaches that audience, which means, in the case of Thrasher, dealing predominantly with the final publication.

So where does that leave Thrasher's manuscript in relationship to *Skid Row Eskimo*? To focus solely on Thrasher's original prison writings would be to disregard the communitist potential of residential school survival narratives. At the same time, to focus solely on the published narrative would be to ignore the politics embedded in the situation of Thrasher's literary agency and his actual writings. Therefore, I will use the manuscript to assist in understanding *Skid Row Eskimo*, showing how the literary arsenal Thrasher employs in the eventual publication is clarified and elucidated by the much longer prison manuscript.

THRASHER: TWO-WAY ETHNOGRAPHER

Skid Row Eskimo opens with a gesture toward the ethnographic trope of the 'Vanishing Indian': "*Listen to the North Wind. It has come to take us away. The name, Inuvialuit,*[49] *will only be heard in the wind. The land will still be there, the moon will still shine, the Northern Lights will still be bright, and the Midnight Sun will still be seen. But we will be gone forever ...*" (iii). This epigram from Thrasher's original manuscript seems to situate the tale that will follow within a metanarrative of the tragic but inevitable corrosion of primitive cultures and peoples in the face of an overwhelming modern civilization. By the autobiography's final pages, many of the forces conspiring to hasten the physical and cultural destruction of the Inuit have been made explicit. *Skid Row Eskimo*'s penultimate paragraph reads:

> Oil explorations have resulted in the deaths of thousands of fish which were left to drift down the Mackenzie River. These same explorations have destroyed thousands of miles of timber in trapping country. The ships that will carry oil in the Arctic will destroy our trapping and hunting on the ice. Water and air pollution will eventually destroy the foxes, seals and polar bears. The fish and the whales will be gone from the Arctic Ocean. Finally the Eskimos will be gone. (164)

A cursory glance at these bookends might lead one to assume that the body of Thrasher's narrative consists largely of anthropological data: customs, traditions, linguistic and spiritual materials copied down and saved from extinction by a sensitive archivist before the original source culture is "*gone forever.*" Thrasher, however, struggles against the 'inevitable extinction' model throughout his narrative, invoking and manipulating anthropological discourse to ensure the survival of Inuit culture, rather than to document its demise.

Thrasher indeed self-identifies as a kind of ethnographer, but his subject population is not solely, as one might expect, the Indigenous inhabitants of the Arctic, of whom he has intimate knowledge as a cultural insider; it is also the colonial population of the South, from whom he fears encroachment and assimilation. In his manuscript, Thrasher clarifies the motivation behind this reversal of traditional ethnographic roles, stating, "I am studying the white man and his world because he is out of control" (316), and also, "I study them like they study us" (289). Recognizing that the survival of Inuit culture depends not only on the availability of Inuit cultural knowledge, but also on keen analysis of those outside forces that would promote the termination of such knowledge, Thrasher endeavours to record in his autobiography observations about the nature of 'white culture.' Narratively constructing his encounters with Euro-Canada through ethnographic tropes, Thrasher commences his investigation of 'white culture' through an examination of the residential school.

Although missionary presence within remote northern communities was no longer uncommon during Thrasher's youth, the experience of residential schooling for Inuit children still was. Within his narrative, Thrasher depicts the Aklavik school as an alien environment to which the reader must be conditioned. He recalls "trembling at the edge of the property, refusing to take one more step into that strange, forbidding world of mission school" (3), before being "dragged, kicking and screaming" by the nuns "into the big school house" (4). He goes on to explain to the uninitiated—possibly Inuit—reader the unique behaviours exhibited within this alien world, supplying cultural context to render them comprehensible. For example, he relates how any student caught complaining about the school's food would be forced by the nuns to "drink a whole can of cod liver oil, to do penance for committing something they called a venial sin. That was smaller than a mortal sin, and something else called a sacrilege was even bigger than a mortal sin" (14). He elaborates on the importance of these distinctions within the school's cosmology: "You never went to Hell on venials" (14). Thrasher continues: "We were told [by the nuns] not to play with the girls, because that would be a sin.... I was taught not to look at girls, and not to look at dogs mating. But I had seen these things long before I went to school. I had seen people in the sex act when I was as young as three years of age. I knew exactly what it was, and how to do it, by the time I was six" (14–15). Thrasher invokes pre-residential school experiences from his Inuit family life to explain, by contrast, the cultural context of the Aklavik school. Stressing the difference between the social and spiritual systems of the (semi-) traditional Inuit and the Roman Catholic Euro-Canadian (as evidenced within the residential school setting), Thrasher inaugurates his discussion of the non-Inuit 'Other.' To more closely analyze his subject population, Thrasher-as-ethnographer ultimately submits to conditions of exile in the South, which enables him to report back to an implied Inuit readership regarding his perceptions of white culture and perhaps assist that readership to better arm itself against colonial violation in an increasingly cosmopolitan North.[50] Although his departure from the North isn't entirely voluntary, within his narrative Thrasher can self-identify as an intrepid anthropologist, like Boas or Radin, who leaves behind his comfortable cultural surround to analyze a different social system—one he finds on Edmonton's skid row.

Thrasher's southern "fieldwork" experience in many ways emulates the "archetypal quest pattern" Renée Hulan identifies in traditional ethnography:

> The hero (ethnographer) becomes separated from her or his own society in order to enter an alien world, and the rest of the story develops around the initiation into that world. The initiation required by fieldwork entails a transformation from cultural "outsider" to cultural "insider" whereby the ethnographer gains the knowledge necessary to enter the subject culture. Upon return, the hero shares experience with readers either by creating the feeling of "being there" that makes the field experience the readers' experience or by establishing intimacy with readers through a self-conscious, confessional form in which the ethnographer acts as storyteller.[51]

Thrasher's inaugural view of the "alien" world of Edmonton is of "millions of beautiful lights" (71), seen through the tiny window of a C-46 transport plane. Invoking the exotic, he notes, "I had never seen anything like that in my life" (72). Thrasher's research of "white man's ways" (*ms.* 289) is quickly limited to a particular subculture of the indigent and addicted, from which he gains most of his insights. His "introduction to civilization was Skid Row. I met the pimps and prostitutes. I met the bums, bootleggers and muggers. I met the street fighters and their broads, dope addicts and pushers and hustlers" (79). Skilfully manipulating the anthropological binary between civilization and savagery, Thrasher identifies negative aspects of Euro-Canadian existence as embodiments of white culture through synecdoche. Thus skid row is described as a locus of civilization, and venereal disease, "which was all over town," is described in the manuscript as "civilization and you can't stop progress" (142).

Initially unaccustomed to the new surroundings, Thrasher improperly imitates what he thinks are "white man's ways." He recalls, "I slicked my hair down with Noxzema Face Cream. I brushed my teeth with shaving lather. I used to wash my face with mouthwash. I couldn't read labels at all, and I ended up chewing laxatives like candy" (75). Over the following chapters, Thrasher documents his slow acquisition of cultural knowledge and eventual admission into skid row society. Casting off his "outsider" status, Thrasher ultimately claims to have "learn[ed] the dirty tricks of Skid Row" (94), and even to have "learned how to pick up cigarette butts like a genuine bum" (95). Confirming his new-found cultural awareness, Thrasher includes a 'how-to' passage, akin to those found in anthropological works, regarding the creation of a rubbing alcohol cocktail: "You pour water into a bottle till it is about two-thirds full. Then you pour in enough of that pure alcohol until it turns white inside. Then you drink it" (95). By the time he comes to compose his narrative, Thrasher can write from the perspective of a fully initiated skid row dweller; having earned his stripes, he documents the cultural climate of skid row from a position of authority, which remains the essential critical requirement of traditional anthropology. As Hulan predicts, in his vivid retelling of experiences such as being beaten and mugged, Thrasher "create[s] the feeling of 'being there' that makes the field experience the readers' experience." He also establishes intimacy with his readers through remarkably frank confessions of personal vice and moral trepidation, drawing his readers closer to the perils and horrors of skid row existence.

Thrasher, however, is never able to return to the North and so complete the "initiatory quest" required of the ethnographic hero. In fact, he writes from a penitentiary in the South, unable to escape the contaminating influence of the skid row culture he has researched and hopes to detail. Unlike the ethnographers Hulan describes, Thrasher cannot construct an entirely triumphant narrative identity in relation to the 'Other,' but is, rather, bound to his exile in a position of subjection. So, although waxing heroic from time to time (and displaying authorial control over ethnographic techniques),[52] Thrasher presents his narrative self most often in the role of *victim*, a significant reversal of authorial position in standard ethnography. He states near the end of *Skid Row Eskimo*, "My story is a little like that ... about a man, an innocent, who tried to join the march of civilization without knowing of the dangers that could trip and squash him" (161–62). Furthermore, Thrasher configures his early period as "cultural outsider" as key to his eventual victimization: "You can never tell who you'll meet on Skid Row, or what they're up to. They see a simple Eskimo who knows nothing of frame-up artists, bookies, loan sharks, crooked ticket-sellers, bootleggers, pimps, prostitutes, queers, muggers, and they prey on you" (97). Meticulously documenting his systematic subjection to the nefarious forces of skid row, Thrasher strives to spare other Inuit his own unpleasant fate. He "hope[s] the younger generation of my people read my story. They will be easy targets, like me, if they are not warned. They should be told, not only about the good side of life in the South, but about the other part" (xi), "so they don't end up like me, in a white man's cage" (132). Portraying the supposedly 'civilized' and 'civilizing' experience as corrosive rather than ennobling, Thrasher resigns to "humble my self for my people," "putting [down] every thing of my experiences in the south country ... [so that] they will know what kind of society to keep away from to be safe" (ms. 218).

Thrasher's construction of narrative identity is complicated by the narrative goal he articulates throughout the preceding quotations. Although he appears to self-identify as victim, his explicit objective of protecting a vulnerable Inuit populous from the clutches of a violating non-Native presence presumes a level of empowerment incompatible with simple victimhood. Literary scholar Dale S. Blake adeptly recognizes this complex area of representation through which Thrasher "constructs himself as ... victimized, but still powerful."[53] For Blake, Thrasher is "an autobiographical rebel who retains agency from a position of relative powerlessness" and "who ensures imaginative survival in difficult conditions.... [He] writes as one who possesses agency, [and] even the power to change others' lives as well as his own."[54] The agency Thrasher accesses *as writer* undermines the completeness of his identification as victim, even though what he writes may be a story of colonial victimization. Thrasher's narrative voice highlights his incapacity to be *solely* a victim or to be *entirely* powerless, regardless of post-colonialist metanarratives to the contrary. The declaration with which Thrasher begins his narrative, "We have been silent too long" (xi)—hearkening back, as it does, to the colonial stereotype of the habitually passive Inuit with which Thrasher will grapple throughout the autobiography—effectively breaks the silence it would lament. "We have been silent too long" is a political performative utterance, which poses as an admission of weakness while claiming discursive power.

The mask of absolute victimhood, donned strategically and sporadically by Thrasher throughout the narrative, conceals an enduring agency that strikes at the heart of what I will call the battle between supposedly violable and inviolable systems. According to colonial metanarratives, Christian spiritual systems are closed, whole, and complete, and therefore inviolable to outside influence. Indigenous spiritual systems, on the other hand, are open, in process, and incomplete, and therefore violable. James (Sakéj) Youngblood Henderson calls this perception "Eurocentric diffusionism," a relational paradigm that "asserts that the normal and natural way that the non-European world progresses—or changes for the better, modernizes, and so on—is by the diffusion (spread) of innovative, progressive ideas from Europe, which flow into it as air flows into a vacuum."[55] In this model of contact situations, Indigenous cultures invariably adapt to the pressures of white culture, which itself remains intact and whole. Supported by Christianity's supposed evidential status via the written "Word" (in relation to oral Indigenous theology), these *perceived* binaries mediated non-Native relations with the Inuit throughout Thrasher's lifetime. The government's assumption that the Inuit were open to unfaltering Euro-Canadian influence is manifest in Thrasher's experiences of residential school, displacement for job training, and incarceration. Within these many carceral spaces, Thrasher would confront the façade of inviolable Euro-Canadian power—or, á la Vizenor, "simulations" of inviolable Euro-Canadian power—and, in return, would play with the façade of Inuit powerlessness and vulnerability to change. In the words of Homi K. Bhabha, quoted earlier, such authorial play on Thrasher's part "is a form of power that is exercised at the very limits of identity and authority, in the mocking spirit of mask and image."[56]

I would argue that Thrasher exploits the subject position of victim not simply, as he states, to "warn" his Inuit readership of possible dangers, but also to expose the capacity for Indigenous strength in light of Euro-Canadian assumptions regarding their inherent weakness. In a shrewd tactical manoeuvre, Thrasher does not simply reverse the violable/inviolable paradigm and assume an impenetrable stance against the often violent forces of assimilation and hegemony. Given the carceral conditions from which he writes, his alcoholism, and the corrosive byproducts of residential schooling, such a stance would be difficult to pull off.[57] Rather, using the notion of "powerful victim" as a provocative tool, Thrasher discursively penetrates the cracks and fissures of colonial ideology to reveal that the Christian systems imposed on the Inuit as 'natural' and 'inevitable' are themselves incomplete and violable. At the same time, he champions the adaptive capacity of Inuit traditionalism as itself empowering and, in this way, encourages his Inuit readership to claim control of their culture and the future of the North. In his manuscript, he argues that the "Eskimo people will never survive to a far future if he is always led by a string like the white men are doing now" (468–69). He adds,

"No one knows what the Eskimo people want or what the Eskimo people should do to adapt to the new culture socially [better] than an Eskimo himself. It is just like the alcoholic. Who knows more about alcoholism than the alcoholic himself. No doctor psychiatrist or any one can explain alcoholism better than a sober alcoholic who has had the natural experience and has suffered through it" (507–08).

In the final 200 pages of his manuscript, Thrasher moves away from personal reminiscence to address the social, economic, and political problems affecting his people. Having detailed what he perceives to be the important events of his life, he turns his attention to the broader context in which those events occurred, extrapolating the significance of colonial history to his own life story and arguing for changes to Inuit relations with the churches and the Canadian government. Some of this rich material can be found in the final chapter of *Skid Row Eskimo*, but Deagle and Mettrick understandably edited out a great deal due to its perceived incoherence with non-Native expectations of autobiography and constraints related to publishing. Although Thrasher attends in this section to a wide range of subjects related to Inuit cultural survival, I will focus specifically on his discussions of Christianity and education.

Thrasher was keenly aware that the government and the churches were wielding education as a weapon in the decimation of Inuit culture. Not only did residential schooling seek to teach Inuit students Euro-Canadian ways, but it also sought to undermine and overwrite their connection to Inuit ways. Thrasher writes in his manuscript:

> This thing of being educated in English bothered me. Every time I'd go home from school I saw older boys that went to the school and when they were left to make a living they were even more ignorant than when they first went to school. They couldn't survive without a job and jobs in those years were next to none. There were summer jobs on handling freight labor and deck hand work on the ships but in the winter teen age boys who should be able to trap and hunt had to rely on their parents. I saw many boys turn that way. They got their education in school then could not make any use of it. Some children also forgot how to speak in Eskimo from too many years in school. Then when they got home they couldn't communicate in any way with their own parents. (83–84)

As Thrasher accurately asserts, the efforts of residential schools to kill the Inuit and save the man, so to speak, engendered catastrophic crises of identity among large numbers of Inuit students:

> Many Eskimo people who get educated are full of shame of their status. They don't tell anyone they are Eskimo. Soon in later years you can walk up to an Eskimo and look at him. All you will see in him is a blank expression of what his people were. He will be highly educated in the white way but his past will be dead. If we don't try to save our traditional culture our people won't even have to die off to disappear we do not want to get lost in civilization. (*ms.* 260)

Eerily envisaging a plausible future, Thrasher acutely diagnoses the culturally genocidal impulse upon which residential schools—including the Roman Catholic school in Aklavik, which Thrasher attended prior to the 1955 northern initiative—were initially founded. As noted in chapter 1, the government used residential school, in the words of Duncan Campbell Scott, to "'get rid of the Indian problem'" by "'absorb[ing]'" Native children "'into the body politic,'" until "'there [would be] no Indian question, and no Indian Department.'"[58] As Thrasher illustrates, the physical elimination of the Inuit would be unnecessary to ensure their "disappear[ance]" as long as they would cease to identify *as Inuit* in the absence of their "traditional culture." The death Thrasher foresees and attempts to subvert, then, is not simply the death of the Inuit past, but the death of the Inuit people as a distinct and enduring cultural group. In the absence of a shared culture, language, and heritage—all of which residential schooling sought to exterminate—the Inuit would become distinguishable from non-Native Canadians in biology alone, which Thrasher alludes to in the "blank" face of the Eskimo. The "expression of what his people were," discernable on the Eskimo's face, represents the physical manifestation of a unique cultural history, but its "blank[ness]" suggests the Eskimo's unwillingness and/or inability to claim that history; it is no longer lived and endorsed, so it cannot be animated, but must persist solely as a biological archive. It is a cultural history—comprised of linguistic, spiritual, oral, and traditional elements—that is no longer embraced and enacted, and is therefore "dead."

Thrasher's narrative struggles against this ominous potentiality. Proclaiming, "I will be one who will try in writing to fight against the loss of our traditional culture" (*ms.* 193), Thrasher strives not only to nourish traditional Inuit knowledge, but also to destabilize the authority of assimilative forces by critiquing the ways in which Christianity has been, and continues to be, inflicted upon Inuit people. A Christian himself, Thrasher is not necessarily averse to the evangelical presentation of Christian dogma to Inuit audiences, but, rather, against the advancement of Christianity in a unidirectional manner in accordance with a violable/inviolable paradigm. The problem, as Thrasher sees it, is not that the Inuit came into contact with Christianity, but that the forces of Christianity presumed for the Inuit no agency in the process of cultural negotiation that would ensue.[59]

Characteristically couching scathing criticism behind a mask of powerlessness, Thrasher writes:

> I may be a stupid Eskimo but I have my rights to believe in what I want to. I am using my faith in the old Eskimo culture as a higher power to help me in my fight against alcohol and the wrongs of the new culture. My people have lost faith in themselves. The Eskimo do not know that going into the new faiths they have lost a very valuable spiritual faith in themselves. In the old ways we used to follow our spiritual inspirations which was very simple because it came out of our own tradition. The new faith of the churches are too confusion filled. Too many sacraments. Too many sins invented. Too many strict rules to follow. We were taught to suffer for our sins by inflicting self injury by whipping each other in 1946. The nuns believed in inquisition. We were the sinful pagans. To reform the Eskimo you have to give him back his self confidence. He has to gain back his old faith in himself. The church makes us feel as though we are of no use unless we get taken in by them. Then we have to depend on the churches preachings. We lost our primitive but helpful spiritual beliefs which kept us well. Our own beliefs were called sinful, dirty and savage pagan rites. Every church on earth preaches of false prophets. (*ms.* 404–05)

At the core of Thrasher's remonstration is a disparity of power he perceives between the Christian churches and the Inuit people whom they supposedly serve. Thrasher articulates his concern in terms of "faith." At its highest level of commitment, the Christian derivation of "faith" involves a divestiture of individual agency to God's will. To have "faith" is to humble oneself before the Higher Power, thereby, in effect, foregoing one's own (small 'p') power. According to Thrasher, this concession becomes dangerous for the Inuit due to the intervening influence of the clergy. Because the Christian churches—particularly the Catholic Church—function according to hierarchical relations of absolute authority to absolute obedience, much as the priests and pastors must unwaveringly obey the will of God, so too can they expect and solicit the unwavering obedience of their flocks. Such surrogate power seized by fallible humans under the auspices of church authority can lead to the invention of sins, the manipulation of rules, and the extraction of unwarranted punishments, all of which control and disempower the congregation.

Within an Indigenous context, the danger embedded in church power relations is often exacerbated by racism and cultural progressivism. Bearing the burden of the churches' xenophobic mistrust of other spiritual systems, Inuit Christians must renounce their cultural past and therefore disclaim aspects of who they are. To have "faith" in the Christian churches, in this case, involves conceding "faith" in oneself, and potentially the agency to make change and improve personal, social, political, and cultural conditions. By "going into the new faiths," the Inuit lose what Thrasher calls "a very valuable spiritual faith in themselves." This "spiritual faith" involves the cultural pride and individual autonomy that form the precondition for Inuit self-determination in the North. Significantly, Thrasher begins articulating the need for regeneration of Inuit pride in subtle acquiescence to the dominant paradigm of non-Inuit control: "To reform the Eskimo you have to give him back his self confidence."[60] Here the "you" seems to imply that the agency Thrasher desires for the Inuit must be granted them by an outside force, thereby qualifying the extent of that agency from its very inception. But Thrasher immediately rephrases the statement—which, I must stress, is Thrasher's primary mode of personal editing throughout the manuscript: not crossing out, erasing, and rewriting, but, rather, correcting himself in subsequent sentences[61]— to suggest the need for the Inuit themselves to actualize their agency, saying "*he* has to gain back his old faith in himself."

Thrasher then demonstrates the reclamation of individual spiritual autonomy for which he argues by cutting out the intermediary influence of preachers and church authorities. A Roman Catholic by birth and through schooling, Thrasher describes his conversion in 1955 to the Pentecostal faith (which, he argues, allows him far more interpretive agency and spiritual freedom):

> One thing was new to me my first real Christian worship. I believed in God and this new experience of prayer on your own was new…. This new experience of church got me deep. I used to think of them as Holy Rollers as they were called by the Catholic Church. When I went right down to bible facts I found out this was only a true Christian kind of worship. I knew the bible and bible History. This was old gospel worship. I was a

catholic but the catholic church can't help me out here so I took the Bibles way just plain Christian worship. It was great I knew some gospel songs since my childhood. I believed the Lord was my saviour so I accepted Christ in the simple Christian way. I felt the power of God come through in the church service room to explain it.... I was praying in my way. (*ms.* 123)

Demystifying the simulation of infallible church authority, Thrasher exercises his ability to interpret spirituality in his own way, according to his understanding of the Bible and of traditional Inuit culture. He strips down the violable/inviolable paradigm, showing Christianity to be malleable and adaptable, provided the individual actualizes her or his interpretive agency and individual autonomy. Thrasher melds the two spiritual systems to create a Christianity that is sensitive to Inuit spirituality and cultural history—or, better yet, to create an Inuit spirituality that is practicable in relation to the Bible. Tongue in cheek, he calls himself "a primitive pagan savage," while simultaneously declaring himself "a Christian through the Pentecostal faith. I chose the best part of the old time religion.... Along with that ... some parts of the Eskimo spiritual culture taken in with my knowledge of what the Holy Bible can give me" (*ms.* 408). With a typically humorous flourish that further undermines the dogmatic façade he has been attacking, Thrasher elsewhere proclaims: "I take my own way in getting spiritual help by going to my own simple Eskimo beliefs and taking the bible in my hand. When I read a bible just the thoughts of the old time religion is good enough for me. Amen" (406–07).

LINGUISTIC PLAY IN *SKID ROW ESKIMO*

The concise and relentlessly autobiographical final product Thrasher's editors and publishers envisaged for *Skid Row Eskimo* considerably limited the author's capacity to argue overtly against Christian hegemony. There simply would be no room in a 164-page life story documenting Thrasher's infancy to his prison life for inclusion of the extensive and detailed expostulations from the manuscript. One can also assume such extravagant argumentation would be too costly for a small press to reproduce. So, with Thrasher's consent, Deagle and Mettrick omitted hundreds of pages of didactic material in favour of content more readily aligned with standard autobiography. This does not mean, however, that Thrasher's assault on Christian domination did not find its way into *Skid Row Eskimo*, that it was completely annexed to the twelve-page final chapter and the cutting-room floor. Despite editorial intervention, Thrasher maintained the "power," in

Kathleen Sands's words, "to use the collaborative process to express difference, to use the narrative events to [his] own ends, and ... to actively resist the collector[s'] cultural and ideological agenda."[62] Thrasher's critique of Christian proselytization via the violable/inviolable paradigm indeed emerges in *Skid Row Eskimo* but in a more covert, and therefore perhaps more seductive, form. Unable to argue directly and at length, Thrasher's attack is subsumed within his narration of childhood and youth, which mobilizes the play of language to corrode the totalizing power of the Christian institutions.

Thrasher employs two main approaches. Like Basil Johnston's *Indian School Days* and many other survival narratives, *Skid Row Eskimo* celebrates the small acts of defiance that actualize the transgressive agency retained by students within even the most oppressive and authoritarian environments. More uniquely, Thrasher chips away at the foundations of church authority by desanctifying the sacred with humour. He injects a playfulness into his reminiscences that penetrates the solemnity of religious authority and, in effect, satirizes the system of assimilative control. His account of an incident in 1949 offers an example of both methods:

> On July 21st, I turned twelve years old.
> A few weeks later, I was back at school, being accused of sinning again with girls in the basement of the school. There were two of us in the basement with four girls. All we were doing was throwing potatoes and having fun, but Sister Cote gave us hell. She lined us boys up against the wall and showed us what she thought of girls.
> "Winnie, Wilma, Rosie, Mary, Jean, Marjie, Lucy, Annabelle ..." she shouted. "This is what I think of them ..."
> She spat on the floor and stamped her foot on it.
> She didn't have to do that. I was still too young to be having any serious thoughts about girls. And anyway, I was too holy. Sometimes I'd steal into the chapel and pray like hell, all by myself. (45)

The actual behaviour leading to Thrasher's punishment was indeed in defiance of the school's code of conduct. While the boys were permitted to work alongside the girls to help maintain the school, they were not allowed to play together as such and certainly not to throw food stuffs surreptitiously beyond the surveillance of the nuns. In this respect, the youthful indiscretion Thrasher describes is a form of (innocent and harmless) resistance to authority.

However, Sister Cote misinterprets this transgression of institutional rules as a transgression of divine law, painting simple misbehaviour as 'sin.' To illustrate the foulness of the sexual activity of which the children were charged, Sister Cote spits on the ground—an odd and uncanny image that suggests symbolic ejaculation. Stamping her foot on the excretion, she dramatizes that profane male sexual emissions must be stifled, thwarted, and stamped out, much like the licentious young girls who supposedly solicit them. Yet all this theatricality on the instructor's part is exposed in Thrasher's telling as ludicrous, in light of the absence of any such sexual transgression and Thrasher's admission that he was "still too young to be having any serious thoughts about girls," anyway. The ridiculousness of the exchange is heightened by Thrasher's ironic declaration that "anyway, I was too holy"—which hearkens back to his account of receiving an award for holiness three pages earlier. Recalling the award, Thrasher explains that he had been "caught drawing a little devil-figure and had to stay after class, but I guess I made amends because I got a Sacred Heart badge for being holy" (42). Thrasher's containment of this 'honour' within a sentence that details his drawing pictures of the Prince of Darkness exposes the arbitrariness of residential school implementation of reward and punishment according to a divine dichotomy of holiness vs. sin that gestures toward the absolute.

Furthermore, the qualification, "I guess," calls into question both the punishment extracted for the drawing and the award granted for "being holy," suggesting neither is based on a keen awareness of divine law and individual behaviour. The randomness of Sister Cote's invocation of "sin" to justify an unwarranted punishment similarly undermines the strength of her religious authority. "I was too holy" functions as verbal irony because both author and reader are aware by this point just how questionable the criteria for holiness have become. Because both Thrasher and his audience are in on the joke, rather than signalling personal evaluation according to divine hierarchies, Thrasher's use of the term 'holiness' serves to overturn those hierarchies themselves. Thrasher then punctuates the absurdity of it all with the marvellous admission: "Sometimes I'd steal into the chapel and pray *like hell*, all by myself." Continuing his ironic assault on Christian codes, Thrasher enunciates the extremity of his 'holiness' by describing fervent prayer as being "like hell," thereby throwing divine signification into further disarray. Uniting the sacred and the profane, Thrasher undermines the sanctity of both prayer and chapel, violating church power through a language game. And he does it "all by [him]self," thereby removing both Thrasher the author and "Thrasher" the character from the tentacles of church authority and establishing an, albeit fleeting, spiritual autonomy.

Such overt use of verbal irony and literary satire to critique church authority and colonial imposition occurs sparingly in *Skid Row Eskimo*. However, less direct forms of linguistic play through genre manipulation and allegory continue the countervailing program of the manuscript. Thrasher's criticism of residential school's culturally genocidal objective, for instance, survives in the published text, merely requiring more energetic analysis to distinguish in the absence of some of the manuscript's argumentative context. Shortly after arriving at the Aklavik school, Thrasher and his classmates go on a camp-out, during which one of the students tells the unsanctioned Inuit "legend of ... Iliapaluk, an orphan who lived with his grandmother, Ananaa, in the bush country" (16). One day Iliapaluk discovers that someone has stolen the snares on which he and his grandmother depend for meat and survival. They go to the village and the old woman, who possesses "the magic power [the Inuit] call Angatkolik," warns the people "not to make fun of a poor orphan boy. She [tells] them she [will] give whoever took Iliapaluk's snares a chance to return them to him" (16). However, no one comes forward. The two go home and the grandmother takes roe from a fish the boy has hooked and covers herself "from head to toe." They then return to village:

> When they arrived, she told the boy to call everyone out of their houses. When he had done this, the old woman began talking to them.
>
> "I will touch all of you, one by one," she said. "If you are good people, do not be afraid. Only the liar will get hurt."
>
> She touched everyone, until she got to a man who suddenly dropped dead.
>
> He was the thief. He had the snares.
>
> Then the grandmother told the people, "Whatever you do, do not ever steal from an orphan who has no mother, and who fights hard to live. He only has those little strings to live on, and when you take them away, he can starve and die." (16–17)

The recitation of this tale is again an exercise of cultural resistance, this time by revisiting traditional Inuit orature while on brief respite from the carceral space of Aklavik Residential School. The telling of the tale, complete with magical powers and sorcerous vengeance, is itself an act of defiance, animating a tradition the Aklavik school is attempting to suffocate. Yet, upon closer examination, there is more to it. The choice of tale is itself significant, something that Thrasher plays up in his retelling. Having lost his own mother at the age of two, Thrasher is himself "an orphan who has no mother" and has fought "hard to live." Also, he relates having set a snare and "caught a whisky-jack" on the very excursion during which the tale is told, suggesting a personal identification with the young trapper Iliapaluk. And the tale's implications can resonate even more broadly. Given the context in which the tale is told—an outing at a Roman Catholic residential school for Eskimos—the role of the victimized orphan could easily apply to the entire student body. For what is residential schooling other than an institutional violation of the parent/child relationship, which creates orphaned children and, by official governmental decree, recasts them as wards of the state?

For an allegorical connection between the Aklavik students and the orphan Iliapaluk to make sense within Thrasher's narrative, however, one must account for what is stolen from the children and how it is reclaimed. By immediately following the tale with the statement, "Story telling was a part of life in the North" (17), Thrasher helps clarify its allegorical function. While Iliapaluk's loss of the snares represents a threat to his *physical* survival, it is the potential loss of the students' connection to Inuit heritage as embodied by oral storytelling that threatens their *cultural* survival. Unwilling to become the "blank expression[s] of what [their] people were" Thrasher forecasts morosely in his manuscript, the students need to re-engage with traditional Inuit culture to stave off residential school-induced acculturation. For just as the grandmother's magic power allows Iliapaluk's snares to be restored to him, it is the unnamed student's unsanctioned telling of the legend of Iliapaluk that helps remind Thrasher of his culture's narrative tradition, symbolically restoring valuable cultural material to his life and the narrative. Thrasher suggests this progression by moving on in the following paragraph to discuss his grandfather, Old Apakark, "the greatest [storyteller] of them all" (17).

The Iliapaluk tale is thus instructive in two ways: first, it argues for the importance of sustaining Inuit culture—here the oral tradition—in the face of Christian hegemony, and, second, it illustrates how that oral tradition can be used to analyze the very hegemonic systems it faces. Anticipating the work of Creek scholar Craig Womack, Thrasher refuses to "overlook the fact that [oral] stories may also function as post-colonial critique, in addition to explanation of the spiritual and material origins of the culture."[63] Nowhere in his narrative does Thrasher didactically assert that the violation of familial bonds enacted through residential school policy was wrong. He implies this instead by expressing some of his early longings for motherly affection while in the Aklavik school and articulating his desire to leave the institution and hunt and fish with his father, but nowhere does he render a precise declaration. Yet, through the Iliapaluk tale, Thrasher allegorically proclaims that northern residential schooling has created a generation of Inuit orphans and that its assimilative project of denying those orphans Inuit heritage materials constitutes a crime (at least symbolically) punishable by death. And, as Thrasher relates elsewhere, "to the Eskimo the most severe law to break in the old days was to mistreat an orphan" (*ms.* 239).

In *Skid Row Eskimo*, Thrasher, in effect, 'snares' the reader into recognizing the appalling transgressions inflicted by the church and government. In this way, his playful narrative techniques create—to borrow the title from Eden Robinson's collection of short stories—'traplines' that capture back for his Inuit audience some of the agency of which the churches and the government sought to divest them. Not simply through argumentation, but more subtly through the playful telling of his life story and the creative re-envisaging of his residential school experiences, Thrasher moves toward reclaiming an adaptable Inuit cultural heritage while simultaneously suggesting the inadequacy of a hierarchical and dominating Christianity.

In the later sections of *Skid Row Eskimo*, Thrasher occasionally fashions narrative escapes for his incarcerated self through imaginings of a traditional Inuit family life on the Arctic tundra. His initial recourse to this idyllic imaginative space occurs the evening he is charged with murder: "That night, I dreamed of a future that would never come" (111). Italicized to accentuate its spectral quality, the passage emphasizes the warmth, security, and joy of traditional Inuit family life through its juxtaposition with the harsh northern weather outside the imagined Thrasher family's igloo—"*The North Wind blows outside. A blizzard*"—while Thrasher and his dream-wife "*warm each other with our love until our hearts beats are out of control. Sweet, sweet love.... Life is beautiful. All is love and happiness ...*" (112). Later, Thrasher continues his longing depiction of a now improbable familial existence:

> *I tell my family a story of my Atatak, my grandfather.... They curl up in one bed against the cold, naked. Their bodies and the fur hides keep them warm....*
>
> *Here in the igloo, my children want to hear Unipkarq, a story. I pick up my Krilaun, Eskimo drum. I sing of how I make my kayak, my canoe. I sing of how I make my Angooni, my paddle. I sing of how I will paddle my kayak....*
>
> *My woman tells me it is time to sleep. The children are asleep already, and they dream of my songs and my stories.* (159)

The poignancy of Thrasher's dream-narrative is heightened by its impossibility, given his exile in the South and, more crucially, his imprisonment. Strategically placed near the narrative's conclusion and after the reader has fully digested the events and circumstances of Thrasher's life, this potential "future" will "never come," it seems, due to colonial impositions on the Inuit like residential schooling. Thrasher suggests such a conclusion in the sentence with which he follows the dream-narrative: "Now our young people are put in schools to learn the white man's language and customs while our culture dies" (159). Effectively orphaned—and thereby denied first-hand experience of natural parenting patterns—and subjected to the assimilative technologies of the Aklavik Residential School, how could Thrasher expect to achieve such a nourishing and culturally endorsable family life as that presented in the dream-narrative, other than through the vehicle of his imagination?

Thrasher's anger and sadness at this apparent impossibility are, however, complicated by a factor that goes unacknowledged in *Skid Row Eskimo*'s final pages: Thrasher's unwillingness to be a husband or father. Although the dream-narrative is presented as an ideal that is tragically unattainable, Thrasher did indeed have opportunities during his life to at least attempt to create a functional family unit, and he passed them all up. Shortly after returning from his training in the South, Thrasher received "the news" in Inuvik "that I was the father of a boy." However, he admits, "my uncle and auntie from a reindeer station adopted my son. His name is Ronnie. I used to go and visit him when he was little. The last time I saw him, he was five" (81). That was fifteen years prior to Thrasher's writing. In Edmonton, Thrasher recalls meeting an Inuit prostitute named "river bank Mary," whom he might have "got pregnant." When she "said she would give her baby [his] name," Thrasher "took off to Calgary" (*ms.* 174). Similarly, Thrasher recalls being told in the mid-1960s that he "had two children at Foxe Basin, another two at Tuk, and one at Reindeer Depot. Two more girls had me marked, too, so in May 1967, when I got my chance, I moved South again" (90). The irony is that while Thrasher narratively upholds the traditional Inuit family unit as an ideal, he actively avoided every chance to approximate that ideal in life by parenting his own children. In fact, he fled the North—where a traditional Inuit family lifestyle would seem most plausible—to escape the constraints of familial responsibility.

Elsewhere Thrasher criticizes non-Inuit men for shirking parental duties toward children they have fathered with Inuit women. He writes in the manuscript:

When the white man comes north on oil exploration jobs or any other jobs. In their pastime out side of work most men go for sex contact with the Eskimo girls.... [who] are left unmarried with white babies. The white men disappear south as usual always.... When a whole bunch of fatherless children are left behind nothing is done. These children grow up on welfare and what little the mother can make. While the father is in a big city bragging about his exploits in the north. (272–73)

Late in *Skid Row Eskimo*—just three pages after the dream-narrative—Thrasher relates on a more personal note, "Two of my sisters have illegitimate children by white men who have disappeared, so I have cute little blue-eyed nephews and nieces. We don't discriminate against these children. We give them the family name. They will grow up, with our own children" (162). They will indeed grow up like Thrasher's "own children": fatherless. Thrasher neglects to acknowledge in these attacks on non-Inuit men that he is not so different from white men who "hunt down [Inuit] women for pleasure" (162) and then abandon them. He too has impregnated Inuit women and then "disappeared" to the South. He too has "bragg[ed]" about his sexual "exploits in the north" (in a narrative that exhaustively details his various sexual excursions). Much like both the white absentee fathers he criticizes and the residential school system he allegorically undermines, Thrasher has created orphans in the North, a perplexing realization that complicates his narrative authority and the political function of his text.

Whether we interpret Thrasher's neglect of parental obligations as incongruous with his criticism of residential school violations of the traditional Inuit family and culture—both allegorical (*Skid Row Eskimo*) and argumentative (*Manuscript*)—depends largely on how we conceive of the relationship among text, context, and authorial voice. If we classify *Skid Row Eskimo* as an argumentative text, completely under authorial control, and carefully articulated to convince its audience of well-reasoned claims, then Thrasher's lack of self-reflexivity on this matter might corrode his critical credibility and so the text's validity. However, *Skid Row Eskimo* is neither a straightforward expostulation nor a piece of academic historical criticism. It is an intricate and flawed narrative life story, composed, edited, and materially produced amid complex conditions in an historically specific context. It presents not an isolatable thesis, but, rather, many provocative points relevant to (but not necessarily corroborated by) the life being documented. Lives are not lived to provide evidence for eventual claims within as-yet-to-be-written autobiographies. Instead, the autobiographical occasion provides an opportunity for the author to make claims regarding her or his history in retrospect, so the idea that Thrasher must be bound to have practised what he ultimately preaches is both critically unsound and restrictive.

Also, within the specific context of the residential school survival narrative, Thrasher's failure to live up to traditional Inuit parental obligations might actually support, rather than undermine, his claims about the destructiveness of residential school familial intervention. As is widely recognized, the seeds of neglect, abuse, and other forms of intimate violence within many Native families and communities are to be found in earlier residential school experiences. As Constance Deiter argues in her study of residential schooling's intergenerational impact, "the loss of being parented in a loving home leads, of course, to poor to non-existent parenting skills in the children who are now adults."[64] Survivor David Neels agrees, calling residential school "the source of our people's ... child abandonment."[65] Residential school constituted a profound disruption in the natural progression of family development, whereby the child learns familial responsibility through enduring contact with parents and elders. One of the resounding questions with which Native Canadians have had to grapple in its wake has been: how do those who have not been parented become healthy parents?

Furthermore, the adverse effects of residential school's orphaning of Indigenous children have been augmented by the patriarchal ideology with which residential school policy was enforced. The coercive ideological surround into which these children were thrust proclaimed men's dominance over women, the filthiness of the corporeal form, and the inherent sinfulness of sexuality, all of which conspired to engender catastrophic crises of identity, sexuality, and social role among many students. Near the close of *Halfbreed*, Métis author Maria Campbell comes to the realization that "the [non-Native] system that fucked me up fucked up our men even worse. The missionaries had impressed upon us the feeling that women were a source of evil."[66] Beyond being separated from their mothers and fathers—from whom they might have attained a healthy understanding of maleness and femaleness—the students were forbidden to socialize with the opposite sex, other than with the (supposedly asexual) nuns and priests. The first experience Thrasher recalls of his arrival at the Aklavik school was being separated from the female students, and, when his younger sisters were old enough to attend school in subsequent years, Thrasher was forbidden to spend time with them, despite the fact that he often acted as their caregiver during summer holidays. Such perplexing contradictions were clearly difficult for the children to reconcile, something Thrasher critically acknowledges: "We were told not to play with the girls, because that would ... be a sin. I thought that was strange, because I had played with girls before I came to school. Now they were telling me I shouldn't touch them" (14). Coming from a semi-nomadic youth, during which the family often slept in a single bed and parental sex was not always sheltered from the children's view, to an institutional setting in which girls were not only separated from boys but were derogated as lesser people worthy only of the nuns' disdain, it is unsurprising that Thrasher's view of family roles, relationships, and women would be problematic.

The extent of Thrasher's crisis of gender relations is exemplified by a brief account of his inaugural exploitation of skid row prostitutes. After agreeing to a friend's suggestion, "'Let's get some whores,'" Thrasher recalls: "We found two women. It was the first time I ever saw two women take on six guys at once, and make a lot of money for it in less than an hour. It was quite a surprise. *These nice-looking women had less morality than the most primitive people you could ever find*" (my emphasis, 74–75). Entirely absent from Thrasher's recollection is any self-reflexivity about the "morality" of the men implicated in this sexual act. After all, it was they who solicited and financed the supposedly depraved encounter. Yet, hearkening back to Sister Cote's graphic suggestion about the filthiness of the feminine from his residential school days—"This is what I think of [girls]'" (while spitting on the floor)—Thrasher locates the lack of morality solely in the women, which brings us back to the relationship among text, context, and authorial voice in residential school survival narratives. The difficulty in analyzing discussions of colonial interventions like residential school is that not only has colonialism created social and political conditions that complicate Indigenous authorship, but it has also supplied the ideological backdrop—and indeed the language—in which such discussions often take place. So whereas elsewhere Thrasher laments the colonial conditions that have rendered Indigenous subsistence so difficult that many must rely on criminal activity (like prostitution) to survive, he supplies none of this context to his discussion of the two prostitutes, whom he simply subjects to the vexing and highly gendered moral codes he encountered in residential school. To explain this experience, he falls back on the conceptions of morality taught to him by the nuns, even employing a specious evaluation of the women according to notions of primitivism (similar to those wielded in residential school denigration of Indigenous culture and history). Grasping for means of articulating his post-residential school experience, he remains mired in the sexist ideology and racist language he was burdened with therein.

Anthony Thrasher is a writer torn by colonial history, alcoholism, and institutionalization. Although he argues eloquently for the resilience of Inuit culture against the hegemonic power of Christianity, Thrasher could never actualize this empowering potential and free himself from the perplexed and misogynist ideological aftermath of his residential school experiences. As a result, while recognizing the beauty of a traditional Inuit familial existence, Thrasher serially abandoned his own children, perpetuating the cycle of neglect initiated for him in Aklavik Residential School. However, this negates neither *Skid Row Eskimo*'s political potential nor its evocative force. Quite the contrary: this tension renders *Skid Row Eskimo* all the more valuable a resource. Thrasher's autobiography represents not only how residential schooling is implicated in the corrosion of Inuit cultural and familial existence, but also how it has influenced the ideological and discursive fields through which Inuit survivors must express their outrage at colonial interventions. *Skid Row Eskimo* remains an enormously important (albeit sadly neglected) text because it both argues against colonial imposition and embodies the effects of such imposition within the texture of its narrative. Thus, Thrasher's impassioned allegorical and ironic pleas against residential schooling's criminal violation of Inuit family and culture remain undiminished by the misery of his incapacity to parent, connect, and love—in fact, this incapacity constitutes the most powerful form of evidence.

Although Thrasher's is largely a tale of victimhood, it illuminates the potential for Inuit empowerment even when its author must concede his own inability to actualize it. Employing an ethnographic model, Thrasher interrogates for his Inuit audience the intricacies of an imperialistic Euro-Canadian culture to the South, thereby providing valuable information with which to arm against further encroachment. Also, as I argued in relation to the manuscript, Thrasher demystifies the illusory nature of Christianity's inviolable façade to reveal how traditional Inuit culture can be adapted to the former without inevitable cultural loss or compulsory assimilation. Thrasher's valuable provocations endure in *Skid Row Eskimo* through what I have called linguistic play: the ironic, satirical, and at times allegorical overturning of colonial master-narratives to open up spaces for potential reflection, empowerment, and change. *Skid Row Eskimo* is not just a warning to an Inuit readership of "what to watch out for" in cultural negotiations with non-Inuit Canada, but is also an indication of how that audience might actualize its agency to make change and stop the cycle of familial and cultural breakdown that colonial imposition, and, in particular, residential schooling, began. It is a narrative of survivance by an author survived by his own empowering words.

Indian Residential Schools

Today on television I heard a discussion
Of residential schools across the country.
I saw a man talk about sex abuse done to him
He even had a hard time saying it.
I was in one of the schools, my daughter too
There was physical abuse where I was
Not sex but mind mistreatment.
To me there was one individual who did this
As always there are certain people who do.
The rest of the nuns were tolerable
The priest in my time a kind man.

My daughter says she didn't have it hard
But again only one person did her wrong
And upon seeing her in later years
This person hugged her and cried
My daughter knew the forgiving song.

I know for a fact people who came from schools
Have turned into productive persons.
Even women who had it hard have become nuns
And men from across the country their dreams realized.
In my case I've nobody to blame for being there
I put myself where I would receive training
The four years have given me strength
My life to this day has gained courage
I know who I am, and my people are the prize.

From *Song of Rita Joe: Autobiography of a Mi'kmaq Poet* (1996)
by Rita Joe (Mi'kmaq)
Survivor: Shubenacadie Residential School,
Shubenacadie, Nova Scotia

CHAPTER 4

"Analyze, if you wish, but listen": The Affirmatist Literary Methodology of Rita Joe

"Fanon ... shows clearly that this irrepressible [anti-colonial] violence is neither sound and fury, nor the resurrection of savage instincts, nor even the effect of resentment: it is man recreating himself. I think we understood this truth at one time, but we have forgotten it—that no gentleness can efface the marks of violence; only violence itself can destroy them."
Jean-Paul Sartre,
"Preface" to *The Wretched of the Earth*

"I was at war—but it was a gentle war"
Rita Joe,
Song of Rita Joe

Early in *Indian School Days* (1988), Ojibway writer Basil Johnston signals his book's divergence from the dominant body of Indigenous writing on residential school history by responding to "the inevitable question, 'Is there a place for residential schools in the educational system?'" with "a qualified yes."[1] Although tempered by the addendum, "but under vastly different terms, conditions and formats from those that existed in the residential school as I first encountered it" (12), Johnston's statement nevertheless differs in kind rather than in degree from Roland Chrisjohn's and Sherri Young's contention that the schools' "*very existence*, in however benign a form, constituted an abomination."[2] According to Johnston, "you can't credit [the] schools with everything, nor can you blame [the] schools for everything."[3] In fact, Johnston acknowledges that "some" of his contemporaries at Garnier Residential School "have said, 'It was probably the best thing that could have happened to me'" (*Indian School Days*, 12). Adopting in *Indian School Days* what Deena Rymhs calls a "mild, nostalgic tone"[4] in place of a possible critical/academic one, Johnston neither condemns nor commends in absolute terms the residential school system and those by whom it was implemented. He explicitly endeavours to be "as accurate as memory and effort and bias will allow" and also to be "fair" (11), but he pointedly leaves moral, ethical, and political judgments to his readers.[5]

Johnston's narrative treatment of individual instructors and overseers is similarly unique. Reviewer Lisa Emmerich deems it "especially well done" because "it offers a poignant counterpoint to the familiar pairing of well meaning, ethnocentric assimilation efforts and the student alienation that policy frequently produced."[6] Because so much writing on residential schooling has been devoted to bringing to public attention the horrific conditions and attendant abuse within residential schools, writing that recognizes the positive influence of instructor-guardians is sparse. Yet Johnston takes the time to acknowledge the kindness and expertise of several overseers, even dedicating *Indian School Days* to, among others, "all the prefects and priests and teachers who tried to instruct us and made possible the events herein recorded."[7] He notes the "considerable hindsight" and great "foresight" (164) of Father Superior R.J. Oliver, who believed "the boys deserved a better and broader training than they had hitherto received" (165) and was instrumental in revamping the school's antiquated vocational training methodology in an effort to produce better educated and more readily employable graduates. Johnston similarly lauds Mr. Sammon as "not only a gifted teacher, but a dedicated one as well. ... In terms of dedication, when dedication was the hallmark of teachers, Mr. Sammon was among the most dedicated. For him giving extra help was not merely an option, it was mandatory" (189). With respect to Brother O'Keeffe, Johnston states, "Of all the staff, priests included, [he] was probably the most gifted and accomplished. ... The boys who studied under Brother O'Keeffe were twice fortunate; once, to have learned reading, writing and arithmetic from him, and again to have heard him narrate stories. There was not a boy who was not influenced or enriched by Brother O'Keeffe's knowledge and love of and reverence for the word" (64). According to Johnston—a much sought-after orator in his own right—"It was delicious to listen to Brother O'Keeffe speak English the way it ought to be spoken" (66). Johnston further declares of Brother Voison, affectionately known to the boys as "'Choiman,'" that "no priest or brother, then or before, was as respected and as well liked by the boys as he. To them there was not a mean bone in the man's body or a mean thought in his mind. The boys who worked for 'Choiman' in the barn were convinced that he would do anything for them" (232).

Such praise of unique individuals who managed to transcend the oppressive and acculturative mandate of the residential school system is perhaps less surprising than Johnston's willingness to deal even-handedly even with those who did not. Johnston acknowledges early on that "if the priests and brothers, but especially the prefects, could not extend the warmth, sympathy and affection that were necessary [for the emotional well-being of the students], it was because their system, the system of the Jesuits, prevented them from doing so" (7). Johnston argues that even those who "possessed a degree of compassion ... were helpless to show their sympathy in a tangible way, for [they], too, were under the close and keen observation of the Father Superior and 'the Minister,' the administrator of the school. During their regency, the prefects ... had to demonstrate that they had the stuff to be Jesuits" (44), which, as Johnston mentions elsewhere, involved "renounc[ing] the world and worldliness" and "repudiat[ing] wordly feelings and demonstrations of emotion" (7). Recognizing that the governmental and religious systems that conspired in residential school policy circumscribed these individuals' capacity to nurture, Johnston does not wish to condemn either the prefects, who had the most direct contact with the students, or the priests and lay teachers, for their failure to attend to the emotional needs of the institutionally orphaned children.[8] In this way, Johnston gestures towards exonerating them of their uncompassionate, dehumanizing, and even at times abusive behaviour.

Johnston is certainly not the only commentator to temper blame toward individual perpetrators in an effort to recognize systemic neglect and the ways in which "the system [itself] was ... abusive."[9] For example, in *A National Crime*, John Milloy painstakingly argues that because the residential school system was at its core "a creature of the federal government" (xiii), all individual transgressions must be understood within an overarching framework of governmental culpability. In a similar vein, Chrisjohn and Young are careful to avoid what they call "methodological individualism," focusing too narrowly on the negative actions of individuals, so as not to divert attention away from the systemic failings that created climates of oppression and cultures of abuse within the residential schools.

Johnston's explanations of overseer behaviour, however, are not so readily reconciled with a strategic campaign against the residential school system entire. For one thing, as mentioned above, Johnston sees "a place" for Native residential schooling "in the educational system" (12). For another, *Indian School Days* is pointedly not an argumentative treatise. In an interview with Hartmut Lutz, Johnston explains, "See, I don't like doing what has already been done. It is simply a repetition. I want to do something a little different. Something that hasn't been done before. This is the main reason why I took [a humorous] direction. Also, the former inmates of [the residential school in] Spanish were the ones who suggested which stories were to be included."[10] Adopting the fondly nostalgic tone of evenings the author spent with his former classmates "recalling not the dark and dismal, but the incidents that brought a little cheer and relief to a bleak existence" (*Indian School Days*, 11), Johnston intentionally avoids a critical scholarly prose, favouring what Rymhs calls the "discursive elasticity" of "the memoir."[11] Employing an anecdotal and episodic narrative style with a minimum of editorial commentary, Johnston lets the exploits of his contemporaries speak for themselves, refusing to extract from them 'evidence' to be accumulated and repackaged in a bold denunciation of residential school policy.

Johnston's reticence to sermonize and condemn clearly runs counter to academic expectations regarding survivor accounts of residential school, as evidenced by historian Menno Boldt's scathing review of *Indian School Days* in *Canadian Literature*. Boldt writes:

> Basil Johnston was a victim of [residential school] policy. But, contrary to the claims of the publisher, Johnston does not view his experience in the framework of government policy. There is no analysis of tyranny and oppression. He does not meditate on the meaning or consequence of government policy for his people or himself. The Indian school experience described by Johnston does not symbolize a consequential political issue nor is it linked to the present condition of Canada's Indian people.[12]

Although Boldt does concede that "it is not obligatory that a book about Indian school days must contain social and political analysis and commentary," he still considers Johnston's book a "loss" and contends that "the author has evaded or repressed the true meaning of his experience" (312). The irony in this critique is that in order to castigate Johnston for not analyzing the "racism and ethnocentrism" (311) of a system that sought to turn him "into 'a white kid'" (312), Boldt employs an evaluative framework, conditioned by academic expectations, that is obviously Eurocentric. What Boldt fails to recognize in his evaluation is that scholarly research dedicated to linking personal trauma encountered in residential school to, on the one hand, governmental and church policy, and, on the other hand, social and political movements for healing and redress is merely one possible approach to dealing with the residential school legacy. And it is important to note that the idea that the social, political, or spiritual significance of a story—be it a legend or a life-narrative—ought to be isolated and explicated didactically is not necessarily endorsed by the Ojibway or other traditional Indigenous cultures. Johnston's failure, in Boldt's eyes, it seems, was to write as a storyteller about "the roguish behaviour of the students"[13] rather than as a historian about the intricacies of governmental policy and its effects; in other words, he failed by not conforming to the argumentative imperatives of an academic paradigm.

Johnston deliberately takes an alternative approach in *Indian School Days*, one that diverts attention away from the system itself and its non-Native instruments of control and oppression and focuses on the students, without whose "spirit," Johnston exults, "everyday would have passed according to schedule, and there would have been no story" (47). In this way Johnston proposes, as does K. Tsianina Lomawaima in the Native American context, that "boarding school culture … was created and sustained by students much more than by teachers or staff."[14] Perhaps more provocatively, by positing what Jamie S. Scott calls "an ambiguity of matter and method"[15] in place of more standard academic discourse, Johnston "assert[s] interpretive sovereignty over his experiences," rendering *Indian School Days* "a much more resistant text than it might appear."[16] As Rymhs concludes, "Retelling this segment of his life in a way that resists cultural scripts is one of the ways that Johnston recuperates, or 'repossesses,' his past."[17] Significantly, the cultural scripts to which Rymhs refers include not only the assimilationist storyline concocted by the Department of Indian Affairs and church bodies bent on proselytization—the storyline in which Native students would, through education, cast off 'antiquated' beliefs and traditions and allow themselves to be absorbed into the Canadian body politic—but also the reverse view that would paint residential schooling as monolithically evil and all those involved in its operation as racist abusers bent on acculturation and genocide.[18]

I have begun with *Indian School Days* because Johnston's reluctance to highlight the negative aspects of his residential school experience provokes the question that will chart this chapter's course: can non-condemnatory discussions of residential school history participate in the struggles for healing, justice, and political and monetary redress in which Native individuals and communities are currently embroiled? In other words, can positive renderings of residential school life evoke a viable emancipatory politics? In the case of *Indian School Days*, as both Rymhs and Scott argue in far greater detail than I offer here, Johnston's "refusal to play upon the guilt-ridden posture of ... white neo-colonial fiction"[19] involves an actualization of autonomous Indigenous memory that can be readily harnessed by Native movements striving to assert their control over residential school history, and, ultimately, over their tribal futures through sovereignty and self-determination. Thus, Johnston's work has enormous, although perhaps covert, empowering potential.

But what of a writer who deliberately *conceals* the negative side of her or his memories of colonial collision? In her autobiography, Mi'kmaq poet Rita Joe explicitly avoids devoting narrative attention to either the negative and immoral actions of others or her own most personally traumatic experiences; she certainly touches on these in passing but refuses to allow them to figure prominently in her narrative. Joe focuses narrative attention overwhelmingly on positive aspects of her life to the exclusion of fully developed discussions of personal trauma, from violent foster homes to residential school to years of spousal abuse. Early on in *Song of Rita Joe*, she acknowledges having "had some negative experiences" at Shubenacadie Indian Residential School, but she declares: "I do not like to dwell on the negative if I can help it. The positive outlook that I have worked on for so long now turns me off the negative. I look for the good."[20] Joe even admits to having entreated former Shubenacadie classmate Isabelle Knockwood, whose own book, *Out of the Depths* (1992), absolutely blisters with, to my mind, justified rage over the treatment of Native students in the school, to "write a sequel" to the book that would focus on "some of the positive things" (48). Similarly, when approached by the CBC to be involved with a documentary on residential schools, "Right away [Joe] told [them], 'If I do go on the air about residential schools, it will not be negative. It will be *positive*" (emphasis original).[21]

As much as I am reluctant to coin a term within a critical discourse that already lacks clarity due to the complexities of cultural collision and the multilingual nature of Aboriginal authorship throughout North America, I enlist the term "affirmatism" to describe Joe's literary methodology, in recognition of the absence of appropriate existing terminology. To identify Joe's peculiar (and strategic) artistic positioning and its basis in an ideological commitment to focusing on and building from what the author has so often called "the positive," I initially considered referring to her literary methodology as "positivism"; however, this risked being confused with the Victorian philosophical position of the same name, which argues that all knowledge, to be considered valid, must be tested against natural science-based empirical investigation. Alternatively, "affirmatism" is developed from "affirm," in the sense of "to assert positively." Joe's literary creations are affirmations not only of the power of the positive, but also of the crucial role of the Native author in engaging history and rendering it fruitful in the struggle toward empowerment. They are active assertions, not passive dismissals of the negative. Furthermore, I've settled on "affirmatism" rather than "affirmativism" in order to avoid unnecessary overlap with "affirmative action"—although clearly Joe's work has much to say in relation to racial and gender concerns—and also as a nod toward Jace Weaver's theory of communitism, which, as I argue below, is a valuable critical tool in relation to Joe's poetry and prose.

Joe's description in *Song of Rita Joe* of how, despite having no visitors of her own, she used to glean happiness from the visits other children at the Shubenacadie residential school received from their relatives, offers an initial example of affirmatism in action. Joe explains:

> The way I used to think of it was this: I knew a lot of people from different reserves, so if somebody had a mother or a father or a cousin coming to visit them, I often knew who their relations were. I could talk to them about who I knew and, in that way, I would get to have a little portion of the visit, too.
>
> It is like that with everything in my life. I look for an honourable image to create. (54–55)

The affirmatist stance invoked by Joe in this anecdote is neither a trite attempt to 'look on the bright side' nor an example of stoic Christian endurance. Joe does not accept the loneliness of her orphaned condition, but, rather, actively pursues a scenario in which she can achieve some joy. She *creates* conditions of happiness for herself and others through any means at her disposal, here the company of strangers who are familiar with friends. Born out of an ideological commitment to affirming the positive, Joe's affirmatist literary methodology is similarly not a negation of the negative but a creation of the positive through strategic attention and artistry. The doctrinal statement, "I look for an honourable image to create," contains exploratory and creative elements, neither of which is passive. Joe actively seeks out the "good" and with that "good" "create[s]" the "honourable image" through which empowerment becomes possible. Without the creative intervention of the affirmatist artist, the "good," it would seem, is not transformed into the personally and politically effective "honourable image," but, instead, remains an anomalous blip on the historical path of dominance and oppression.

My investigation into the political potential of Joe's affirmatist literary methodology necessarily takes place at the intersection of politics, narrative, and criticism. As an example of how easily the critic's own politics can obscure discussions of authorial stance and textual significance, note Jamie S. Scott's reference to Joe's "nuanced picture of the residential school"[22] below. Offered as evidence of Joe's complex understanding of both the good and bad aspects of residential schooling, Scott quotes the author as follows:

> "If you think that for two, sometimes three generations, people, families were being broken up, and they don't even *learn*, some of the kids, that their parents love them! What do you expect them to do when they are parents? So, I think some of the problems, or a lot of the problems that we see today, are really the result of the residential schools. And that must never happen again!...
>
> "But let me tell you about the positive part that I have tried to research.
>
> "The positive part of the residential school—and I will say that across the nation!—the positive part was: the people that came from it, the good ones, learned a lot from there. And so many people have gone on, and they have become chiefs, counsellors, and social workers, and they went on to learn!" (153)

The problem with Scott's use of this quotation is that he attributes it all to Joe when, in fact, the first paragraph was stated entirely by German scholar Hartmut Lutz, who was interviewing Joe at the time. That leaves Joe speaking solely about the "positive part," rather than addressing both sides of the residential school coin. Scott's misquoting suggests the critic's difficulty digesting the possibility that Joe views residential school as a *predominantly positive experience* rather than as containing *some positive aspects*, and connects back to Boldt's dismissal of Johnston's work.[23] While Scott misreads Joe perhaps because of a particular anti-colonial critical argument, Boldt's supposedly anti-colonial critical discourse, far more dangerously, denigrates Johnston's survivor testimony in a way that, once again, places ultimate authority beyond Native control. Boldt's outrageous claim that Johnston "has ... repressed the true meaning of his experience"—which implies, of course, that Boldt *does* understand that true meaning—betrays the resilience of paternalism in critical discourse on Native issues. Boldt's intervention in Johnston's life story suggests, along with Elizabeth Furniss, that "certain groups in society"—here non-Native historians rather than Indian agents and residential school principals—"know what is in Native peoples' best interests" better than Natives themselves.[24] The rhetoric is familiar enough: Native people don't understand the significance of their confrontations with colonial power, so those trained by Western academic institutions to analyze such confrontations must decipher these confrontations on their behalf.

Particularly in light of the massive attack on Indigenous autonomy and personal freedom perpetrated by residential schooling, I question the legitimacy of scholarly judgments that measure only by one system the way Native survivors recall and retell their experiences. As Gerald Vizenor, I think correctly, declares: "No one in our time has the right of consciousness to renounce the courage and humour of Native students in boarding schools.... No one has the right to erase the virtues and reason of their parents, or the ardent manners of certain teachers."[25] However, this does not mean that the significance of survivor narratives is not up for debate or that there is no role for the critic in engaging these issues. As Robert Allen Warrior states: "The tendency to find in the work of ... American Indian writers something worthy of unmitigated praise ... stand[s] in the way of sincere disagreement and engagement."[26] I do not intend to leave Joe's work unanalyzed or to avoid difficult questions about its (actual and potential) political effectiveness; however, as a literary critic I do not have the right to dictate the framework for discussion to the author. In other words, while I intend to fully analyze Joe's literary remembrances and to assess their potential impact on the socio-political reality of Native Canada struggling to deal with the adverse legacy of residential schooling, I am not in an ethical position to postulate how Joe *ought* to have conducted her autobiography. I can evaluate the textual survival narrative available within the public domain and what it has the potential to do, but I haven't the right (nor the expertise) to judge *how* the survivor remembers, to judge her process of remembering.[27]

MI'KMAQ HISTORY: AN OVERVIEW

Fated by geography to endure the initial wave of European colonialism on what would become Canada's eastern coast, the Mi'kmaq have undergone an arduous, protracted, and often traumatic post-contact history. Having experienced European settlement within their ancestral domains from the 1520s onward, the Mi'kmaq were among the first Indigenous nations to acquire foreign implements, to engage in nation-to-nation relations with the European monarchies, to accept Christian baptism in large numbers, to take up arms in the colonial wars, and to suffer the agonies of dispossession, relocation, poverty, and persecution. The Mi'kmaq experience of colonialism has been lengthy and the extent of their acculturation severe. Mi'kmaq scholar Bonita Lawrence suggests that by the mid-twentieth century, the Mi'kmaq "language was almost the only thing left, after 500 years of forced changes, to keep the people strong *as* Mi'kmaq."[28] Yet, despite the extremity of their colonial experience, the Mi'kmaq have remained resilient, consistently manifesting a combination of resistance, adaptation, and accommodation that has aided their physical and cultural survival. Thus, remarkably, despite being "among the earliest in Canada to be colonized by Europeans," the Mi'kmaq "are still to be found in their ancestral lands (although admittedly on only a tiny fraction of what had once been theirs), and retain a lively sense of their cultural identity."[29]

Mi'kmaq colonial history, replete with hard-fought triumphs and manifold indignities, in many ways prefigures colonization as it would take place throughout the country. Yet, in other key ways, it remains unique among tribal histories in Canada. Much of its distinctive character emerges from the tribe's early relationships with the French and the Catholic Church. In the course of the sixteenth century, the Mi'kmaq developed strong ties with French traders and officials who settled in Mikmaki—"the name the Mikmaq ... gave to their national territory," also known as Megummaage.[30] Gaining early access to European tools and implements, the Mi'kmaq employed their "strategic coastal position [and] seafaring skills ... to become middlemen in the fur trade,"[31] thereby developing a means of profiting from the newcomers without abandoning their traditional migratory patterns. The catastrophic effects of early disease contagion, however, left the Mi'kmaq far more dependent on trade relations than perhaps they had intended. According to the calculations of cultural anthropologist Harald Prins, "the Mi'kmaq suffered a mortality rate of 75 to 90 percent [during the first] one hundred years of direct contact," plummeting to a nadir of around 2000 people in the seventeenth century.[32] Although initially easing the devastating environmental effects trade-induced overtrapping would eventually produce, the 'Great Dying' tore asunder the extended familial and clan-based food-gathering systems that had hitherto allowed the Mi'kmaq to ensure their survival throughout the four seasons. With a grossly depleted hunting and fishing force, a high percentage of the population unable to travel on either land or water, and a large contingency diverted from their traditional roles by the need to tend to the sick and dying, the Mi'kmaq became heavily reliant on modes of subsistence available through trade with the French. The Mi'kmaq maintained their migratory lifeways for centuries after contact, but the conditions created by the Great Dying pushed the French and the Mi'kmaq toward interdependency and close alliance from an early date.

Mi'kmaq reliance on the French, however, was far from unidirectional. By 1663 there were only 3000 French settlers in all of Canada and just 500 in Acadia, compared to the more than 50 000 Protestant settlers strewn throughout New England, leaving the French dependent on the Mi'kmaq and other Wabanaki allies for economic and military stability.[33] The small size of the French Acadian settlement, which neither threatened traditional migratory patterns nor dispossessed the Mi'kmaq of large portions of their land, further encouraged the Mi'kmaq to engage the foreigners in diplomatic relations. Each determined to avail itself of the other's assets, and united against British expansionism, the French and Mi'kmaq developed during the early colonial period what Prins terms "a symbiotic relationship": "The migratory Mi'kmaqs specialized as market hunters and could count on the French for crops, manufactured goods, and arms. The sedentary French Acadians focused on their farms, the fisheries, or the fur trade; they relied on Mi'kmaqs for furs and eventually turned to Mi'kmaq warriors as valued allies during the colonial wars."[34]

The unique nature of Mi'kmaq/French relations during the first two centuries of colonial intervention in pre-Canada was epitomized by the peculiar condition of an enduring Indigenous sovereignty within French-claimed domains. On the one hand, as Cornelius Jaenen notes, "It seems evident that the French never doubted their right to acquire lands not already under Christian control," and thus perceived themselves as rightful owners of Mikmaki (which they renamed Acadia) under international law.[35] However, on the other hand, because, as Prins claims in *The Mi'kmaq*, "the land was vast and the French were few" (134), the French did not extend their claims to Acadian soil against the Indigenous inhabitants, but, rather, harnessed Mi'kmaq sovereignty within Acadia against the potential intrusion of the British. As Brian Slattery argues, the French Crown's "'rights to the soil were … held, not to the exclusion of the Indigenous peoples, but through them.'"[36] In what Jaenen terms in "French Sovereignty" the "innovative dualism of native self-determination under French sovereignty" (30), the French pursued a colonial policy in Acadia that recognized Native nationhood while maintaining Crown sovereign authority over the land in an abstract sense.

111

Although essentially of a nation-to-nation nature, the relationship between the French and Mi'kmaq was cemented in more intimate forums. The French indeed refrained from attempting the complete assimilation of the Mi'kmaq, but, as Daniel Paul notes, "religious conversion was ... one area where the French did work singlemindedly and achieve results."[37] In 1610 Mi'kmaq Grand Chief Membertou became the first Indigenous chief in pre-Canada to accept baptism, an event Rita Joe celebrates in the poem "Mouipeltu' (Membertou)": "And on the ways across the sky / I walk the ways my people meet / Leading the way again and again through Christianity / My name Mouipeltu' / A Grand Chief." Joe addends the explanatory note: "*(Grand Chief Membertou was the first Micmac to be baptized to the Catholic faith, June 24, 1610—the first aboriginal people in Canada to be Christians).*"[38] Membertou's conversion—which precipitated the conversion of the majority of the Mi'kmaq by the middle of the seventeenth century—did not, however, represent the simple bending of Indigenous leadership to the coercive colonial will, but, rather, symbolized coterminous developments in both Mi'kmaq/French relations and Mi'kmaq/Catholic spiritual thought. As Chickasaw scholar James (Sakéj) Youngblood Henderson argues in his book, *The Mikmaw Concordat*, the 1610 conversions invoked "ancient Aboriginal rituals to harmonize with the keeper of European spirituality" in a celebration that "combined Mikmaq and Catholic" elements.[39] During the festivities, "the Mikmaq presented the Church with sacred wampum belts of agreement, and the great chief and his extended family, about 140 Mikmaq, participated in the Catholic ritual of initiation—baptism."[40]

What distinguishes Mi'kmaq acceptance of Catholicism in the seventeenth century is not simply its earliness in colonial history. Henderson argues it was "seen by the Mikmaq as enfold[ing] within their existing belief system" (90). In this respect, according to Henderson, conversion represented an evolution rather than a revolution in Mi'kmaq spiritual thought. Certain aspects of pre-contact Mi'kmaq spiritual practice were adapted to Catholic worship, rather than discarded, and many Mi'kmaq have continued to practise a form of religious syncretism to the present. Furthermore, as Henderson argues, through "The Concordat of Mikmaki," which dates back to Membertou's era, the Mi'kmaq established a unique relationship with the "Holy See representing the Catholic Church" (87) that effectively ended, in Henderson's words, "all discussion of the French King's pretensions of authority over the Mi'kmaq" (89–90). Under the aegis of the Concordat, the Mi'kmaq

> synthesized their Aboriginal beliefs with Catholic teachings and developed
> a distinctive Mi'kmaq.... spiritual republic, a theocracy. The allied people

refused to blindly accept either Roman or French Catholicism or the priests' exclusive authority. Authority, for the Mi'kmaq, remained a manifestation of human character and integrity through experience rather than the mere ceremony of ordination. The maintenance of their worldview was an essential part of their heritage of freedoms and rights. (91)

Although it is beyond the range of this chapter to engage Henderson's argument in detail,[41] it is crucial to note here that the Mi'kmaq adopted (largely by consensus) an internally endorsable and culturally adapted form of Catholicism early in their colonial history and that many ultimately guarded that Catholicism as an integral aspect of a distinct Mi'kmaq cultural identity over time.

With the signing of the Treaty of Utrecht in 1713—which ceded French Acadia to the British (in whose hands it became Nova Scotia), while allowing the French to retain what would later become Cape Breton and Prince Edward Island and their adjacent mainland areas—Mi'kmaq colonial conditions altered drastically. Although the French had maintained nation-to-nation relations with the Mi'kmaq since the early 1500s, they made no effort to include their Indigenous allies in the terms of the treaty. Similarly, because the British perceived the French to have extinguished Aboriginal title to Acadia a priori, they foresaw (or claimed there to be) no need to negotiate with the Mi'kmaq during their acquisition of Maritime lands. However, because French colonial policy had never sought Mi'kmaq removal from, or relocation within, Acadia through signed treaties, but, rather, established proxy authority over the area through nation-to-nation alliance, the Mi'kmaq found themselves after 1713 in the bizarre and unenviable position of being without land rights in their own territory under British colonial law. As Dickason asserts, "when the British took over Acadia, they had a long history of recognition of aboriginal land rights, in contrast to the French, who had never formally acknowledged such rights, except where it was useful for annoying the British."[42] Yet, in this case, the British conveniently ignored Aboriginal title—which they elsewhere treated as inherent until officially ceded through treaty—as a problem belonging to the previous colonial authority, of consequence to neither the British Crown nor its settlers.

The establishment of British colonial rule in Mi'kmaq lands inaugurated a new and debilitating stage in Mi'kmaq history. The "symbiotic" relationship forged with the small and generally propitious French settler population was supplanted by a relationship of "subordination and domination"[43] with the immense and growing multitude of British settlers. As the British began building towns on traditional

113

Mi'kmaq hunting grounds, roads on and across traditional Mi'kmaq migratory routes, and ports along the Mi'kmaq coastline, the Mi'kmaq became "squatters on their own lands and poachers of their own game."[44] The situation was exacerbated in the 1780s by the influx of some 32 000 British Loyalists fleeing the American Revolutionary War, reducing the Mi'kmaq to a mere five percent of the total population of Nova Scotia. Although lands were eventually set aside for Mi'kmaq use by the British colonial government, these were non-coastal and largely undesirable, procured by "government grants or legislative acts, not by negotiated treaties,"[45] meaning authority over those lands continued to reside with the colonial government rather than with the Indigenous inhabitants. Such dispensation of land to the Mi'kmaq exemplified the changes by which the Indigenous of Mikmaki were encumbered: no longer were they internationally perceived as the independent nation that had negotiated alliances with the French and the Catholic Church and maintained its migratory lifestyle and sovereignty within a colonial setting, and yet neither had they become the common tribal nation that strategically cedes its land rights to the British in return for a reserved land base and economic and political concessions; the Mi'kmaq were a neither/nor pariah, perceived by the colonial government as completely under its authority and subordinate to its will, while beset on all sides by an ever-growing settler population, to whose concerns that government routinely capitulated.

Countless tyrannies of the majority occurred over the following two centuries in Nova Scotia. Prins remarks that "pandering to white constituents went so far that in 1859 the Committee for Indian Affairs 'proposed that [Indian] lands which had been trespassed upon be sold to the violators at varying sums.'"[46] A more encompassing example occurred in the 1940s when the Nova Scotia government, with the support of the Department of Indian Affairs, embarked on an abortive process of centralization that sought to relocate all Maritime Mi'kmaq from sundry communities and small reserves to two large reserves at Eskasoni and Shubenacadie. Explicitly designed to render supervision and control by the Indian Agent easier and less costly while simultaneously offering better economic opportunities for the direly impoverished Mi'kmaq, the policy of centralization was at the same time a move toward segregation put in place to speed the removal of Natives from within and around white settlements. J. Ralph Kirk, Member of Parliament for Antigonish-Guysborough, wrote to Director of Indian Affairs R.A. Hoey on 15 November 1944, "'I have had inquiries from some of my constituents, expressing the hope that the Indians living in the neighbourhood of Bayfield, N.S. would be moved away from there soon, and this leads me to inquire as to the present status of the Department's plans in this connection.'"[47] In response, Hoey wrote: "'With the hope of improving conditions, plans were made toward consolidation and centralization of the reserves in the knowledge, may I say, that under such a plan we would be able to offer the Indian better educational and vocational facilities.... It was felt that we would also *improve the amenities of the White communities which are not improved by the immediate presence of isolated groups of Indians*'" (my emphasis).[48]

The irony behind centralization, which ultimately failed due to staunch Mi'kmaq resistance, was that it was instituted on the heels of Nova Scotia residential school policy. Shubenacadie Indian Residential School (est. 1929), like all residential schools of its time, had as its supposed objective facilitating the 'cultural progression' of Indigenous students so that they could be assimilated into the body politic as more or less equal citizens. The goal of assimilationist integration clearly runs counter to the segregationist thrust of centralization policy, but this should, by now, come as no surprise. Residential school policy has always been similarly perplexed with its 'cultural progressivist' agenda dogged by endemic racism; never has the political goal of assimilating the Native population, and thereby abolishing their distinct rights, truly contained the social corollary of ignoring ethnic difference and abandoning white perceptions regarding the inferiority of Native blood,[49] nor has it striven to ease the divide between white economic superiority and Indigenous poverty.

The brief historical narrative above sets the stage for how Rita Joe and her contemporaries would come to understand their residential school experiences in the mid-1900s, after the Mi'kmaq had endured over two centuries of British colonial and Canadian state rule. French colonial recognition of Mi'kmaq self-determination and nationhood had become a distant memory. By this point, even the election of Mi'kmaq band leaders and council members was subject to the outside validation of the Indian Agent, as was the determination of individual band membership and Indian status. Relocated and marginalized, without even recourse to the legal foundation of treaty rights available to most other Native nations in Canada—although treaty rights, of course, have not always saved other Native peoples from illegitimate seizure, removal, and outright theft—the Mi'kmaq persisted in the first half of the twentieth century in varying states of extreme poverty, powerlessness, and alienation, which constitute the necessary context in which to understand the life and literature of Rita Joe.

THE COLONIAL EXPERIENCE OF RITA JOE

Joe was born in Whycocomagh, Cape Breton, in 1932, the youngest of five surviving children. Her father, Josie Gould Bernard, was in his late fifties or early
sixties when he married Joe's mother, Annie Googoo, who was sixteen at the time
and significantly younger than some of Josie's children from two previous mar-
riages. Despite being "very poor," like most Mi'kmaq at the time, Joe describes in
Song of Rita Joe having "a loving family" in which "everybody was soft-spoken and
gentle."[50] With Josie making axe handles and working odd jobs, and Annie fishing,
gathering plants, and tending to the children, the family managed to subsist below
the poverty line until Annie's death during childbirth in 1937.[51] Like Anthony
Thrasher, Joe was profoundly affected by the loss of a mother at an extremely
young age, left to "visualize" their times together "like hazy motion pictures of
years gone by" (*Song*, 18). Predeceased by a third wife and now in his seventies,
Josie found himself unable to hold the family together. Josie kept two of his sons
in residential school, left the third with Annie's parents, and maintained guard-
ianship solely of Annabel, Rita's older sister, who was nine or ten at the time and
to whom fell the responsibilities of "cooking, washing, sewing and other chores
for [her] father" (24). Rita, still only five, was placed in a series of Native (predominantly Mi'kmaq) foster homes in the Nova Scotia area. Moving from home
to home and community to community "for six months, maybe three months,
maybe a year, two months, a month, two weeks" (24), Joe was never able, during
her seven years in foster care, to set down the surrogate familial roots that might
have sustained her during later years of hardship.

As with everything else, Joe strives in her autobiography "to recall the good stories" from "each foster home" (24). At times, however, the extremity of the trauma
she experienced overwhelms her narrative recourse to positivity. She was fed and
clothed, although seldom adequately, and she did receive love from "a lot of good
mothers" (25)—albeit what she calls "indifferent love: no touching, except on
the head" (25). Lonesome, dejected, and desperate for affection, Joe came to accept "whatever morsel of praise or love" her foster parents gave her, ultimately
"work[ing] hard for that affection—very hard" (25). Despite her efforts, however,
Joe seldom attained a healthy balance of tenderness, sustenance, and protection.
Joe learned early that "when you live in a foster home, you … don't do anything
wrong and you don't give anyone an excuse to scold you or beat you or whatever.
When I was still very little I learned to be a good girl, to always help" (29) and to
always "do what I was told, no matter how unusual I thought the request" (27–28).

In one home this included making homebrew for alcoholic foster parents and even drinking her vile concoction when the foster mother threatened her: "'If you don't drink it,' … 'I'll throw you out of the house'" (42). Later that night, the ten- or eleven-year-old was found passed out in a vomit-soaked quilt on the snowy front yard.

Joe first experienced the pain of physical abuse in her inaugural foster placement at the home of her half-sister Susie. Although providing an often caring sisterly presence, Susie "had a strong hand" and a "mean" husband (26). Joe recalls: "When [the husband] hit me, I would land across the room" (26). In another home, Joe ran afoul of a foster father who "had a reputation for hurting children for the sake of his own twisted desires" (30). Joe writes of this experience:

> I remember suffering abuse at that house, from the man. When the man asked me to do something that was not pleasant and I objected to it, he said, 'But you do it so good.' That approval meant something to me. When you're in a foster home, you do what you're told. If you're told you're doing something right, you do it again—and again and again, no matter how negative or impossible or bad or ugly it is.…
>
> In order to get away from the man who abused me, I would go upstairs in his house. There was a little crawlspace there; the entrance was about as big as my face and head are today—it was not very big. I used to crawl into it and go to the end. Nobody could come after me because nobody could fit in that crawlspace—only me. I used to go as far as I could, and then fall asleep. (30–31)

Joe's depiction of this abuse establishes certain techniques that constitute what I call her affirmatist literary methodology, a literary posture that endeavours to frame memory and experience in ways that guard both the author and her primary audience from possible (re)traumatization through writing/reading. In many ways, Joe strives for rigorous and faithful reportage throughout *Song of Rita Joe*, explicitly resolving to "tell the truth" and to "talk openly" about "things that have hurt [her]" (138). In some cases, however, by revisiting trauma through narrative, Joe risks subjecting herself to the perils of revictimization and further identity fragmentation (the exact opposite of the consummation of individual identity in which life-writing is supposed to take part). Addressing this danger, Joe writes:

> It's hard for me to describe what it was like when I was little. Words sometimes will not come to me; it's as if they're stuck inside. Some of the hurt was too great, so I just bundled it up and put the little bundles away.

> Those bundles are still on the shelf today and I cannot open some of them.
> If I open them, I will cry, I will get hurt. So that's why I leave the bundles
> alone. It's hard enough to survive knowing that they are there. (32)

To navigate this potential danger while still accommodating her desire "not … to
erase what had happened in [her] life" (138), Joe mobilizes her ideological attachment to a "positive outlook" (137) in a manner that constitutes the heart of her
literary methodology.

Joe uncovers ways of engaging traumatic history that potentially retain their
political expediency without threatening to place reader or author too close to the
details of the violence they announce. Significantly, Joe frames her recollection of
what appears to be sexual abuse not in terms of violent imposition, but in terms
of love and love's loss. Clearly, the abuse was an act of violence, not love, but it was
conducted by virtue of the perpetrator's exploitation of vulnerability created by
the victim's largely loveless childhood. Joe courageously confronts the role of the
child's desire for affection in her exploitation, suggesting, "If you get praised for
doing [something], you want that praise. I always looked for praise and approval
when I was little. I hunted for it" (31).

Beyond the child's need for love, Joe also focuses on the ways in which the abuse
affected the loving relationship she enjoyed with the foster mother in whose home
the abuse occurred:

> Again and again, my love for my foster mother meant so much to me
> that I was willing to shut my mind to the harm the man inflicted, and hope
> that things would end with his death. This didn't happen, so the abuse
> went on … until I told another little girl, and she told her mother, and the
> matter was looked into by people on the reservation.… It broke my heart
> when my foster mother blamed me for what had happened, although I was
> only seven years old. I expressed my love for her, but she shut me out with
> an angry burst of words: "*Mu wela'luksiwun* (You have no gratitude)." I
> cried and wondered if I should have kept my mouth shut. I missed her love
> more than anything else. (30–31)

The pain of the abuse is not most acute in the memory of its physical dimension,
but in its intercession in, and contamination of, the one loving relationship sustaining Joe at the time. In fact, Joe devotes as much text to the loss of the mother's
love as she does to the abuse itself.

Joe's interpretive approach marginalizes both the abuser—who is never named and is referred to only as "the man" and "her husband" rather than the potential 'my foster father'[52]—and the abuse act itself, which is alluded to but never described. It mobilizes narrative energy toward analysis of the condition of love, even within the most debilitating of circumstances. And yet it never leaves the audience any question about the extremity of the trauma with which it deals. The pervasive atmosphere of fear, neglect, and abuse in which Joe found herself throughout her foster years constituted the context in which she, at the age of twelve, *placed herself* in residential school. Unlike other survivors discussed in this book, who were forcibly removed at the behest of Indian Agents or the clergy, Joe decided for her own protection to enter Shubenacadie Indian Residential School in 1944. Such anomalously self-determined enrolment has occasionally been a source of derision among some members of Joe's Mi'kmaq community. Joe recalls one resident of Eskasoni mocking in a full auditorium: "'Rita put herself in that place,' ... and she laughed. Some other people laughed too. But there was another individual in the group who said, 'Rita had bundles of hurt to carry when she was little, so she put herself in there for safekeeping'" (49). Therein lies the contextual complexity surrounding Joe's experience of residential schooling: she entered a harsh environment, which so many have come to lament, compelled by personal anguish and fear rather than authoritarian decree; her understanding of what would ensue was undoubtedly conditioned by the miserable reality it superseded.

Clearly, all residential school experiences are to some degree conditioned by the circumstances that precede them, but we must be careful not to oversimplify this connection. Basil Johnston argues that even though some students at St. Peter Claver's Indian Residential School came from broken homes, their "sense of hurt and alienation was not in any proportion diminished." In Johnston's estimation, "Most of the [students] were already hurt; they were orphans, waifs, cast-offs, exiles from family and home, who needed less of a heavy hand, a heavy foot, heavy words, and more of affection, approbation, companionship, praise, guidance, trust, laughter, regard, love, tenderness."[53] Joe quotes her husband Frank, making a similar plea: "'Some of us didn't have fathers or mothers, and when you knock down people like that, they become demoralized.'"[54] In this sense, the more difficult the child's pre-residential school experience, the more potentially traumatic residential schooling might be. As Regional Director of Indian Affairs F.B. McKinnon noted in the 1960s, the Shubenacadie School was developed "'as an educational facility and not a child caring institution'" and had "neither the appropriate resources nor staff to meet the needs of child caring problems."[55] Thus, despite the fact that many students were, in McKinnon's words, "'exhibiting serious psycho-social problems'"[56] that were presumably the by-products of the Mi'kmaq colonial legacy, dealing with them remained beyond the school's capabilities.

In *Out of the Depths*, Knockwood presents a scathing portrait of the abusive and neglectful environment Mi'kmaq children encountered at Shubenacadie Indian Residential School. Emerging from archival research, authorial memory, and copious interviews with fellow survivors, Knockwood's book exhaustively details the violence with which Shubenacadie's assimilationist mandate was enforced and the brutality of some of those entrusted with children's care and education. As elsewhere, from their entry into the school, the children were beaten for speaking their Native language. Knockwood recalls, "When little children first arrived at the school we would see bruises on their throats and cheeks that told us that they had been caught speaking Mi'kmaw. Once we saw the bruises begin to fade, we knew they'd stopped talking" (98). Many were forcibly humiliated for their female bodies,[57] while others were assaulted physically and/or sexually.[58] Although admitting that "not all the nuns at the school were cruel," Knockwood identifies as "profoundly confusing" the condition that many of those "directly in charge of both girls and boys, far from being examples of Christian love and forgiveness, were ... objects of terror. What continues to mystify many of those who entered the school is the depth of some nuns' hatred for the children" (45). Knockwood provides ample evidence to support this claim, including one nun force-feeding a desperately ill child the food she had just regurgitated (87–88) and another nun employing a strap across a child's hands on a daily basis to teach her to "count to thirty" (82).

While Joe presents a more positive view of the Shubenacadie school, Knockwood provides an extensive inventory of its violence. Unable to "understand why the hurt and shame of seeing and hearing the cries of abused Mi'kmaw children, many of them orphans, does not go away or heal," Knockwood strives through "the act of writing ... [to] help [herself] and others to come up with some answers" (7). Elsewhere, Knockwood explains: "'The reason I wrote the book was to heal the people who were in there. There's a lot of healing that has to be done. Many negative feelings that we carry around are because of that place.'"[59] Following Grand Chief of the Assembly of First Nations Phil Fontaine and other advocates of disclosure as the primary mechanism through which to achieve individual and communal healing, *Out of the Depths* endeavours to "heal" its Mi'kmaq audience by giving public voice to the trauma experienced by Shubenacadie students. Fontaine, the first Native leader to speak publicly about residential school abuse, argued in 1991 that "the only way" for the Native community to overcome the history of residential schooling is to "talk about our collective experience. It should never leave our memory and non-aboriginal people should know what was done to our people." He added that the ultimate "motive for disclosure is to stop our people from killing themselves."[60]

The healing power of disclosure is perhaps given its most potent fictive endorsement in Teetl'it Gwich'in author Robert Arthur Alexie's *Porcupines and China Dolls*, which portrays the act of disclosure by three victims of sexual abuse at residential school as a mythic battle between Native warriors and the demons haunting their community. "As they slowly gather courage in the telling," writes reviewer James Grainger, "the victims are transformed into the warrior heroes of legend."[61] Alexie portrays Chief David reaching "deep down into the very depths of his tormented and fucked-up soul" and pulling "out the rage, anger, hate, sorrow and sadness by their roots and [throwing] them on the floor for the world to see."[62] Chief David then proceeds "to choke the little fuckers like they deserved it," before declaring, "'I'm tired of runnin.' This is where it ends. Right here an' right now. This is where we make the change for ourselves an' for our children. I will run no more!'"[63] In Alexie's work, as in Knockwood's, survivors of residential school abuse are encouraged to confront and vocalize their traumatic experiences in the service of personal and communal healing.

Perhaps the most damning testimony in *Out of the Depths* comes from none other than Rita Joe. Joe recalled the following incident during an interview with Knockwood in the late 1980s. In punishment for having called the nun "swine,"

> Sister took Mary Agnes near the big boys' table and began to smack her around, all the while hollering at her. She kept smacking her, smacking, smacking until Mary Agnes' back was on the boys' table—smack right in the face. The other Sister was peering over the fat Sister who was pinching and hitting. Mary Agnes struck out, and her right fist landed on the other Sister's face. Then the two of them got into it. After they were done beating her, the fat one pushed Mary Agnes all the way to the scullery.... her eye, her mouth and nose were bloody.... The kitchen Sister [saw her and] said, 'You march right up to Father Brown and show him what they have done'. ... Father Brown was hollering and talking real loud. He was so angry! It

was the first time I had ever heard a priest swear. And we heard her crying. Later when I tried to find out I was told that she was taken to the infirmary on the third floor. She stayed in that infirmary from that time on. Then we [heard] she was taken to the hospital. Then, sometime later, we [heard] that she was dead. The incident was so fresh in my mind that when Sister announced that she died because her bones were too big for her heart, I didn't believe her. (107–08)

As astonishing as is the violence herein depicted, just as shocking is Joe's decision not to describe the incident in her autobiography, a decision that signals her methodological divergence from the disclosure-based approach of Knockwood. She indeed alludes to the beating of a girl in *Song of Rita Joe*, but she does so in order to illustrate the kindness of Father Brown rather than to indict the guilty parties. She writes: "Father Brown.... was a gentle man. I only heard him raise his voice once, when he was angry that one of the girls had been severely beaten" (50). Never does she describe the "severe" beating the girl received (and she herself witnessed) or mention that the girl likely died from her wounds. She concisely states that a beating took place and moves on to other matters.

The essential difference between the work of Knockwood and Joe is not of intent but strategy. Both authors promote what Jace Weaver calls "communitist values" by attempting "to participate in the healing of the sense of grief and exile felt by Native communities and the pained individuals in them."[64] Like Knockwood, Joe contends that the "basic reason for [her] writing and speaking is to bring honour to [her] people" (*Song*, 157) and to help them triumph over the indignities of colonial history. However, unlike Knockwood, Joe believes that "if one wishes to be healed, one must dwell on the positive" (14). Joe does not presume that announcing to the world the suffering she and others endured at Shubenacadie will necessarily speed their healing. In fact, Joe admits "'hat[ing] to remember those bad stories'" and preferring "'to dwell on the good ones.'"[65] Of course, as Joe admits, this is not always as easy as it sounds. Recalling how Knockwood challenged her to think of a single positive story from their years at Shubenacadie, Joe writes, "So there we sat, in a room with a tape recorder between us, and it was a long while before I could bring up a good story" (*Song*, 49). She continues later: "It is like that with everything in my life. I look for an honourable image to create. Sometimes—with many things that happened at school—I have had to search for a long time, but when I find it, it is good" (55).

Joe's willingness to downplay the negative renders her work vulnerable to attack from more aggressively anti-colonial Native critical factions who conceivably might confront the author with any of the following questions: Is such authorial self-censoring appropriate, given what Fontaine and others view passionately as the essential role of disclosure in saving Indigenous lives and communities? Is Joe's positivity not a form of historical erasure, marginalizing suffering, sweeping criminal behaviour under the carpet, and offering an incomplete picture of the oppressive forces of government and church? Could Joe's stance not be perceived as politically debilitating, socially regressive, and even historically inaccurate? Does it not play into the hands of dominance?

In his review of Joe's autobiography, David Newhouse gestures toward some explanations of the political potential of the author's positive stance. In response to Joe's comment, at one point in the book, that she and her husband "must 'forgive and forget' the things that happened to them while growing up at the Shubenacadie Indian School," Newhouse disagrees, insisting "we must forgive, but we must not forget. And *Song of Rita Joe* will help us not forget."[66] The peculiar nature of Joe's literary methodology is to advocate a turn away from the painful past that, rather than erasing that past, seeks to build a positive future from its ashes. As Newhouse illustrates, while Joe's affirmatism appears to endorse the complete abnegation of negative history—and the "forgive and forget" comment certainly supports such a suggestion—the text itself simply doesn't allow that the negative didn't occur.[67] In fact, Joe repeatedly acknowledges throughout *Song of Rita Joe* the hardships she endured in foster care, in residential school, and in marriage;[68] she just determines not to "dwell" on them. One comes away from reading *Song of Rita Joe* struck by the extent of the trauma she has endured and by her capacity to prevent that trauma from (pre)occupying her consciousness. Knockwood and Joe adopt in their work what might be crudely referred to as contrasting 'victim' and 'survivor' postures.[69] For Knockwood the act of speaking her victimhood provides a level of narrative control over traumatic personal history that creates the conditions in which healing might occur. Joe, on the other hand, refuses to proclaim herself a victim, despite the injuries she has endured, thereby creating a narrative voice that already assumes itself empowered. Joe believes augmenting through literary attention those historical relations (or moments of interaction) among individuals, communities, tribes, and nations that have been positive to be the most effective means of promoting the social, political, and spiritual health of her Mi'kmaq audience.

Joe told the predominantly Native audience during her acceptance of a National Aboriginal Achievement Award—the award, among many she has received, that she "values most"[70]—that "no matter from what circumstances you come ..., and no matter from what culture, or how poor you are, everybody can do this"—by which I interpret her to mean achieve success, spiritual health, and community admiration and support. "You just have to put your effort into it and be positive. Don't try to work on the negative stuff."[71] Implicit in Joe's heterodox advice is a belief that focusing on past trauma risks binding oneself to its negativity and thereby stalling rather than encouraging personal healing. The crucial point here is that Joe's affirmatist literary methodology is not a denial of the negative past, but is, rather, a strategic focusing of narrative attention on positive aspects of personal experience, upon which a peaceful and empowered future might be built. In this way, Joe's reticence to include certain details about her residential school experience in *Song of Rita Joe* should be viewed, I would argue, as different in kind rather than in degree from the type of censorship that Shubenacadie administrators solicited (often by threat) from their students in order to hide their own abusive behaviour. Knockwood recalls

> Sister Superior coming into our classroom to lecture us about loyalty to the school and how it was our responsibility to keep its reputation good and not bring disgrace to it and to Father Mackey. "You give the school and your teachers the same loyalty you give your parents. For example, you don't go around telling the whole neighbourhood when your parents have a fight so you do the same thing here. Don't repeat what you've seen and heard about the fights or punishments in the school especially when you go on vacation because we have ways of finding out if you do."[72]

Joe suggests that a narrative focus on the negative things fails to forward the social and political goals she desires of her writing; she suggests that transfixing ourselves with the negative aspects of the past is a dead-end road unless harnessed to a positive outlook for the future.[73]

AN AFFIRMATIST LITERARY METHODOLOGY

Anishinabe writer Gerald Vizenor argues in *Manifest Manners* that Native literatures should "be read as the eternal shadows of the heard rather than *as mere evidence*" (my emphasis)[74] for tribal lifeways or historical reconstructions. Calling distinctly "literary" analyses of Indigenous literatures "a wise departure from the surveillance of the social sciences" (77), Vizenor cautions against the critical reduction of Native literatures to "mere representations" (71) of the historical past. According to Vizenor, "Native American Indian literatures have been overburdened with critical interpretations based on … social science theories that value incoherent foundational representations of tribal experiences" (74) at the expense of postmodern literary interpretations that value the motion and play of language beyond the "burdens of conceptual reference" that bog down the critical "literature of dominance" (71).

Up to this point, I have been discussing Joe's autobiography in terms of its representation and silencing of Shubenacadie experiences (or memories), a critical posture more historical than literary, which surely would provoke Vizenor's ire. As its subtitle declares, *Song of Rita Joe* is the *Autobiography of a Mi'kmaq Poet.* It splices autobiographically charged poetry into the heart of its prose narrative, complicating genre and narrative voice and troubling any pretence that its language straightforwardly represents a somehow factual past. Joe enlists poetry from her previously published collections to expand upon, complicate, and even amend her prose narrative, generating meaning through the dialogic collision of authorial voices: poetic, didactic, and autobiographical. Joe had taken on nearly all the major incidents she relates in *Song of Rita Joe* in one or another of her collections of poetry long before she considered presenting her life story as a linear narrative. As Ruth Holmes Whitehead acknowledges in the book's introduction, Joe "constantly works with her past in her writing,"[75] poetic or otherwise. Her poetry, written largely in the first person, consistently references settings and individuals (often by name) from the author's life, including herself. The poem "I Am an Indian on This Land" illustrates the open and exposed authorial position from which Joe tends to compose:

> Today I will share what is mine
> Today I give you my heart
> This is all we own.
> Today I show.
> Hello everybody, my name is Rita Joe. (69)

Joe is omnipresent in her poetry, as authorial voice and often as speaker and even subject matter, although these presences are sometimes veiled in the nuances of poetic diction and craft.

In an autobiographical essay entitled "Neon Scars," Hopi/Miwok poet Wendy Rose illustrates the vexing relationship that can inhere for the artist between autobiography and poetry:

> Everything I have ever written is fundamentally autobiographical, no matter what the topic or style; to state my life now in an orderly way with clear language is actually to restate, simplified, what has already been said. If I could just come right out and state it like that, as a matter of fact, I would not have needed poetry. If I could look my childhood in the eye and describe it, I would not have had to veil those memories in metaphor. If I had grown up with a comfortable identity, I would not need to explain myself from one or another persona.[76]

Having devoted such meticulous attention to struggling with and rendering her personal history through poetry, Joe, like Rose, recognizes the limitations of expression and effect offered by standard, linear prose, autobiography. Joe invokes seventy-eight poems or segments of poems throughout *Song of Rita Joe*'s 160 pages, penetrating the realist style of standard autobiography with the play of verse. Significantly, Joe's poetic insertions, although always thematically appropriate and often directly related by content to the sections in which they are found, are almost never naturalized into the narrative through editorial commentary or authorial discussion. The poems persist on their own in the midst of the narrative, often without breaks or section indicators, with no introduction by the author and no attendant analysis. In short, Joe refuses to interpret on the reader's behalf, refuses to rob her reader of interpretive agency. Neither, however, is the narrative bent to the will of the poetry; the prose does not simply fill the gaps left between autobiographical poems, but rather proceeds independently of the poetry with which it is interspersed. Despite the apparent independence, however, each genre influences the other in a strategic manner, creating the fertile tension through which Joe's affirmatist literary methodology functions.

Joe invokes three full poems related to residential schooling in the portion of her autobiography dedicated to the Shubenacadie years: "Indian Residential Schools" from *Lnu and Indians We're Called* (1991),[77] and "I Lost My Talk" and "Hated Structure" from *Song of Eskasoni* (1988).[78] After detailing in the prose narrative the circumstances underlying her decision to place herself in Shubenacadie at the age of twelve, Joe introduces her residential school experiences with "Indian Residential Schools." Expertly contextualizing her discussion of Shubenacadie within (and against) a predominantly negative contemporary discourse of disclosure—beginning "Today on television I heard a discussion / Of residential schools across the country. / I saw a man talk about sex abuse done to him / He even had a hard time saying it" (49)—the poem then shifts discursive attention toward more positive aspects of residential school history. Although the poet[79] admits that "There was physical abuse where I was / Not sex, but mind mistreatment" and that "With me, there was one individual who did this," she insists on bringing to light the "fact" that "people who came from schools / Have turned into productive persons. / Even women who had it hard have become nuns / And men from across the country their dreams realized" (49). She proclaims, "The four years [at residential school] have given me strength. / My life to this day has gained courage. / I know who I am, and my people are the prize" (50). While acknowledging the existence of the negative conditions that have preoccupied public discourse on residential schooling, "Indian Residential Schools" offers an alternative interpretation of residential schooling in relation to positive developments for Native individuals and communities that have emerged in its wake, not declaring residential school a positive experience but recognizing the part it played in creating conditions that have led to some progress.

Joe's willingness in the poem to view residential school experiences in relation to positive effects within Native communities appropriately sets the stage for the prose passage that follows. Although she again admits briefly "that bad things happened" (50) during her time at Shubenacadie, Joe focuses her prose narrative on positive events and relationships that sustained her throughout these potentially alienating years. She talks of the "very kind" Sister Rita, whom the children "all loved" because she "taught" them what they "were supposed to learn," "did not look down" on them, and "even befriended [them]" (51). She speaks of the nun who worked in the laundry and "every day" would give her "a candy or a chocolate or a little gift—perhaps a notebook or pencil or box of crayons," gifts that were "simple" but "very important" (51) to the motherless child's senses of belonging and of being loved. For Joe, "this nun was like a mother figure" (51). "I loved her," she exults, "[and] I still love her today" (51). Joe also tells of an act of selfless kindness that profoundly affected her outlook on her residential school years. (This is the episode Joe eventually remembered when challenged by Knockwood to "think of one good story you can tell about that place.")[80] Having no living parents at the time and siblings either in the army overseas or mired in local poverty, Joe never received parcels from home at Christmas like the other Shubenacadie children, a source of considerable grief which she voiced occasionally to the kind nun from the laundry. After years of bitter disappointment and dejection, Joe finally received a Christmas parcel containing "fruit and candies, a handkerchief, hand lotion and pretty pins for [her] hair" (53). "Oh, I treasured those gifts," Joe writes. "They meant so much to me" (53). Joe told Knockwood that on that day she "was the happiest fifteen-year-old in the world."[81] However, despite being "anxious to see who [the parcel] was from,"[82] Joe found the postmark illegible and no indication of sender inside the box. As Joe makes clear in *Song of Rita Joe*, the package must have been sent by the nun from the laundry. Yet, when confronted about it, all the nun said was, "'Oh, ... somebody must care for you'" (54). According to Joe, "she never took credit for the parcel; she wanted me to feel good" (54). This gesture across the racial divide and the hierarchical chasm separating nun from student helped convince Joe of the power of love and conciliation (as opposed to anger and retaliation) to aid the healing of the wounded, a realization integral to her development of an affirmatist writing posture.

Joe's abrupt turn from these discussions of kindness to a poem dealing with the trauma of institutionalized suffocation of Indigenous language, however, produces a somewhat jarring effect on the reader. "I Lost My Talk" reads:

> I lost my talk
> The talk you took away
> When I was a little girl
> At Shubenacadie school.
>
> You snatched it away;
> I speak like you
> I think like you
> I create like you
> The scrambled ballad, about my word.
>
> Two ways I talk
> Both ways I say,
> Your way is more powerful.
>
> So gently I offer my hand and ask,
> Let me find my talk
> So I can teach you about me. (55)

Although seemingly inconsistent with the glowing portrait of loving supervision provided in the preceding prose, "I Lost My Talk" brings together certain threads that augment and alter the way the prose functions. On the one hand, Joe employs poetry here, as elsewhere in *Song of Rita Joe*, to vent pain and anger in a concise way that does not colonize and exhaust her prose. In a manner of speaking, Joe, like Rose, banishes the negative to poetry, where the reader must unearth its corrosive content through analysis and interpretation, rather than laying it bare for easy consumption through extended description. In this way, periodic poetic struggles with the negative free the autobiographical prose to adopt its positive stance. And yet, "I Lost My Talk" is more than simply a mouthpiece for rage toward the systems of power that stole her Mi'kmaq language—the "you" the speaker "speak[s] like," "think[s] like," and "create[s] like." The poem's development signals a movement in thought that nudges its speaker toward an affirmatist realization while mapping out a strategy for speaking to power.

After pronouncing the divestiture of Native voice by white authority, the speaker concedes that the school's "way" of talking is "more powerful" than the Native way. The power of English, however, is initially exercised in terms of divisive force. English was the primary intellectual context in which Mi'kmaq was "snatched … away" from Shubenacadie children (with the aid of fists, switches, and the strap); it was the imposition that separated the speaker from her tribal tongue. By contrast, Joe positions the return of Mi'kmaq as a triumph of (re)conciliation over division. The final stanza begins with the offering of a hand, a gesture of unification that transcends the rage of the opening stanzas, before attempting to instigate a course of action that will restore to the speaker her "talk." Thus the final stanza promotes both the reunification of the speaker and her language and the unification of the Mi'kmaq and the white. However, the progression from division to reunification is presented through the vehicle of the "scrambled ballad" in English, suggesting the utilitarian function of a colonial language when harnessed in the pursuit of Indigenous self-knowledge. English is "more powerful" in the poem not simply because it has historically participated in the suffocation of Indigenous languages, but also because, unlike Mi'kmaq, it can speak to multiple audiences—including Natives who perhaps learned English in residential school and non-Natives who hold the balance of political power in this country.

In an example of affirmatism in practice, Joe affirms the positive potential of a particular colonial imposition in relation to healing and empowerment without trivializing the pain the process of imposition has caused. Joe mobilizes "the good" aspects of English in a poem that foregrounds the continuing importance of Indigenous languages and the reconciliation of Natives and non-Natives. In this way, the English language, when properly used, becomes for Joe akin to the "magic weapons" the

Okimasis brothers acquire in the fields of drama and dance through their interactions with non-Native Canada in Highway's *Kiss of the Fur Queen*. In both cases the artists' skills with non-Native cultural implements are rendered powerful and empowering when employed in the analysis and invigoration of Indigenous cultures.

Given Joe's speaker's deduction that the non-Native way is "more powerful," it is unsurprising that the movement toward conciliation is presented as a plea: the speaker "ask[s]" the implied non-Native audience, "Let me find my talk / So I can teach you about me." However, Joe's precise crafting of the poem's final two lines troubles the conclusiveness of this non-Native authority. The onus in these lines is on the speaker, not the audience. (As Joe writes in one of her most famous poems: "I am the Indian / And the burden / Lies yet with me.")[83] She does not ask to be given her language back, but, rather, asks for the freedom to "find" it herself, an important distinction that acknowledges how Native agency is restricted by the neo-colonial power structure. Joe's "let me find my talk" is not so much deference to non-Native authority as a call for the slackening of forces that seek to circumscribe Native agency. The speaker claims a degree of power in a non-threatening, conciliatory yet deter-mined, position.[84] She becomes the active party by the end of "I Lost My Talk"—a far cry from the victim of thieving non-Native schoolmasters who "snatched" her talk in an earlier stanza—a progression consummated by the reversal implicated in the speaker's intention to "teach you about me." In contrast to the residential school set-ting, in which teaching was the context for disempowerment, trauma, and separation, the final stanza presents teaching *by the Native speaker* as a vehicle for empowerment, healing, and unification, articulating in the process the ideological horizon of the poet's affirmatism. Joe does not adopt a vengeful posture that would seek to revisit the trauma experienced in residential school back on non-Natives. Joe's affirmatism is always a tool for conciliation, *not* division.

Furthermore, the poem acts as evidence that Mi'kmaq thought is neither extinct nor incapable of reaching through the written word. As much as the poem mimics a non-Native "ballad" structure, its words attest to Mi'kmaq experiences of residential school while potentially engendering positive responses; and as much as the final line pronounces the speaker's intention to "teach" the audience about herself in the event that her "talk" can be found, clearly the poem has already taught us about her, thereby initiating the process of conciliation and empowerment the poem appears only to call for. In "I Lost My Talk," Joe salvages an archive of the "good" from her traumatic past—the love of and skill with English poetry—which she mobilizes in her struggle to transcend the negative effects of the residential school legacy. She complicates the predominantly positive prose representation of Shubenacadie experiences that precedes the poem to show not only that "the good" doesn't necessarily exist in isolation from trauma, but also that "the good" must be engaged creatively to achieve its full potency in the struggle toward empowerment.

After "I Lost My Talk," the prose narrative turns to Joe's departure from Shubenacadie at the age of sixteen. Building on the impulse toward autonomous empowerment introduced by the preceding poem, Joe describes the feeling of "freedom" she experienced as the "train pulled away" (56) from Shubenacadie:

> I made a vow to myself that nobody was going to tell me what to do again. I was finally grown up, and nobody would ever hurt me again; nobody would ever tell me when to eat, wash, go to bed or go to the bathroom. Most of all, the spiritual part of me would be my own. If I was going to commit a sin, I would commit it with my own free will.
>
> The confinement of my will had been going on for so long that I cried just until the school was out of sight. Then I began to giggle—and I sat there, giggling, to my heart's content. (56)

After tending to depict her Shubenacadie experience through its positive elements, from loving nuns, to gracious gifts, to the "freedom of reading" (53), Joe finally turns her narrative to the suffocating regimentation of residential school life, but she does so in the affirmatist frame of emancipation. Joe's first extended discussion of how the "confinement" of residential school left her "aching to have [her] freedom" (56) occurs in relation to the joyous moment of her graduation; thus, narrative focus is diverted toward the newly acquired personal freedom that will nourish the young woman's Mi'kmaq identity and eventually her poetic voice, and away from the traumatic oppression that had heretofore kept her identity and voice at bay.

Joe continues interrogating the relationship among personal freedom, creativity, and empowerment in the section's final poem, which links the physical building that housed the Shubenacadie school to the systemic regimentation the students endured therein—hence the two meanings of the poem's title, "Hated Structure." Like "I Lost My Talk," "Hated Structure" paints a darker picture of residential schooling than that found in the surrounding prose. For the adult speaker returning to the site of childhood trauma, the deserted Shubenacadie schoolbuilding is "A reminder to many senses / To respond like demented ones" (57). In it she sees "a deluge of misery / ... Where the children lived in laughter, or abuse" (57). The speaker stops short, however, of re-entering the building, preferring to expostulate its lingering meaning from outside its oppressive walls:

> I had no wish to enter
> Nor to walk the halls.
> I had no wish to feel the floors
> Where I felt fear
> A beating heart of episodes
> I care not to recall.
> The structure stands as if to say:
> I was just a base for theory
> To bend the will of children
> I remind
> Until I fall. (58)

At first glance, "Hated Structure" appears a surprising poem with which to conclude Joe's autobiographical discussion of residential schooling, considering the author's ideological commitment to the positive. "Hated Structure" is surely Joe's most scathing poetic indictment of residential school policy. It performs the opposite of the goal Joe once voiced of telling the world "the positive part of the residential school,"[85] and yet it is the last thing Joe has her reader encounter before moving on to "Song of My Youth." The reason behind such seemingly counterintuitive arrangement, I would argue, brings us back to the struggle between regimentation and freedom.

At its essence, residential schooling was institutionalized divestiture of Indigenous autonomy. It sought to control all aspects of Native children's lives, from the language they spoke, to the clothes they wore, to the games they played, to the God they worshipped. The speaker intuits this oppressive force to be manifest in the physical structure of the Shubenacadie building. The poem's final words, however, signal a mitigation of the speaker's potential retraumatization through the transfer of control from building/system to individual. The building "remind[s]" of childhood trauma only until it "fall[s]," and, as coastal Mi'kmaq readers of Song of Eskasoni would have known in 1988 and readers of the autobiography are made aware, the school had recently been torn down. With the absence of the physical structure that embodied the regimented disciplinary impulse of the system, gone is the compulsion to relive the traumatic experiences that system produced. The speaker is now presumed free from the bodily coercion of the system and also from the tyranny of memory.

And yet, the potential freedom augured by the building's eventual demolition asserts its relevance throughout the poem, even in the building's presence. On a literal level, "Hated Structure" tells of a time when the school still stood; it tells of what the speaker felt as she wandered its circumference, and, even before the school's demolition, the speaker asserts control over how she will remember the period in her life the school represents. She chooses neither to "enter / Nor to walk the halls"; she actively guards against a possible rush of memories she "care[s] not to recall." Much like "I Lost My Talk," "Hated Structure" evidences its speaker's personal empowerment. The delicate crafting of the poetry bespeaks the poet's control over the motion of memory and its representation in the same moment the speaker is shown battling the return of living recollections—the "beating heart of episodes"—and determining their place in her consciousness.

"Hated Structure" executes Joe's affirmatist literary methodology by liberating the speaker/poet to render history and memory in a manner consistent with the ideals of a positive and empowered future. The poem asserts narrative control over a traumatic history so that it can be dealt with in a manner injurious to neither author nor reader. Control over memories and representations of the past forms a precondition for empowerment. For Joe, the primary means of asserting such control is art, by building from the past in a manner of the artist's choosing rather than as dictated by traumatic memory and psychological symptomology. One must rule or be ruled by the negatives she or he has endured. By purging much of the negative in carefully wrought, highly fertile poems (which are themselves acts of defiance and empowerment), Joe is able to orient her life-narrative toward positive elements that promote reconciliation, respect, and mutual love between Natives and non-Natives. Joe's affirmatist literary methodology works dialogically: the positive thrust of the prose narrative is modified and enhanced by the implications of the poetry, while the poetry is enlivened with shadows of "the good" cast upon it by the prose.

Affirmatism is a tool with which to struggle toward empowerment and healing; it is neither the destination nor the ultimate solution. It does not completely annex trauma, but it does provide a strategy for engaging the negative past that gestures toward a more personally and communally healthy future. This being said, Joe is not free, in absolute terms, from the victimization of her past by virtue of her literature. She admits, "Being a survivor means that you don't go crazy or blow your top. At times, it was very hard to survive. The experiences of my childhood, I'm reliving them yet—and I won't stop reliving them until I die."[86] Yet, Joe's regular interactions with those childhood experiences in the controlled and autonomous context of creative literature have left her less at the mercy of memory than she might otherwise be. The end of *Song of Rita Joe* depicts a gloriously content grandmother who has overcome adversity to achieve a harmonious and loving place at the centre of her community. Joe writes:

My life is in Eskasoni, with my friends and my children and grandchildren. The more my grandchildren come to visit, the more I love them. And it is not only my own grandchildren—all the children call me grandma. Even older people call me "*Su'kwis* (Auntie)." I love that. Who could ask for more? Being a survivor has made me build a brave heart—what we would call a *kinap*. Our tradition tells of the men who are *kinaps*, but I think there must be women *kinaps*, too. I leave behind the memory of an orphan child, picking herself up from the misery of being nobody, moving little grains of sand until she could talk about the first nations of the land. (169)

Here, "leave behind" must refer to producing an archive of, rather than discarding, the "memory" of the "orphan child," because it seems through the course of *Song of Rita Joe* that it is indeed the act of "talk[ing]" and writing about the orphan child's history according to the methodological practices of affirmatism that has created the foundation on which the author now stands. Joe has created conditions that promote her own happiness, both through her actions and her literary endeavours. The question remains, however, of whether Joe's affirmatism is effective for others as well. Will it aid in the healing and empowerment of the Mi'kmaq community in the wake of Shubenacadie and half a millennium of colonialism?

Clearly, *Song of Rita Joe* will not be invoked in courtrooms. It will not provide evidence to provoke punitive vengeance against institutional perpetrators or help gain for Shubenacadie survivors monetary reparations from the federal government and the Catholic Church. *Song of Rita Joe* dances well outside the standard frames for revisiting residential school experiences, and therein lies its empowering potential. The authorial power Joe exhibits in her autobiography offers a remarkably fertile model for the empowerment of Mi'kmaq readers because it depends on neither government apologies and remunerations nor church-led conferences and healing circles; in fact, it requires nothing from white authority at all. *Song of Rita Joe* is the exercise of its author's own empowerment, a pure expression of Indigenous sovereignty, which charts a course that others might follow in efforts toward autonomy and healing. *Song of Rita Joe* does not demand that all Mi'kmaq readers adopt the author's affirmatist position. In fact, it encourages others along the paths of their choosing because, at its essence, Joe's affirmatism is a call for individual engagement with personal history, an act that must always remain autonomous, while nonetheless functioning according to a communitist impulse.

A polyphony of Native voices raised in the service of empowerment and survivance is immeasurably preferable to the siphoning of Native resistance into a finite number of preordained categories, often the creation of non-Native scholars and 'experts.' Robert Allen Warrior says, "Unifying categories … obscure crucial differences in a discourse much in need of recognizing the variety of contemporary American Indian experiences. Cohesion, on this reading, is neither beneficial, possible, or necessary."[87] Since Shubenacadie's closing in 1967, non-Native academics have claimed a degree of control over the dissemination and interpretation of Native works that unfortunately mimics the control over language and voice inflicted by residential schools. An example of this control is the way academic discourse has created certain expectations about how Indigenous survivors of residential school ought to remember their experiences in government/church captivity through narrative (recall Boldt on Johnston and Scott on Joe). As Métis author Marilyn Dumont argues, "There is a connection between domination and representation.… [T]he misrepresentation of me makes me doubt my experience, devalue my reality and tempts me to collude in an image which in the end disempowers me."[88] For some, residential school was the most horrifying and debilitating of possible experiences, but this does not *de facto* make it so for *all* survivors. Joe had a difficult time at residential school, but one that was conditioned by even more difficult foster experiences and by certain loving relationships she was able to forge at Shubenacadie. She declares, "Still, today, I do not regret going into the residential school,"[89] and there are absolutely no moral grounds from which to insist that she should. Her experiences are her own and if we, as readers and critics, deny her representation of them, then we collude in her oppression. Again, as Dumont illustrates, "if I, as a native person, engage in the denial of my own image then I am participating in just another variety of internalized colonialism which blinds me and fosters my disempowerment."[90]

Late in her autobiography, Joe recites "one of the [most] important things" she attempted to instil in her children: "We are the ones who know about ourselves. 'Don't fear declaring anything … because you are the ones who know. You may not be an expert, but you do know'" (96). The power of this statement is everywhere in *Song of Rita Joe*, endlessly battling the infection of external control, from residential school to academia and back to Eskasoni. As she gently instructs her readership: "Analyze, if you wish, but listen" (158).

Nitotem

He was tired of having his ears pulled,
squeezed and slapped
by Sister Superior. They bled and
swelled, scabbed and scaled like the brick wall.
Often he didn't hear the Sister shouting
and clapping her orders at him
or the rest of the little boys.
The others, when they could,
would nudge him so he could lip-read Sister's words.

He was embarrassed to undress in front of all the boys
and especially Sister.
At home he always looked out the window
when someone was undressing. Here everyone looked
and laughed at your private parts.
Soon they too were no longer private.

He suffered in silence
in the dark. A hand muffled his mouth
while the other snaked his wiener. He had no
other name, knew no other word. Soon it was no
longer just the hand but the push, just a gentle
push at first, pushing, pushing. Inside the
blanket he sweated and felt the wings
of pleasure, inside his chest the breath burst
pain, pleasure, shame. Shame.
♦♦♦
On the reserve he had already raped two
women, the numbers didn't matter.
Sister Superior was being punished. It was
Father who said it was woman's fault
and that he would go to hell.

He walked, shoulder slightly stooped
and never looked directly at anyone.
When spoken to he mumbled into his chest.
His black hair covered his eyes. He no longer
tried to lip-read, no longer studied the
brick wall.

From *Bear Bones & Feathers* (1994)
by Louise Halfe (Plains Cree)
Survivor: Blue Quills Residential School,
St. Paul, Alberta

CHAPTER 5

From Trickster Poetics to Transgressive Politics: Substantiating Survivance in Tomson Highway's *Kiss of the Fur Queen*

"… a literature is taking shape and acquiring strength, a literature that does not lull its readers to sleep, but rather awakens them; that does not propose to bury our dead, but to immortalize them; that refuses to stir the ashes but rather attempts to light the fire."
Eduardo Galeano,
"In Defense of the Word"

"My story is a gift. If I give you a gift and you accept that gift, then you don't go and throw that gift in the waste basket. You do something with it."
Anonymous residential school survivor,
Breaking the Silence

Within the context of residential school history, survivor narratives have generally been perceived as performing two political functions. The first involves the creation of healthier communities through the cathartic revisitation of past trauma by individual victims. According to this line of thinking, the extended critical rumination required to compose a residential school narrative allows the writer to purge emotional baggage associated with childhood trauma and achieve some form of closure and healing, which ultimately spills back upon the political unit of the community in the form of a more potentially productive individual. This is the position advocated by Fontaine and Knockwood in the preceding chapter. The second involves providing the testimonial evidence that forms the precondition for litigation against individual abusers as well as the institutional and administrative overseers of the residential school system. Survivor testimonials have formed the backbone of nearly all recent critical challenges to the Canadian government regarding its part in residential schooling.[1] They also underlie the thousands of residential school lawsuits currently before the courts. This chapter examines the capacity for a text that departs significantly from both standard avenues for political effect, Tomson Highway's 1998 *Kiss of the Fur Queen*, to nonetheless perform a significant and identifiable political function.

While Highway has publicly declared, "'I *had* to write this book,'"[2] "'if I couldn't have written it, I would have killed myself,'"[3] *Kiss of the Fur Queen* is difficult to treat solely as purgative 'healing' literature due to its complex and lengthy path from composition to publication. Initially written as an autobiography, *Kiss of the Fur Queen* went through incarnations as a stage play, a made-for-TV movie, and an estimated 800-page epic before being published by Doubleday (a major Canadian press) as a novel less than half that size. Although the writing may have performed various psychologically and spiritually redemptive tasks for its author, the ultimate textual product—subject to editorial intervention, alterations in genre, and processes of material manufacture—can evidence those tasks solely through implication; to borrow a phrase from Gerald Vizenor, they persist as "the tease of shadows in tribal remembrance."[4] Furthermore, *Kiss of the Fur Queen* explicitly distances itself from survivor testimony, stating in its Acknowledgements, "This book, of course, is a novel—all the characters and what happens to them are fictitious" (v). The central questions for this chapter are, therefore, how can a novel that intentionally diverges from the testimonial paradigm, and, as such, cannot aid in the acquisition of retribution and restitution within the existing legal framework, generate political effect beyond the individual healing of its author? And how can that effect be understood and discussed in non-hypothetical terms?

One possible strategy for exploring these questions emerges from the critical work of Anishinabe writer Gerald Vizenor. In his 1994 treatise, *Manifest Manners*, and elsewhere, Vizenor develops the concept of "survivance," which he applies to Indigenous literary works that battle the dominance of colonially imposed simulations and unsettle existing power relations by creatively re-imagining Indigenous culture and identity in the contemporary moment. Conceptualizing the battle over identity within a discursive realm dominated by Baudrillardian simulation, Vizenor divides narrative acts between those forged in the interest of ongoing domination of Indigenous peoples by Euro-North America—what he calls "manifest manners"—and those forged in the interest of Indigenous cultural integrity and survival—what he calls "survivance." In a world contaminated by the duplicitous tales of foreign parties about colonial history, and even about Native identity, it becomes essential for what he calls the "postindian warrior" to creatively reimagine her or his reality.[5] By controlling the self-image and imaginatively reinventing viable ways of being Native through narrative, postindian warriors defy the impositions of the dominant culture and, most importantly, define their identities for themselves: "touch" themselves "into being with words."[6]

In Vizenorian terms, Highway's departure from a testimonial paradigm can thus be construed as politically charged in its actualization of narrative agency and its staunch refusal to emulate what Vizenor calls in *Manifest Manners* "the surveillance of the social sciences" (77). Highway refuses in the novel to be constrained by a fact-based historiographic relationship to residential school experience; his writing acquiesces neither to the colonial storyline of inevitable assimilation crafted through residential school institutionalization nor the post-colonial storyline of inevitable victimhood crafted through revisionist history—both examples of Vizenor's "manifest manners." In this way, Highway's narrative posture in *Kiss of the Fur Queen* embodies the principles of Vizenor's "survivance." Yet, what remain difficult to articulate with any sense of accuracy using Vizenor's critical methodology are the political effects initiated by Highway's artistic departure. The language of postmodern simulation in which Vizenor renders his theory tends to frustrate critical attempts to clarify the relationship between literature and life, between the simulations embedded in literary creations and actual lived experience within an extra-textual reality. In fact, given Vizenor's contention that "there isn't any center to the world but a story,"[7] it appears difficult to articulate a distinction between the lived and the literary at all.

Vizenor argues in *Manifest Manners* that "some simulations are survivance, but post-indian warriors are wounded by the real. The warriors of simulations are worried more by the real than other enemies of reference. Simulations are the substitutes of the real, and those who pose with the absence of the real must fear the rush of the real in their stories" (23). What becomes unclear in this formulation is the status of the "real" in response to narratives of survivance. Presumably the bleak and oppressive "real" to which Vizenor refers has been created, or at least influenced, by the simulations of dominance. The simulations of survivance, on the other hand, seek to "substitute" for this unpalatable "real" by which the postindian is "wounded." This substitution, however, seems ultimately trapped in simulation as the postindian simulator must "fear the rush of the real" in her or his narrative simulations (perhaps even in those of survivance). Because the postindian warrior strives invariably against the "real," it becomes unclear how that "real" can be affected by her or his simulations. In much the same way that Baudrillard departs from the premise that simulations affect reality to argue ultimately that reality itself is a pure simulacrum,[8] Vizenor seems to be stymied in the realm of the image, unable to articulate the necessary bridge on the far side of his counter-discursive program.

Certain critics, however, have identified in Vizenor's work a keen, although covert, recognition of the boundaries between the real and the simulated. Barry E. Laga, for example, notes in his review of *Manifest Manners* that Vizenor's work presupposes a "tribal real" by analyzing how it "has been replaced, misconstrued, and superseded by simulations of the unreal."[9] Similarly, Colin Samson argues that Vizenor's "sympathy is always with the active and dynamic real, rather than the simulation, the sense of a native presence, rather than the markers of its absence."[10] Samson views Vizenor as distinguishing between static conceptions of "the real," simulated in the service of domination, and the flexible and fluid reality of daily existence for Native people. "The real as an 'it' is a simulation," he claims. "What is labelled as 'real,' what is concluded to be 'fact,' what is produced as the trump card over all other forms of making sense of the world, simulates the real experience of people" (60). Thus, according to Samson, it is the attempt to "fix" reality through language—to identify it as a *thing*—that impairs our understanding of "real experience." When ongoing experience is arrested as a noun, it becomes, in Samson's reading of Vizenor, a simulation. But this begets the question: how, then, do we speak of the "tribal real"? If conducting our analysis through the imperfect vehicle of language dooms us to, at best, perpetually misrepresenting and, at worst, perversely simulating "the real," how can we adeptly address political problems affecting "the real experience[s]" of Native North Americans?

As Krupat argues, "Although it is no longer possible to believe that we can literally represent 'reality,' 'history,' or 'truth,' it still makes a difference whether one chooses or refuses to take it as axiomatic that there is, nonetheless, an aprioristic material reality, of whose history we can more or less speak, in a manner positing truth as a value."[11] While discourse mediates our interactions with corporeal reality, it remains crucial—particularly given the extremity of conditions in many Native communities and among many in the Indigenous diaspora—to acknowledge reality's existence, impossible though it may be to pin down and understand fully. Simulation only gains meaning through its relations with the 'real.'

In "Trickster Discourse," Vizenor speaks of "the imagination of tribal stories, and the power of tribal stories to heal. Stories that enlighten and relieve and relive. Stories that create as they're being told. And stories that overturn the burdens of our human existence."[12] Unless we are willing to explicate the course of survivance, to show what stories "create" through their telling, to trace the genealogies of "enlighten[ing]" and of "heal[ing]," and to interrogate the process through which "human existence" is unburdened, we, as critics, risk imprisoning survivance in parentheses, painting it as hypothetical through speculation. To take survivance seriously, critics must be willing to intercede in the semiotic fog of Beaudrillardian simulation and make explicit the connections between the hyperreality of text and the political and social reality of Indigenous North America. Far from destabilizing the notion that published literature and narrative in general can alter the world, this position affirms the political nature of literature by refusing to take it as a given; it calls upon the critic to legitimate her or his reading of a particular text as political and to trace out in meaningful ways the implications of such a classification. *Kiss of the Fur Queen* enacts a significant imaginative intervention into a discursive environment dominated by simulations designed to "fix" residential school experiences in an historical discourse that maintains non-Native authority. It is, as such, a narrative of survivance. However, straining against the limitations of Vizenorian analysis, this chapter seeks to account for the tangible effects Highway's novel has had on, and augurs for, Native individuals and communities struggling against the adverse legacy of over a century of residential schooling in Canada.

Highway's political positioning has always seemed cause for debate among scholars. In his literary work and public statements, the author has consistently remained a vocal advocate of Indigenous rights in the face of ongoing political, spiritual, and economic oppression. However, he has always done so as a "proud" Canadian citizen, often voicing admiration for his country both at home and abroad.[13] In an article for the *Imperial Oil Review* entitled "My Canada," Highway asks, "Is Canada a successful experiment in racial harmony and peaceful coexistence?" His answer: "Yes, I would say so proudly."[14] Similarly, in a 1995 *Toronto Star* article in which he is asked to speculate about Canada's future, Highway writes, "It's a wonderful privilege to be bilingual and trilingual. It bespeaks of a highly intelligent society, a rich society. I'm proud to be part of this society."[15] Although his praise in these examples is pointedly directed toward social manifestations of multiculturalism rather than specific political institutions, Highway is a difficult figure to situate among the radical fringe of Native activists who would self-identify as 'anti-Canadian' and would adopt what Kanien'kehaka scholar Taiaiake Alfred has called in *Peace, Power, Righteousness* "a 'contentious' posture in relation to the state."[16] Highway, in fact, might be considered among those Native people who Alfred claims mistakenly "*imagine* themselves to be Canadians" (my emphasis, xxi). Holder of three honorary degrees, member of the Order of Canada, and winner of numerous major arts awards, Highway has been embraced to an unprecedented degree by non-Native political institutions, the media, and the Canadian public; he therefore finds himself in the awkward position of writing as an outsider about outsider issues from *within* the mainstream Canadian arts community.

Highway's seemingly conflicted political position has influenced criticisms of his work from two different directions: one suggesting that Highway's attentiveness to a political program compromises his artistry, and the other suggesting that his artistry undermines his work's political effectiveness. In "Nanabush's Return,"[17] Albert Braz argues that Highway is "less ... a bard than ... a cultural and spiritual leader" (143), who "at times allows his politics to undermine the aesthetic unity of his works" (153). With respect to the Rez plays, Braz takes particular exception to what he perceives as Highway's "overtly political conception of Nanabush," which he claims "is achieved through an oversimplification, if not falsification, of both [Native and Christian] traditions" (154). For Braz, Highway's ultimate goal of "replac[ing] Christ at the centre of Native consciousness with his Aboriginal counterpart, the Trickster" (143) leads to serious flaws in the plays' messages, their artistic quality, and their depictions of Native and non-Native cultures. On the other hand, Alan Filewod, in two extremely ambitious articles from the early 1990s, argues that the material context of commercial productions of Highway's plays transforms the author's anti-colonial sentiments into "a more comfortable message [for non-Native audiences] that native culture still survives [and] is growing stronger."[18] According to Filewod, by positioning both Native and non-Native audience members to identify with the Native protagonists, the plays "[permit] the colonizer to assume the posture of the colonized. It is inevitable that we should come to Highway's plays through an identification with the oppressed characters rather than an awareness of our place as colonizer."[19] "Put simply," Filewod continues, "[Highway] lets the Anglo audience off the hook."[20] For Filewod, Highway's plays stifle rather than generate political action because they are so easily absorbed into the cultural agenda of the non-Native majority, which desires to see itself as sympathetic, "sophisticated," and "multicultural,"[21] while anxiously avoiding its implicatedness in the history of oppression Highway's plays document.

Although I haven't room to engage Braz's and Filewod's arguments in depth,[22] I wish to note both critics' identification of a tension among narrative, politics, and spirituality in Highway's art. Braz claims that Highway's politicization of Nana-bush causes the political to overwhelm the spiritual, compromising the audience's understanding of Native and non-Native spiritual systems. Filewod "fear[s] ... that so long as Highway narrates the native struggles as a process of spiritual re-generation audiences will be less accepting of an angrier voice that narrates the struggle in terms of political action" ("Averting," 22). Considering spiritual regen-eration apolitical, Filewod worries about the future of arts-based Indigenous resis-tance if dominated by spiritual concerns. The problem with both these positions is that they presuppose a disjuncture between the political and the spiritual that Highway's work has consistently striven against. In the Rez plays, as in *Kiss of the Fur Queen*, spiritual regeneration is highly politicized; it is portrayed as a political act. In fact, the term "politicized" is poorly chosen as it implies that the spiritual must be altered to render it political, whereas many Native critics have argued that Indigenous spirituality is always already political. In his study of Creek literature *Red on Red*,[23] Muskogee scholar Craig Womack argues that there is "always an in-terrelationship between the political and spiritual" (53). For Womack the "oral tradition has always contained within it [a] level of political critique" (57) and "traditionalism has always been a complicated matrix of social, religious, political, and cultural aspects" (59). Because spirituality was integral to the political orga-nization of most, if not all, pre-contact Indigenous communities, the concept of political action as non-spiritual seems, in an Indigenist sense, externally imposed.

Within the context of residential school history, to which we now return, the dif-ficulty of disentangling the spiritual from the political becomes all too apparent. The violent spiritual imposition enacted by residential schooling occurred at the behest of the Canadian government; thus, any Native reaction to that imposi-tion that seeks to rejuvenate Indigenous spirituality is political insofar as it strives against the assimilative and culturally genocidal program of the former Canadian government and the citizenry for which it stood. In the current political environ-ment, as different government, religious, and Indigenous bodies work to sort out the aftermath of residential schooling, Native spirituality has emerged as a viable form of political protest. With most avenues for what might be termed conven-tional political action—such as litigation, recourse to the Royal Commission on Aboriginal Peoples, and protest through the Assembly of First Nations—presided over by individuals or institutions with close ties to the government from which

Indigenous peoples demand retribution, a search for alternative means of political action, including spiritual regeneration, is occurring.

The existing body of public discourse on the residential school legacy—what I will call 'legacy discourse'—has, for the most part, argued toward a small number of specific strategies for dealing with residential schooling's adverse effects. Largely dominated by government and church interests, yet occasionally penetrated by Aboriginal and non-Aboriginal criticisms, legacy discourse has generally sought partial solutions to residential schooling's aftermath that limit the government and the churches' pecuniary responsibility. Although legacy discourse has evolved significantly since residential schooling became a source of public debate in the early 1980s, the parameters for discussion have remained largely intact, merely shifting in response to further disclosure, historical evidence, and vocal protest. The far more sympathetic and apologetic rhetoric of current legacy discourse still carries with it a finite number of options for political (re)action, most of which maintain the authority of a culpable Canadian government. The political effectiveness of Highway's novel resides not in its provision of support and evidence for existing avenues of compensation within legacy discourse, as might be provided by a testimonial account, but in its criticism and reimagining of legacy discourse itself. Taking into account Taiaiake Alfred's arguments that "the idea that Indigenous peoples can find justice within the colonial legal framework" is a "myth," and that "attempting to decolonize without addressing the structural imperatives of the colonial system is clearly futile,"[24] *Kiss of the Fur Queen* can be read as an alternative to existing legacy discourse, rather than as working within its existing parameters.

Although the novel is readily aligned with what might be termed a liberal body of texts whose transgressive potential is recuperated into mainstream thought by hopeful messages of possibility for those willing to strive against the odds[25]—after all, *Kiss of the Fur Queen* narrates the story of two Cree brothers who triumph over their traumatic past through hard work, dedication, and spiritual reflection—the purpose of this chapter is to show that, in fact, Highway employs a radical politics predicated on a complete reconfiguration of ideology. By attacking the ideological and systemic underpinnings of the discourse that has framed and is framing governmental and some tribal response to the social, political, economic, and spiritual consequences of residential schooling, Highway presents alternatives to current compensation strategies that seek not only economic and legal restitution, but also the reinvigoration of modes of thought, spirituality, and being with the world that residential schooling sought to extinguish. Highway states in a recent interview, "'All those things [abuse, marital dysfunction, alcoholism, etc.] create a terrible confusion and I think I wrote this novel as one, hopefully, among a whole series of novels and plays and other works of art, addressing the basic issue of religion, spirituality, because I think this is at the origin of all these problems.'"[26] In the pages that follow, I will situate Highway's spiritually charged narrative account among more overtly political discussions of retribution and reconciliation current at the time of its composition, examining how the novel interrogates the inadequacies of existing vocabularies within the evolving legacy discourse and posits a unique vision of where an energetically decolonized legacy discourse might lead.

Two intimately connected conditions of possibility for Indigenous empowerment should emerge from legacy discourse: first, the development of "the resources and economic base"[27] that will free Indigenous communities from economic dependence; and, second, the reclamation of Indigenous modes of pedagogy, spirituality, and governance by Aboriginal communities. While the acquisition of the former relies heavily on Indigenous success within the "colonial legal framework" of litigation, the latter bears the potential to reconceptualize creatively the relations between Aboriginal people and the government of Canada. Although Highway has "lent his name to an organization now forming to sue the church and the Department of Indian Affairs"[28] and thus construes the utilitarian necessity of legal intervention, *Kiss of the Fur Queen* lays the ideological groundwork required to render productive, in terms of Indigenous empowerment, the restitution gained through litigation. Highway explores the capacity for Indigenous education, storytelling, and what Alfred calls "self-conscious traditionalism"[29] to aid in purging the poisonous effects of residential school extant in misogynist band politics and crippling lateral violence within Native communities. This argument is quite the opposite of Eva Tihanyi's, who has claimed that *Kiss of the Fur Queen* "is no political treatise" but is rather "a celebration of a Cree family, a language, a way of being with the world";[30] *Kiss of the Fur Queen* is political precisely because of its celebration of Indigenous family, spirituality, language, and culture within the context of a specific legacy discourse to which it speaks.

In *Victims of Benevolence*, Elizabeth Furniss cogently identifies the "larger problem" underlying the residential school system: "certain groups in society have presumed to know what is in Native peoples' best interests, and ... these groups have held, and continue to hold, the power and authority to interfere in Native peoples' lives and to enforce conditions that Native people oppose."[31] Although speaking more broadly about the ideological backdrop to structures governing the relations between non-Native Canada and Native people, Furniss cuts to the heart of contemporary criticisms of legacy discourse: "While Indian education policies may have changed, and many today agree that the residential school system is an unfortunate incident in Canadian history, the premises that have legitimized the coercive intervention of government and church officials into Native lives still persist" (109). Over the twenty-five years since the residential school issue first gained public currency, the federal government has shown remarkable resilience in setting and maintaining the parameters for discussion regarding retribution, reconciliation, and healing of residential school transgressions. In a form of discursive domination that mimics the institutional control inflicted by the schools themselves, the government has striven to set the path toward dealing with this sordid history, suggesting that once again it "knows best" how to deal with the difficulties besetting Native people.

As is widely recognized, the residential school issue entered the domain of contestable public knowledge only after the disclosure by Aboriginal victims in the 1980s of sexual abuse suffered at the hands of staff and administrators. Reacting to the displacement of residential school discourse from obscure academic and political spheres into the public arena, the federal government initially sought to maintain discursive focus on these specific instances of abuse, which, in effect, pre-empted systemic analysis of how the conditions of residential schools not only fostered the likelihood of such abuse, but were abusive themselves. Isolating the source of the problem in distinct violations of the Criminal Code, a process Roland Chrisjohn and Sherri Young have identified as "methodological individualism," the government effectively ensured that the negative effects of residential school remained the responsibility of anomalous sadists and perverts who slipped through the cracks of an otherwise altruistic system.

As a protected document internal to the Department of Indian Affairs and Northern Development (DIAND) suggests, the government was careful to "'be seen as responding [to the disclosure of residential school trauma] in a way that liability [was] not admitted, but that it [was] recognizing the sequelae of these events.'"[32] Emerging in the early 1990s, roughly coterminous with the initial apologies of some of the churches, a second tactic for strategic evasion involved focusing public attention on a discourse of healing that situated Aboriginal people, in whom the problems of residential school would be supposedly manifest, as the primary objects of study, rather than the system of acculturative violence itself. Rather than

146

institute a full public inquiry, DIAND desired "'to work closely with First Nations to address this problem at the community level and to begin the healing process.'"[33] As Bernard Schissel and Terry Wotherspoon have noted, "'Residential School Syndrome' became the mantra of a society hoping to gain political absolution by treating its victims as sick and in need of care and therapy."[34] Milloy has termed this a "focus on the 'now' of the problem: Aboriginal people [are] now 'sick,' not savage, in need of psychological, rather than theological, salvation."[35] Rhetorically diverting attention from residential schooling as a technology of acculturative violence toward an opportunistic discourse of "healing" for individuals, the government railroaded administrative and pecuniary action toward a counselling and 'rehabilitation' network that maintained non-Native control.[36]

By the late 1990s, these specific tactics of evasion gave way, in the face of overwhelming dissent by Native and non-Native critics and activists, and a changing political landscape ushered in by Oka and Meech Lake, to a strategic recognition of qualified culpability and a call for the study of residential school history. Offering an official apology in 1998, over half a decade after the Catholic Church's influential "An Apology to the First Nations of Canada by the Oblate Conference of Canada," the government began funding historical studies and testimonials designed to detail the 'truth' of residential school history. The government focused discursive attention on the past while DIAND and band council systems of governance remained intact, virtually untouched by increasing critical attention to Aboriginal history. The government's recent position thus emphasizes the connection between historical residential schooling and negative conditions among contemporary First Nations people. However, at the same time, it presumes a disjuncture between an historical Canadian government responsible, in part, for residential school transgressions and the current government purportedly committed to dealing with their effects. Chrisjohn thus synthesizes governmental manipulation of legacy discourse:

> Nominal funds are available for therapeutic rehabilitation of victims. Institutional perpetrators of offences (be they priests, teachers, administrators, or what have you) are passed off as aberrant individuals who do not reflect the basic 'good-heartedness' that motivated the organization. And even more insidiously, since there are no residential schools in the old sense any more, abuses are 'all in the past' and no present systemic changes are necessary.[37]

Largely due to the diligent criticism of scholar-activists like Chrisjohn and Young, Milloy, and Haig-Brown, and grass-roots dissent from within Native communities, the current stage of legacy discourse is the least guarded, the most open to Aboriginal input, and the most potentially empowering to Native communities and individuals. Indeed, the official apology and the multi-billion-dollar Reconciliation and Compensation Agreement established between the federal government and representatives of First Nations in November 2005 signal profound alterations in government strategy on the residential school matter. However, ongoing governmental influence and the resilience of Euro-Canadian models for dispute resolution present reason for pause. For example, current emphasis on the 'truth' of residential school history, for better or worse, is intimately bound to Euro-Canadian legal epistemology. The unearthing and public dissemination of actual encounters with the residential school system, although crucial to any thorough understanding of Indigenous Canada today, whether by Natives or non-Natives, is based on proof as a supposed imperative.[38] Yet we are quickly approaching a moment in legacy discourse, predicted by Chrisjohn and Young, in which the vast body of historical evidence will indisputably acknowledge that residential schools, "in however benign a form, constituted an abomination,"[39] rendering further proof unnecessary beyond the context of specific legal action. In other words, the fact-finding mission of historicizing residential schooling is nearing the horizon of its necessity unless mobilized in the progressive reinvention of relations between Aboriginal people and the Canadian government.[40] To paraphrase George Orwell, whoever controls the past may control the future, but in this circumstance, when the uncovering of residential history is given official sanction by the Canadian government who actually finances its research and its retelling, is there any substantial disturbance to the balance of power? Is the future of Indigenous Canada not still externally controlled by the currently powerful?

Among the most promising recent developments in dealing with the residential school legacy is the Alternative Dispute Resolution (ADR) program, instituted jointly by the government, the churches, and tribal authorities. Organized by broadly conceived Indigenous ideals of balance and harmony rather than a Euro-Canadian framework of adversarial litigation, without ignoring the continued need for material retribution, ADR seeks to divert residential school claims from the courts and achieve individual and community healing through a "true and equal partnership" among the three parties. According to *Reconciliation and Healing: Alternative Resolution Strategies for Dealing with Residential School Claims*,

Those expected to use an alternative process, the survivors and the institutions affected, must be equally and mutually involved in designing it. A key issue for many survivors is the lack of control they had over their lives at the residential schools. Therefore, the starting point of the process is the recognition of the ability of survivors to care for themselves by settling problems in a joint effort with other parties. Working with their own support mechanisms including administrative resources and personnel, and advisors (family, community, professional), and with government and churches as equals to design a resolution process can be an important part of the healing process.[41]

Clearly, Indigenous involvement in devising and implementing these important projects on individual reserves bespeaks a form of agency distinct from the oppressive regimentation of residential school; however, the extent of that agency remains circumscribed by the fiscal power of DIAND and the churches who are financing the projects and are "equally" involved in their creation. Furthermore, given the historical victimization of Aboriginal survivors by both of the other "partners," one wonders why "equal" representation is desired or even ethical. Why should the government and churches have substantial say in the atonement required for crimes committed by their earlier incarnations?

In *Peace, Power, Righteousness*, Taiaiake Alfred argues forcefully for the extrication of Indigenous resistance from the "context of the law as structured by the state" (47). Although speaking about Indigenous governance more broadly than about the specific issue of residential school compensation, Alfred's work has a great deal to say about searching beyond the modes of resistance offered by the Canadian government. Contending that the desire to "'promote change from within'" is "fundamentally naive" (32) and that arguing "on behalf of Indigenous nationhood within the dominant Western paradigm is self-defeating" (58), Alfred identifies "two [possible] approaches to the future: one that seeks to resurrect a form of Indigenous nationhood (a traditional objective); and another that attempts to achieve partial recognition of a right of self-government within the legal and structural confines of the state (an assimilative goal)" (99).

At the heart of Alfred's critique of Indigenous politics is his identification of a form of socio-political schizophrenia within Native communities: "Native American community life today is framed by two value systems that are fundamentally opposed. One, still rooted in traditional teachings, structures social and cultural relations; the other, imposed by the state, structures politics" (1). As I mentioned above, most Indigenous communities in what would become Canada possessed highly integrated spiritual, social, and political structures prior to European settlement. The imposition of the band council system by DIAND, along with the division of certain tribes and the amalgamation of others during the relocation to reserves, completely reconfigured tribal politics according to European paradigms, compromising consensus decision making, gender equality, traditional spiritual influence, and many other features of Indigenous governance. The ensuing Native political systems—actually, in Alfred's words, "creatures of the federal government" (70)—are, according to Alfred, incapable of promoting real change based on actual Indigenous thought and tradition. His project in *Peace, Power, Righteousness* is to illustrate the importance of removing Indigenous politics from the yoke of Euro-Canadian political structures and reintegrating tribal traditions in culturally appropriate ways. As an example of such a process, Alfred invokes his home community of Kahnawake, which "did not inherit a pure and unbroken traditional culture—far from it. Choosing to relearn the traditional teachings, over the span of twenty years many worked to recover the most important elements of the Rotinohshonni culture and make them the foundations for politics and governance" (81).

Although extremely important in its willingness to look beyond existing political structures and to seek out alternative avenues for instigating change and actualizing Indigenous empowerment, Alfred's work remains limited by the intercultural complexity of Indigenous Canada as well as such realities as the Indigenous diaspora. Many Indigenous communities contain both Christian residents and residents of traditional tribal affiliation (and often others as well), which makes the possibility of achieving consensus over the integration of tribal tradition with community politics difficult. Alfred himself admits that the form of Indigenous governance he seeks "can be practised only in a decentralized, small-scale environment among people who share a culture" (26); however, levels of cultural commitment inevitably vary within communities. Also, the reality of urban existence renders Alfred's form of tribal governance inapplicable to many Natives alienated from their reserves or home communities. Recognizing the limitations of Alfred's intense focus on particular types of Indigenous leadership and dogmatism regarding Indigenous traditionalism, Métis scholar Kristina Fagan worries that Alfred's approach to Indigenous politics might not be "grounded in the lives of the majority of Aboriginal people." She also astutely concedes, "It would be a mistake to look for Alfred's style of nationalism in Aboriginal writers from across Canada."[42] Furthermore, Alfred's dogmatic stance on the necessity of scrapping

DIAND—albeit well argued and largely convincing—carries with it the corollary of losing governmental economic support, on which many Native communities currently rely. As a result, even if Alfred's ideal community were more of a political possibility, it is highly unlikely it could achieve majority support within many contemporary Indigenous communities. Perhaps this is why Alfred concedes that *Peace, Power, Righteousness* "is concerned not with the process through which self-government is negotiated, but with the end goals and the nature of Indigenous governments, once decolonization has been achieved" (xiii).

Alfred's incitement for Indigenous people to look beyond existing Euro-Canadian-constructed avenues for action and to strategically incorporate traditional tribal-specific thought in their efforts towards empowerment nonetheless bears enormous potential for Native people struggling with the aftermath of residential schooling and other contaminants of history. Alfred states, "Native people need to go beyond the divisive electoral politics and Western-style institutions recommended by most scholars and develop solutions *for themselves* from within their own cultural frameworks, reuniting *for themselves as individuals* with their collectivity" (my emphases, 5). This seems a much more plausible goal than the complete political and economic independence for which Alfred ultimately calls, because it doesn't rest upon communal consensus and geographic isolation. And it retains its political potential. Highway's *Kiss of the Fur Queen* performs the crucial ideological work for Indigenous individuals that *Peace, Power, Righteousness* performs for Indigenous communities. While Alfred urges Indigenous leaders to mine their tribal traditions for more culturally appropriate modes of governance (which are beyond the political sway of the federal government and as such do not replicate the people's oppression), Highway encourages all his Indigenous readers to search their tribal traditions for more healthy and culturally appropriate ways of being and, most importantly, more culturally constructive ways of dealing with the traumatic history of residential schooling than those provided by the federal government.

In the beginning of his book, Alfred argues that "the key to surviving and overcoming [the] crisis is leadership" (xv). While Alfred interprets this to mean political leadership, as Highway represents, such leadership can come from many different directions beyond band councils, chiefs, and the Assembly of First Nations. In *Kiss of the Fur Queen*, Highway enacts the form of cultural introspection on behalf of his Indigenous readership that Alfred argues is necessary for positive change for Indigenous people at this stage in colonial history. In his novel, Highway takes on the pedagogical role Alfred deems necessary. Alfred states:

Among Indigenous peoples, the basic 'texts' are the traditional teachings that form the narrative backbone of each culture. These are the sources of wisdom. But guidance is needed in interpreting and implementing the messages they convey. Our communities lack the solid, well-defined cultural roles for elders and traditional teachers that would aid in the transmission of knowledge and meaning. Thus contemporary scholars, writers, and artists must take on the responsibility of translating the meaning of traditions and providing the guidance required to make those traditions part of the contemporary reality. (135)

CREE MYTHOLOGY AS CONTEXT

It is difficult to trace the evolution of *Kiss of the Fur Queen* from autobiography to novel with complete accuracy; however, Highway's interviews throughout the 1990s provide significant clues that assist in developing an educated trajectory of the novel's development.[43] As Highway told the *Toronto Star*'s Judy Stoffman, "'I thought about writing a non-fiction memoir, but it seemed too far-fetched. … Then I tried to write it as a stage play, then as a movie. I actually did four drafts of script, but my way was blocked. Finally, I did it the only way possible.'"[44] Given the political potential of a memoir documenting sexual abuse within a government- and church-sponsored institution, Highway's initial conception of the story as a "non-fiction memoir" is unsurprising. With scant historical evidence available to substantiate Indigenous calls for justice and recompense in the face of early 1990s governmental evasion tactics, a strictly autobiographical *Kiss of the Fur Queen* would certainly have caused a stir among both Native and non-Native readers. However, as Highway states, "'When I tried to tell them it was an autobiography, people didn't believe it. Two Indian kids from northern Manitoba become a dancer and a concert pianist—forget it! Nobody is going to believe it. It sounds like fiction, so I said OK!'"[45]

Recognizing that his endeavour to publish the autobiographic memoir "was blocked," Highway first sought to rewrite *Kiss of the Fur Queen* as a play. Only a few years after the opening of *Dry Lips Oughta Move to Kapuskasing* and the subsequent publication of both *Dry Lips* and *The Rez Sisters*, theatre remained Highway's most comfortable medium in the early 1990s. However, given that Highway makes reference to the stage play as a viable option only one time in the thirteen-plus interviews he gave throughout the 1990s—suggesting to Judy Steed in March of 1991 that the story of residential school abuse is one "he is going to tell in one of his next plays"[46]—it seems likely he entertained the notion for only a short period. The effect of *Kiss of the Fur Queen* depends a great deal on the juxtaposition of a vast northern landscape with a claustrophobic residential school setting and an alienating urban south, making it difficult from a practical standpoint to stage in the theatre. Thus, as early as June 1992, Highway was contemplating the potential effectiveness of the medium of television: "'For once or twice I'd like to take a show into every living room, every bedroom in [my home reserve of] Brochet and to every reserve in the country. You can only do that with television.'"[47]

Television carried with it the ability to disseminate information to a far greater audience than could be reached by any other medium. In light of the guarded nature of legacy discourse in the early 1990s and Highway's conviction that the "'unforgivable, monstrous evil'" of residential schools "'should be published as the headline of every newspaper every day for 10 years,'"[48] the open-form medium of television seemed by 1992 an extremely attractive option. By October 1993, Kathleen Kenna found Highway "eager to discuss his TV project,"[49] and by April 1994, he was able to provide Paul Gessell a detailed outline of the "four-hour mini-series": "A semi-autobiographical drama of epic proportions, [*Kiss of the Fur Queen*] open[s] with grand shots of caribou herds in the North and mov[es] to lavish scenes of professional theatrical productions in Toronto."[50] Even in 1994, however, the difficulty of confirming a venue for his made-for-TV movie was becoming apparent. As Gessell continues,

> Highway ... seems very reluctant to discuss any aspect of scripts, money, contracts, production dates and other crucial data about ... *Kiss*. As each question is asked, dark clouds gather over his head.... [W]riting ... is a long, agonizing process. Getting [his work] to production sometimes takes just as long and requires as much creativity as the writing.[51]

Although I can't be certain exactly when Highway abandoned his efforts to have *Kiss of the Fur Queen* produced as a television series, it seems probable that he began rewriting it as a novel sometime in late 1995 or early 1996, given the novel's publication date of 1998, the lengthy editing process required to cut the initial 800-page manuscript down to just over 300 pages, and the fact that Highway was still discussing the "television mini-series based on the life of his late brother"[52] as late as February of 1995.

By the time Highway had settled on the story's ultimate form, a great deal had changed in the discursive environment into which he was writing. Many churches had officially apologized for their role in residential schooling and certain influential historical works like J.R. Miller's *Shingwuak's Vision* had received wide publication, causing the need for highly publicized disclosure to wane, although government-supported historicization had yet to begin on a grand scale. Although Highway was pressured to switch media by practical concerns beyond his control, his use of each medium reflects a keen understanding of the evolving legacy discourse with which, I believe, he intended his work to engage. In other words, *Kiss of the Fur Queen* exhibits what Jace Weaver calls a "communitist" impulse in each stage of its development by responding to the needs of the Aboriginal community in its ongoing pursuit of justice and healing regarding the residential school legacy. The early autobiographical version sought to participate in the substantiation of early claims against the government and the churches, and the film version sought to raise awareness and magnify vocal protest through wide dissemination. As Highway turned to fiction as his final medium, he similarly strove to actualize a political effect. While his ability to reach a massive television audience or to consolidate communities through group theatrical performance had been lost, his capacity to explore the redemptive nature of storytelling and the function of narrative in understanding identity, community, and history had been augmented significantly. The relatively private engagement between author and reader, requiring from the latter a considerable investment of time and interpretive energy, allowed Highway to deal far more extensively with Aboriginal heritage materials and to illustrate their ongoing utility in the struggle toward Indigenous empowerment.

Kiss of the Fur Queen is a spiritually charged narrative. It employs tribal-specific spiritual knowledge both symbolically and causally throughout. However, its protagonists know very little about their cultural heritage until they begin in adulthood to actively incorporate Cree spirituality in their art. As such, Highway's semi-omniscient narrator performs the role of spiritual translator for the majority of the text, while his protagonists learn, as the story goes on, to perform this task for themselves. Thus, *Kiss of the Fur Queen* not only argues for the application of Cree spirituality and orature to contemporary engagements with the residential school legacy; it embodies this application in the texture of its narrative. It is an example of the spiritualization of contemporary discourse in practice, providing a prototype for the process it explicitly champions.[53] This process becomes all the more fertile to the informed reader who recognizes the text itself as evidence of a similar process on the part of its author. As Jennifer Preston contends, Highway's work not only represents "the importance of [Indigenous] mythology

... in dealing with the social and spiritual problems on reserves," it "enact[s] this re-creation with, for, and on behalf of [the] community."[54]

Contrary to some critical assumptions, however, for Highway this does not simply mean mining "a solid upbringing in the Cree tradition."[55] Despite the exoticism and air of authentication (presumably for non-Native audiences) within such biographical excerpts as the introduction to *The Rez Sisters*—which cites the author's birth "in a tent ... in the middle of a snowbank ... not 10 feet from the dog-sled in which [his family] travelled in those days," and his "exquisitely beautiful nomadic [youth] among the lakes and forests of remote northwestern Manitoba," during which "Cree was the only language spoken"[56]—Highway's early life was far from untouched by colonialism. As Highway acknowledges, "'there was a great deal of poverty and, yes, awful things happened on [his] reserve'" including the deaths of "'six of [his] brothers and sisters ... before [he] was born.'"[57] Furthermore, Highway was raised in a Christian home, "only learning about Cree mythology in bits and pieces."[58] Not until his "early twenties, as he extricated himself from white, institutionalized education and began working with Native organizations, [did] he bec[o]me more interested in Native mythology."[59]

As a result, *Kiss of the Fur Queen* is not so much about tapping some essential internal source or accessing a personal truth placed under erasure by the forces of evangelical Christianity as it is about interrogating the ideological underpinnings of those very forces, searching for alternatives among more culturally relevant sources and determining for oneself the most endorsable and empowering spiritual, social, and political position from which to speak, think, and act. Precisely because the colonial interventions of Euro-Canada have all but ensured that most Natives have not inherited "a pure and unbroken traditional culture,"[60] the need is paramount, in Alfred's terms, for "a self-conscious traditionalism, an intellectual, social, and political movement that will reinvigorate those values, principles, and other cultural elements that are best suited to the larger contemporary political and economic reality."[61] In *Kiss of the Fur Queen*, Highway validates such a struggle toward traditional knowledge and its relevance to contemporary concerns, recognizing that the 'authenticity' debate, for the most part, exhausted its usefulness years ago.

Kiss of the Fur Queen relates the story of Champion and Ooneemeetoo Okimasis, Cree brothers torn from the loving comfort of their nomadic family life in the far North of Manitoba by obligatory residential schooling in the South. Coming of age in urban centres hundreds of kilometres from their parents and the physical geography of their infancy, the two must develop creative strategies to overcome their cultural alienation and the emotional, intellectual, and spiritual aftermath of abuse incurred at Birch Lake Residential School. Based loosely on the events of Highway's life and that of his younger brother René, who died of an AIDS-related illness in October 1990, shortly before Tomson began writing the book, *Kiss of the Fur Queen* is very much an elegy. Highway points to this function in the novel's Cree-language dedication, "Igwani igoosi, n'seemis"—which translates approximately to "this one's for you, little brother"—and its two epigraphs, one by Chief Seattle of the Squamish, stating, "'Let [the whiteman] deal kindly with my people. For the dead are not powerless'" (ii), and the other taken from a letter by Minister of Indian Affairs Duncan Campbell Scott, alluding to the countervailing potential of René's celebrated career as a ballet dancer: "'Use your utmost endeavours to dissuade the Indians from excessive indulgence in the practice of dancing'" (ii). Both Champion and Ooneemeetoo, like the Highway brothers, take to artistic expression—the former through piano and writing and the latter through dance—initially as a coping mechanism for past trauma and eventually as a means of combating the forces of oppression that have infected not only their own lives but those of thousands of Natives whom they endeavour to influence.

The novel's basic *kunstlerroman* structure is broadened by Highway to encompass the lives of both brothers, rendering *Kiss of the Fur Queen* a portrait of two Cree artists as young men. Highway's choice of third-person omniscient narration allows his audience access to the protagonists' unique, yet mutually implicated, psychological struggles, while further distancing his account from the conventional testimonial model. The anonymous narrator's omniscience, however, is at times undercut by her or his inability or unwillingness to assess the factuality of internal storytelling within the novel. Repeated qualifications like "or so Abraham Okimasis would relate to his two youngest sons years later" (13) and "as … Champion would shamelessly ornament the story years later" (45) destabilize the veracity of other narrative threads throughout. Even Champion's origin as a "spirit baby" (20) fallen to earth and assisted by animal spirits in locating his mother's womb, which the narrator relates with only the slightest hint of irony, is later called into question by its association with a narrative tradition that prizes ornamentation and embellishment. When the midwife arriving to deliver Ooneemeetoo deindividualizes the tale of Champion's birth as a traditional narrative the Okimasis family has "heard at least one hundred times yet would never tire of hearing[,]

156

... embellish[ing] the ancient yarn as only her advanced age [has] earned her the right to do" (32), the reader is left uncertain of the relationship between tale telling and notions of 'factual' history. Was Champion's birth story merely a "yarn" spun by a precocious narrator? Or does the reliability of the narrator's tale remain intact despite the midwife's lavish storytelling techniques? At this point in the novel, it is difficult to tell.

Highway points to the function of potentially fallible narration in his discussion of Ooneemeetoo's baptism, during which the boy is renamed Gabriel. While Gabriel claims to remember the entire ceremony, Champion insists that the younger sibling has merely assimilated Champion's telling of the tale into his imagined memory of events. Through narrative interjection, however, the audience learns that, "*In truth*, it was Kookoos Cook ... who would never tire of telling his nephews the yarn, which, as the years progressed, became ever more outrageous, exaggerated, as is the Cree way of telling stories, of making myth" (my emphasis, 38). Highway's strategic use of "In truth" actually undermines the words' signifying potential, causing them to refer not to the events in question, but to the individual who most enjoys embellishing them. The "truth" resides in Kookoos Cook's enthusiasm and abilities as a storyteller, a Cree storyteller, while the veracity of the story he tells remains forever in question, unapproached and unapproachable by such imperatives as fact or objectivity. Furthermore, the novel's frequent incorporation of traditional Cree tales, as well as its author's highly publicized allegiance to Cree mythmaking, unsettle the audience's confidence in the story's narrative reliability, given Cree storytelling's apparent propensity for "outrageous[ness]" and "exaggerat[ion]." As the above example demonstrates, however, the instability of fact does not negate the continued relevance of individual understandings of past events—particularly, as we shall see, traumatic events—hampered though they may be by the weakness of memory and the inadequacies of cognition.

The novel's central crisis, which will inscribe itself indelibly into the lives of both protagonists, involves the rape of Gabriel by the principal of Birch Lake, Father Lafleur. This horrible act of abuse is told from the perspectives of both brothers: the younger sibling struggling to comprehend the pain and pleasure of an experience for which he has no frame of reference; the older futilely grasping for means to reconcile his inability to save the little brother he had sworn to protect.[62] Even at this crucial point Highway is careful to avoid any pretence of objective reportage. The scene, which commences with Gabriel "furiously engaged" in a dream about square dancing, again troubles the division between lived experience and (anti-historical) subconscious interference when Father Lafleur's stroking of the sleeping boy's penis begins to influence the reverie: "The *undisputed fact* was that Gabriel Okimasis's little body was moving up and down, up and down, producing, in the crux of his being, a sensation so pleasurable that he wanted [his dance partner] to float up and up forever so he could keep jumping up ... and pulling her back down" (my emphasis, 77). Highway explicitly identifies as "fact" that which cannot be corroborated due to its occurrence within a state of altered consciousness, suggesting once again the inadequacy of "fact" as the primary criterion for understanding experience.

Similarly, happening upon the priest's erotic assault *in medias res*, Champion, whose name has been changed by Birch Lake administrators to Jeremiah, struggles against his sleep-addled young consciousness to comprehend what he is seeing:

> He blinked, opened his eyes as wide as they would go. He wanted—needed—to see more clearly.
>
> The bedspread was pulsating, rippling from the centre. No, Jeremiah wailed to himself, *please*. Not him again....
>
> Jeremiah opened his mouth and moved his tongue, but his throat went dry. No sound came except a ringing in his ears. Had this really happened before? Or had it not? But some chamber deep inside his mind slammed permanently shut. It had happened to nobody. He had not seen what he was seeing. (79–80)

Even as Jeremiah overcomes the incapacity of his clouded vision in the darkened dormitory to determine it "*was* him. Again" (79), Highway undermines the authority of the statement by having the boy immediately repress his experience. The "permanent[] shut[ting]" of the chamber in Jeremiah's mind illustrates the difficulty, perhaps impossibility, of determining with any precision the nature of childhood trauma. Neither brother is shown to be in a position to indisputably detail Father Lafleur's assault on Gabriel—the younger brother consumed by sleep and confusion, the older brother subject to the ego-guarding processes of his psyche. Yet the audience is never left with any doubt that the abuse has occurred, which cuts to the heart of *Kiss of the Fur Queen*'s implicit critique of standard historicizing tactics for the residential school legacy. When bound by Euro-Canadian legal definitions of 'truth' and 'fact,' contingent on the improbable attainment of 'evidence,' the crucial cognitive endeavour of revisiting residential school trauma is limited in its capacity to influence people's understandings of the broader causes and implications of residential school transgressions. For this reason, Highway presents the novel's most crucial incident of abuse as factually uncertain, yet with enormous symbolic and evocative force.

Careful to avoid isolating Gabriel's abuse as the anomalous act of a sadistic individual, Highway implicates a system of thought, on whose behalf the cleric functions, in the transgression:

> His face [was] glowing in the moonlight with the intense whiteness of the saints in the catechism book....
>
> Father Lafleur bent, closer and closer, until the crucifix that dangled from his neck came to rest on Gabriel's face. The subtly throbbing motion of the priest's upper body made the naked Jesus Christ—this sliver of silver light, this fleshly Son of God so achingly beautiful—rub his body against the child's lips, over and over and over again. Gabriel had no strength left. The pleasure in his centre welled so deep that he was about to open his mouth and swallow whole the living flesh—in his half-dream state, this man nailed to the cross was a living, breathing man. (78)

In a gross parody of communion, the central symbol of Christian theology assaults Gabriel's lips in the very moment that Father Lafleur's ape-like hands assault his genitalia. Although wielded by the cleric—God's instrument on Earth—the power inflicted on Gabriel belongs to the "living, breathing" Christ, who actively "rub[s] his body against the child's lips," demanding entry. In an almost clichéd illustration of the symbolic rape of Indigenous cultures by evangelical Christianity, Christ endeavours to force himself into the sanctified space of the boy's mouth, presumably preparing him to pay lip-service to the 'true' religion while renouncing the legitimacy of Cree spirituality, and simultaneously replacing the Cree language with a European tongue.

The aspects of Christianity Gabriel internalizes, however, are quite different from those adopted by the boy's proselytized parents, and are directly related to the instrument of torture dangling at his lips. While aggressively averse to many of the Bible's central teachings, Gabriel cannot escape the masochistic predilection for eroticized pain that the ever-suffering Christ, tortured and penetrated, symbolizes. Nurtured by the glory of playing Jesus to an audience of young Aboriginal "Roman centurion[s]" with whips and gravel, and the oft repeated maxim, "*Mea culpa, mea culpa, mea maxima culpa*" (80),[63] Gabriel learns to seek out sensual punishment in a form of bodily abnegation for which there is no non-corporeal plane.

Examining the implications of sexual abuse within a propagandist evangelical environment devoted to indoctrinating victims with the 'truth' of their inherent sinfulness, Highway illustrates how Gabriel eventually "accept[s] the blame" (81). Although he recognizes that Catholicism asks him "to apologize for something beyond [his] control," Gabriel concludes that it is indeed his "most grievous fault" (81). He also comes to accept and crave his punishment.

In contrast to the Christian symbolism inculcated in Gabriel's experience of the rape, Jeremiah's perception of the act is configured in terms of Cree spirituality. Upon leaving his bed to check on his brother, Jeremiah noticed:

> Gabriel was not alone. A dark, hulking figure hovered over him, like a crow. Visible only in silhouette, for all Jeremiah knew it might have been a bear devouring a honey-comb, or the Weetigo feasting on human flesh.
>
> As he stood half-asleep, he thought he could hear the smacking of lips, mastication....
>
> When the beast reared its head, it came face to face, not four feet away, with that of Jeremiah Okimasis. The whites of the beast's eyes grew large, blinked once. Jeremiah stared. It *was* him. Again. (79)

Given Jeremiah's tenuous connection to Cree spirituality and oral history at this point in the story, it is unsurprising that his identification of Father Lafleur as the Weetigo is presented in vague terms—"it might have been ... the Weetigo." In Cree theology the Weetigo is the most terrifying of creatures; referred to by some as a cannibalistic human, by others as a monster or spirit, the Weetigo's defining characteristic is its consumption of human flesh, which renders it an appropriate symbolic tool for interrogating transgressions of the body by a Roman Catholic priest, particularly in light of the Eucharist. However, Jeremiah is not yet well enough armed with Cree spiritual knowledge to draw out the significance of this association. In fact, Highway's strategic wording of the passage makes it unclear whether the association is Jeremiah's or the narrator's. The "for all Jeremiah knew" could stand as a narrative conjecture unrelated to the character's actual imaginings, simply an expression for the incomprehensibility of the scene; yet the term "knew" seems to situate the conjecture within Jeremiah's thoughts. Such uncertainty renders the Weetigo's introduction to the novel evocative rather than conclusive, a signpost whose symbolic fertility waits to be further interrogated.

Emerging from the assimilative grasp of residential school, the Okimasis brothers find themselves in Winnipeg, two of "'only three Indians in a school filled with two thousand white middle-class kids'" (149). Straining against cultural alienation's attendant despair, the brothers for the first time actively revisit the oral archive of their Cree heritage. Marching through Polo Park shopping mall, Jeremiah and Gabriel endeavour to remember their Aunt Black-Eyed Susan's censored tale about the Weetigo and the Weasel, taking turns piecing together this traditional myth, recorded no less than four times in Robert Brightman's ethnographic collection of tales from the Rock Cree of northern Manitoba. Significantly, the boys' reminiscence begins with a question by Jeremiah—"'Remember [the] story ... about the weasel's new fur coat?'" (118)—and then carries on largely in the inquisitive: "'You mean where [the trickster figure] Weesageechak comes down to Earth disguised as a weasel ... [and] crawls up the Weetigo's bumhole?'" (118). According to the tale, after chewing up the Weetigo's entrails, thereby killing the monster, Weesageechak escapes covered in feces. "'Feeling sorry for the hapless trickster,'" continues Jeremiah, "'God dipped him in the river to clean his coat. But he held him by the tail, so its tip stayed dirty'" (121), and, as Gabriel concludes, "'to this day, ... the weasel's coat is white but for the black tip of the tail'" (121).

Highway expertly weaves the telling of this traditional Cree tale with the brothers' inaugural shopping venture in Winnipeg, as they plunge into the city's mecca of consumerism, identified as "the entrails of the beast" (116), to acquire the accoutrements that will mask newly arrived Gabriel's Native otherness. In this metaphorical equation, the brothers become trickster figures and the mall becomes the Weetigo, complicating the earlier connection between the Weetigo and Christianity to suggest capitalist consumerism's implication in the cultural rape of Indigenous people on the continent. Like Weesageechak, the brothers feast in what Highway identifies as "the belly of the beast" (119)—the mall's food court—where they eat so much, "their bellies c[o]me near to bursting" (120). Then when they finally depart, "exulting" that they have recalled a "wicked ... Cree legend[]," "grey and soulless, the mall loom[s] behind them, the rear end of a beast that, having gorged itself, expels its detritus" (121).

Clearly, the boys' shopping adventure is meant to re-enact the journey of Weesageechak to the Weetigo's belly and back; however, significant tensions between the two tales persist. If we take the association of both Father Lafleur and the Polo Park Mall with the Weetigo to suggest a conspiracy between the forces of Christian religion and capitalist economics in the assault on Native cultural identity, then the function of the brothers' excursion to the belly of the beast becomes somewhat different from that of the trickster. The boys don't enter the mall to destroy it, but rather to implicate themselves in its processes. They go there to become more

Euro-Canadian. The white weasel with a black tip of the tail thus becomes, in Highway's contemporary telling, the two Cree brothers, covered by white cultural costumes, with only their faces remaining unmasked. And whereas Weesageechak extricates itself from the dead body of the Weetigo, the Okimasis brothers are, in effect, shit out by the beast—still very much alive, although soulless—whose characteristics now taint their Cree bodies.

Oblivious to the ironies behind their retreat to traditional orature at this particular moment, Jeremiah and Gabriel are not yet prepared to interpret Cree myth in relation to their own lives. Here the tale functions for the brothers as simple comic relief, while it is the narrator who makes the metaphorical associations that become evident to the reader. The brothers cannot even determine with any confidence the tale's meaning. When asked about the purpose behind Weesageechak's murder of the monster, Jeremiah replies, "'*All I remember* is that the Weetigo had to be killed because he ate people....Weesageechak chewed the Weetigo's entrails to smithereens from the inside out'" (my emphasis, 120). Unwittingly mistaking living orature for dogma, Jeremiah settles for what he considers an authoritative past telling of the tale rather than reinterpreting it. He glosses over the spiritually significant 'whys' of the tale to focus on plot details, like Weesageechak's chewing of the entrails. He and Gabriel, in effect, emulate in their retelling of the Cree myth the mindless regurgitation of doctrine required of them at Birch Lake, where they were made to parrot Latin and English phrases while not yet understanding either language: "'Hello merry, mutter of cod, lay for ussinees, now anat tee ower of ower beth, aw, men'" (71). As Sioux author and activist Vine Deloria Jr. has argued,

> Unlike many other religious traditions, tribal religions ... have not been authoritatively set 'once and for always.' Truth is in the ever changing experiences of the community. For the traditional Indian to fail to appreciate this aspect of his heritage is the saddest of heresies. It means the Indian has unwittingly fallen into the trap of Western religion, which seeks to freeze history in an unchanging and authoritative past.[64]

So long as the Okimasis brothers' relationship with Cree orature and spirituality is mediated by the structural imperatives of Roman Catholicism, its relevance to their lives is obscured and its capacity to aid in their healing hindered; they remain mired in the externally imposed ideological systems that have worked historically toward their acculturation and oppression.

The novel's most important Cree tale, the myth that forms its spiritual backdrop, is significantly withheld from the reader until over two-thirds of the way through *Kiss of the Fur Queen*, after Jeremiah has abandoned his dream of becoming a concert pianist and must renegotiate his place in the world. The Son of Ayash[65] myth is introduced to the Okimasis brothers by their father on his deathbed:

> My son'.... 'The world has become too evil. With these magic weapons, make a new world,' said the mother of the hero, the Son of Ayash.... So the Son of Ayash took the weapons and, on a magic water snake, journeyed down into the realm of the human soul, where he met.... [e]vil after evil ... the most fearsome among them the man who ate human flesh.(227)

Unlike the earlier tale concerning the Weetigo and the Weasel, Abraham Okimasis's sparse performance of the Son of Ayash is difficult to treat as axiomatic for two reasons. First, the brevity of the father's telling, urged along by his impending death, belies the complexity and length of other recorded versions of the tale. Second, the profoundly Christian Okimasis patriarch's oral narrative takes place during his final absolution by a Roman Catholic priest, just seconds before he accepts the host for the last time. Regardless of mediation by a Christian man, however, the tribal materials found within the tale remain enormously important to the young Cree audience. The juxtaposition of the Christian and the Indigenous, evident in Abraham's "Cree descant whirring, light as foam, over the [priest's] English dirge" (227), indicates not the inauthenticity of the myth's articulation, but, rather, the essential place of the listener in providing the context and interpretive discourse to render productive the oral materials offered. To make the Son of Ayash myth functional in his own life, Jeremiah must analyze it energetically and thoughtfully, adapting it to his contemporary moment, and retelling it in his own voice and words.

In his 1989 *âcaôôhkîwina and âcimôwina: Traditional Narratives of the Rock Cree Indians*, Robert Brightman provides a more detailed version of the Son of Ayash myth, narrated and translated by Cree elder Caroline Dumas.[66] Like all published versions of the myth, Dumas's begins with the hero's abandonment on an island by a male relative (in Dumas's version, his grandfather; in others, his father or stepfather), and chronicles his journey through many ordeals to return to his mother and remake the wounded world. In Dumas's version, the Son of Ayash (here simply Ayas) is confronted by a benevolent giant serpent who assumes the role of grandmother and assists him in escaping the island. While crossing the water on the serpent's back, however, Ayas reneges on his promise to warn her of impending thunder out of fear she may submerge, causing him to drown, and the serpent is blown apart by lightning the moment Ayas reaches the shore. Awaking the following morning, Ayas goes "down to the shore ... and scoop[s] up the [serpent's] blood with ... two baskets he had made" (106) and places them in a tree so that the serpent can regenerate herself. Pleased with Ayas's willingness to save her, the grandmother serpent forgives his earlier indiscretion and imparts to him the knowledge that will guide him through the many obstacles by which he will be beset en route to his mother—this knowledge embodies the "'magic weapons'" from Abraham's telling. As Brightman asserts, the hero's "dangerous obstacles vary from one version to another" (112); in the Dumas version, these include the "memorably nightmarish" (112) women "who sharpen their elbows to points like knives" (107). With the knowledge provided him by the serpent grandmother, however, and certain spirit and animal guardians along the way, Ayas is ultimately able to reach his destination. According to Brightman, "all versions culminate in Ayas's reunion with his mistreated mother and his destruction of the earth by fire" (112). In Dumas's version, the mother has been repeatedly burned on the face and hands by the grandfather and his wife, who are ultimately destroyed when Ayas shoots his "arrow up in the air.... [and] fire spr[ings] up and burn[s] all over the earth" (110–11).

The hero's initial abandonment on the island clearly resonates with the Okimasis brothers' imposed exile at Birch Lake Residential School and their separation from what Highway has often referred to as an essentially female Cree spiritual system represented by the absent mother. Like the relinquishment of the boys, which occurs in acquiescence to the will of "Father Bouchard" and "*Soonieye-gimow*,"[67] the exile of Ayas takes place because the grandfather figure believes his "spirit guardian" requires the boy as a sacrifice. (Highway picks up on this fundamental violation of parental bonds by naming the Okimasis patriarch after the biblical Abraham.) On the island, however, the hero receives the tools that will enable him to conquer the evils he faces and return home to his mother, which, in the context of the Okimasis brothers' experiences, alludes to the acquisition of valuable skills even in the context of institutionalized abuse. In a 2001 interview, discussing the effects of residential school on his life, Highway stated, "I realize that there is nothing I can do about the [negative and abusive] things that happened. I can only live with the equipment that I have been given and I have been given some extraordinary equipment."[68] For Highway, as for Jeremiah, this "extraordinary equipment"—these "'magic weapons'"—includes language skills, Christian mythological knowledge, and emotional and intellectual depth.

Significantly, however, the "magic weapons" provided the hero in the Ayas myth are not the sole product of the location of exile, but are also mediated by the instructive influence of the "ohkoma" or serpent grandmother, suggesting the importance of traditional knowledge in rendering those weapons functional and empowering. It is not until the Okimasis brothers apply their respective skills for dance and music to a creative examination of Cree spirituality that they achieve purgative release and provoke the self-exploration among their audience required to potentially alter structures of power (as demanded by Alfred above). By collaborating and combining Gabriel's talent for the European art form of ballet and Jeremiah's talent for classical piano in a modern dance performance based on extrapolated Cree teachings, the brothers are able to interact creatively with their own spiritualities and with a body of Cree spiritual knowledge in a manner distinct from the religious regimentation of residential school. Looking out over the crowd at the close of their initial performance,

> Gabriel knew that his magic had worked, for the audience was speaking to some space inside themselves, some void that needed filling, some depthless sky; and this sky was responding. Through the brothers, as one, and through a chamber as vast as the north, an old man's voice passed. 'My son,' it sighed, 'with these magic weapons, make a new world....'" (267)

Employing their talents for distinctly European art forms in the exploration of an entirely different cultural heritage with entirely different ideological foundations, the brothers loosen the structural limitations with which those activities had been imbued and create a space for introspection, something they had been unable to accomplish in their initial introduction to the Son of Ayash myth. Listening to their father's tale through the ideological lens created by a Roman Catholic residential school upbringing, the brothers immediately recognized the apocalyptical implications of the Son of Ayash's destruction of the world by fire. In fact, they "heard" and "remember," spliced into the centre of their father's tale, the priest's reading: "'That my Avenger liveth, and he, at the Last, will take his stand upon the Earth'" (227). Situating the Son of Ayash myth within a Christian framework of divine punishment for sin, this reading suggests the Son of Ayash's "destruction of the earth by fire" to be the righteous vengeance of a wrathful supreme power, rather than, as Abraham would have it and as the brothers ultimately explore in their theatrical work, the creation through art of "'a new world.'" By initially failing to break out of the ideological system imposed on them by the forces of evangelical Christianity, the brothers are not yet able to unlock the empowering capacity of traditional Cree thought, which, as I mentioned, is exactly what Alfred has criticized in the context of Euro-Canadian law: "Attempting to decolonize without addressing the structural imperatives of the colonial system is clearly futile."[69] If the ideological and systemic structures of Euro-Canadian power remain intact, even in the context of tribal revitalization, true Indigenous empowerment will remain a myth.

In order to better elucidate what Highway sees as the perils of this paradox, I will depart briefly from *Kiss of the Fur Queen* to analyze a character from *Dry Lips Oughta Move to Kapuskasing* who paradigmatically fails to break free of an unhealthy non-Native ideological framework and, as such, serves as a warning of what the Okimasis brothers are in danger of becoming.

Among the most complicated and conflicted characters in Highway's theatrical oeuvre is ex-activist-turned-hockey-arena-manager Big Joey McLeod, whose enormous capacity for violence against women influenced significantly the debate in Toronto's *Globe and Mail* during April of 1991 over whether *Dry Lips* is an "unambiguous examination/explanation of misogyny" or is a "play studded with misogyny."[70] What is intriguing about Big Joey's characterization is the extent to which, despite his years as an Indigenous rights activist and his purported desire to "work for the betterment and the advancement of [his] community" (*Dry Lips*, 22), he has internalized destructive aspects of Euro-Canadian ideology.[71] Given Big Joey's affiliation with the American Indian Movement (AIM) and the standoff at Wounded Knee in South Dakota in 1973, this may be unsurprising. Stoh:lo author Lee Maracle, who was active in Indigenous activist movements in the 1970s, is critical of AIM's non-Native approaches to dealing with Native issues in her largely autobiographical *I Am Woman* (1996): "Culturally, the worst, most dominant white male traits were emphasized [by AIM's leadership]. Machismo and the boss mentality were the basis for choosing leaders. This idea of leadership was essentially a European one promulgated by power mongers."[72] She continues, "The AIM leadership looked at the rewards of 'serving the people' with European eyes. Their interpretation of spirituality was rooted in European culture."[73]

The communal trauma forming the psychological backdrop of the play involves the drunken birth of Dickie Bird Halked in a bar seventeen years prior to the play's action, leaving the child, who is related in one way or another to all the play's male characters, mute through foetal alcohol syndrome. As Gitta Honegger explains, "Everyone had a part in that hellish night. Everyone had avoided facing up to the truth of their own irresponsibility, their dependence on the self-perpetuating cycle of the dominant culture's destructive forces."[74] Big Joey, in particular, is culpable because, as it turns out, he is the boy's biological father and had fled the scene of the birth. To explain this and other reprehensible behaviour near the play's conclusion, Big Joey divulges:

> That was me. Wounded Knee, South Dakota, Spring of '73. The FBI. They beat us to the ground. Again and again and again. Ever since that spring, I've had these dreams where blood is spillin' out from my groin, nothin' there but blood and emptiness. It's like ... I lost myself. So when I saw this baby comin' out of Caroline, Black Lady [Dickie Bird's mother] ... Gazelle dancin' ... all this blood ... and I knew it was gonna come ... I ... I tried to stop it ... I freaked out. I don't know what I did ... and I knew it was mine....[75]

Entangled in his quasi-cathartic admission of guilt are the various strands of institutional oppression through the FBI in 1973, paralyzing fear of impotence, and disgust over the sight of womanly blood. The knot nudges both audience and character in the direction of understanding Big Joey's misogyny, but not in a prescriptive way. Big Joey's memory of the ill-fated standoff at Wounded Knee functionally dismantles any illusions of achieving Indigenous independence by overpowering the forces of colonial governments. The powerlessness Big Joey experiences in relation to this realization manifests itself in a recurring dream of "blood ... spillin' out from [his] groin," which, as the addendum "nothin' there but blood and emptiness" implies, Big Joey interprets as an indication of his own impotence.

Big Joey's projection of the source of this powerlessness and impotence onto women, through such statements as, "I hate them! I hate them fuckin' bitches. Because they—our own women—took the power away" (120), reflects not only a masculinist misunderstanding of the phallus as power's source, but also a profound misinterpretation of the spiritual significance of his dream—and, according to Brightman, dreaming is considered "a modality of learning that possesses, for traditional Cree, a validity sometimes exceeding the data of conventional waking perception."[76] In Big Joey's personal analysis of the dream, the "blood and emptiness" in his groin reflect a loss of self. However, he does not consider the possibility that the blood spilling from his groin might indicate, not the destruction of the essence of his maleness, but the awakening of an essential femaleness through symbolic menstruation. As Highway has stated, the play is ultimately about "'the empowerment of the female principle, the reawakening of the feminine in men.'"[77] In most traditional Indigenous cultures, including the Cree and Ojibway who inhabit Wasaychigan Hill, menstruation is perceived as "a spiritually charged occurrence," "central to the understanding of creative female energy"; it is "a sign of the incredible power of the feminine."[78] A symbolic example of this power from Cree orature would be the bloody pool in which the serpent grandmother regenerates herself in Dumas's Ayas myth. Big Joey's revulsion at the sight of Black Lady Halked's pre-birthing fluids, however, evidences a distinctly non-Indigenous association of vaginal fluids with impurity, filth, and contamination (possibly the by-product of Eurocentric education like residential schooling), causing him to reject entirely the possibility of his own creativity. So invested is he in Eurocentric notions of phallic power and feminine impurity that he denies his own creative capacity by abandoning his son.[79]

Desperately grasping for an illusory sense of surrogate power through violence, Big Joey, in effect, reinforces his own impotence by stifling his creativity and continuing to endorse an ideology of confrontation that is based on destruction. Unwilling to interrogate the ideological underpinnings of his misogyny, Big Joey locks himself into a cycle of lateral violence, characterized by *self-imposed* impotence. His two most flagrantly violent acts are significantly failures to intervene (i.e., moments of inaction) rather than overt physical transgressions: his abandonment of Black Lady Halked and their son, and his refusal to intercede in his son's rape of a young female spiritual revitalizationist. These failures are mutually implicated. Big Joey's refusal to acknowledge his son—and thus his own (pro)creativity—underwrites the boy's confusion, which culminates in the violent attack, while the attack itself becomes non-procreative through the use of a crucifix rather than the phallus. In fact, the rape could be considered anti-creative because it bears the capacity to cause its pregnant victim to miscarry, making it a sadistic parody of copulation whose offspring is death rather than life. And throughout, Big Joey stands by as voyeur, refusing to intervene and, according to the stage directions, "*violently*" (100) preventing his companion, Creature Nataways, from intervening. Big Joey's violence, spawned from a profound misinterpretation of feminine creative power as disempowering to Native men, emerges as a further divestiture of personal power through inaction. Interpreting femininity without reference to either Cree or Ojibway traditional teachings, Big Joey escalates lateral violence and denies his own capacity to induce positive change.

The shocking violence of *Dry Lips*, while by implication the product of colonial interventions, is perpetrated by and exacted upon Indigenous people. As is widely recognized, many Indigenous communities endure extraordinarily high levels of violence. Highway himself has stated, "'I come from a reserve in northern Manitoba which is being ripped apart by certain almost indefinable spiritual and social forces that are explosively destructive.'"[80] Also widely recognized is the central position residential school has played in the historical manufacture of cultures of violence within Native communities. As one survivor indicates, "'The boarding schools taught us violence. Violence was emphasized through physical, corporal punishment, strapping, beatings, bruising and control. We learned to understand that this was power and control.'"[81]

For the Okimasis brothers, the latent danger of lateral violence resides primarily in the aftermath of their respective histories of sexual abuse. Sexual violence, in the words of John Milloy,

> was not simply visited on the individual child in school; it spilled back into communities, so that even after the schools were closed it echoed in the lives of subsequent generations of children. A 1989 study sponsored by the Native Women's Association of the Northwest Territories found that eight out of ten girls under the age of eight were victims of sexual abuse, and fifty percent of the boys the same age had been sexually molested.[82]

While Big Joey's failure to interrogate the ideological underpinnings of his own system of thought or to question what he has been "taught" in the world created through colonial encounter ultimately leads to the perpetuation of lateral violence in *Dry Lips*, Highway's depiction of the Okimasis brothers' crisis to combat the potential revisitation of their abuse on others in *Kiss of the Fur Queen* offers the possibility of active mitigation. While, as its epigram suggests, *Dry Lips* serves to "expose" the "poison" of Euro-influenced misogynistic violence "before the healing can take place," *Kiss of the Fur Queen* explores more thoroughly Indigenous alternatives to the ideologies of violence and misogyny, forging avenues for healing and empowerment at which the play can only hint.

The issue of lateral sexual violence is not raised—beyond Gabriel's masochism—until late in the novel, after Jeremiah has devoted himself fully to writing for the theatre and begun adapting Cree oral tales to the stage. At this time, due to the lack of financial stability offered by writing, Jeremiah works a day-job at a centre for Native youth, where he imparts to his students the story of the Son of Ayash he had learned from his father. Restructuring the tale as a "Cree rap with a Latin stamp" (270), thereby illustrating the importance of adapting myth creatively to suit the needs of a contemporary audience (here children), Jeremiah explains: "Our hero, the Son of Ayash, has to be careful, for he is entering the dark place of the human soul where he will meet evil creatures like ... the Weetigo" (271). Responding to a small boy's inquiry, Jeremiah continues: "A Weetigo is a monster who eats little boys ... like you" (271). After class, the child returns to divulge the traumatic reality behind his interest in the Weetigo. Hugging Jeremiah, "the hot face buried in his groin," the child declares, "'A Weetigo ate me'" (271). To the teacher's shock and dismay, the child then enacts the monster's trademark mastication, biting into his teacher's "faded blue denim" and causing "a needle longer than an arm" to shoot up Jeremiah's spine. "In a panic, [the teacher] disengaged himself and squatted, his eyes inches from the six-year-old's. He had a raging hard-on" (271).

It is no coincidence that the place the Son of Ayash is entering in the song is "the dark place of the human soul," as in this moment the mythic battle between the Son of Ayash and the Weetigo is reconceptualized as one waged within the self. While Jeremiah's sexual abuse at residential school resonates with the more recent abuse of the child in his care, it is his latent capacity to become an abuser in the present, signalled by his unwanted arousal, that bears the weight of ultimate significance for the story. After battling a "vortex screaming with monsters" (272) that the confrontation with pedophiliac abuse conjures from his past, Jeremiah bursts into the office of the Friendship Centre's director, anxious to determine the whereabouts of the child's tormentor. After it is ascertained that "the perpetrator ... is being charged ... and, hopefully, ... will be jailed," Highway concludes the chapter by stating, "For Jeremiah, jail was nowhere near enough" (272). Although directed at the child's abuser, this line elucidates the precariousness of Jeremiah's own position, in the wake of the return of his repressed past. If Jeremiah cannot negotiate a way of dealing with his capacity to abuse, he will need to segregate himself from the community or doom himself to superimposing the role of victimizer over the role of victim.

In the very next sentence, however, Highway identifies the productive path Jeremiah must take, a path with enormous potential for empowerment and regeneration. Hearkening back to the initial portrayal of abuse in the novel, wherein Father Lafleur was mistaken for both "a bear devouring a honeycomb" and "the

Weetigo feasting on human flesh," Jeremiah is described as "hunched at a type-writer," "like a bear with a honeypot" (273). Significantly, the story Jeremiah strives to compose in the aftermath of his crisis with the child is the Son of Ayash myth, adapted to his own experiences. He writes of himself at age nine sitting with his brother "at the stern of their father's blue canoe" (274), but he does so in the language of myth he had just imparted to his students: "*eehee, Ayash oogoosisa*" (274). He entwines both his distant past and the recent trauma in a mythic discourse he can ultimately control as writer. Thus, he actively prevents himself from feasting on others like the Weetigo—whether "feasting" refers to sexual exploitation or other forms of more covert violence—seeking instead emotional, spiritual, and psychological nourishment in the creative process. Rather than being consumed by past trauma, and passing it on to others, Jeremiah channels his anguish into creative work that will not only aid his personal healing, but will provide the cultural materials for a broader Indigenous empowerment.

Significantly, Highway places this crisis, as well as its resolution, within the context of a culturally enabling pedagogical environment, a place wherein the future is nurtured. In stark contrast to the residential school setting that looms so heavily over the novel, the Muskoosis Club at which Jeremiah both teaches and writes offers the potential for personal and cultural growth on Native terms, defined for and by each individual in the contemporary moment. Thus, in the instant in which he imparts to a younger generation its inheritance of cultural stories, and thereby provides a potential vocabulary for the articulation of selfhood, Jeremiah determines the identity he will claim, an identity characterized by creativity, not violence. In this way, Jeremiah predicts a course of action Highway would himself undertake upon completing the novel. Between 2001 and 2003, Highway completed a trilogy of children's stories written in both English and Cree. Responding to a need he identifies in *Kiss of the Fur Queen* for Indigenous youth to be able to access their tribal languages and tribal spiritual systems, Highway wrote *Caribou Song* (2001), *Dragonfly Kites* (2002), and *Fox on the Ice* (2003), which retell portions of the Okimasis brothers' story.[83] Thus, Highway's project as a writer, like Jeremiah's, is not simply to produce politically relevant work for a knowledgeable literary audience, but also to stimulate a thirst for knowledge (Indigenous and otherwise) among Indigenous youth. Although their life histories have included the complex and often violent interaction of disparately empowered cultural and spiritual systems, as tellers of stories, Highway and his character Jeremiah can reflect upon their experiences according to the codes they choose in processes of creative self-definition. Like Highway, Jeremiah reconceptualizes his life in narrative terms of Cree spirituality and traditional orature, made relevant to the contemporary moment through creative adaptation, invention, and augmentation, a process that affords him the creative weaponry to defeat the Weetigo of his past.

In his powerful analysis of creative literature's relevance to political struggle, entitled "In Defense of the Word," Uruguayan author Eduardo Galeano writes:

> At times ... written work radiates an influence much greater than is apparent; at times, it answers—years in advance—the questions and needs of the collectivity, if the writer has known how to experience them first, through inner doubts and agonies. Writing springs from the wounded consciousness of the writer and is projected onto the world; the act of creation is an act of solidarity.[84]

Written between 1992 and 1998, Highway's *Kiss of the Fur Queen* provides valuable insight into the "needs" of the Indigenous "collectivity" within the geographic space of Canada at an important impasse in residential school legacy discourse in 2006, the year in which I am writing. Highway has stated, "I wrote [*Kiss of the Fur Queen*] for a Cree readership ... I hope to reach the kids in the mall in Saskatoon and Winnipeg."[85] Although the novel is multifarious, offering manifold insights to readers from diverse backgrounds both within Canada and without, as I hope I have shown, it speaks with particular force to an Indigenous audience struggling to deal with the awful legacy of Canada's residential school system. While the large-scale, government-backed historicization of the residential school legacy had only recently begun when *Kiss of the Fur Queen* was first published, the novel speaks directly to the limitations, in terms of Indigenous empowerment, of the fact-finding pursuit as it is understood in Euro-Canadian legal and historical terms. Similarly, it recognizes, far ahead of most analysts and critics, that while litigation can provide Indigenous communities and individuals with much-needed resources, those resources will never actualize Indigenous empowerment without serious reconsideration of the unhealthy and distinctly non-Indigenous ideological basis of structures that continue to mediate Indigenous relations with the government of Canada.

Highway's novel criticizes the capacity for a predominantly past-focused healing mission, like that structured by contemporary legacy discourse (through litigation and historicization), to alleviate the very real oppression of Indigenous people in this country. In order to render historical knowledge and monetary gains productive in terms of post-residential school Indigenous empowerment, Highway argues, tribal values—analyzed, interpreted, adapted, and adopted—must be reinvigorated in Indigenous communities (including urban Indigenous communities) to provide the foundation for alternative conceptions of the position of First Nations vis-à-vis the state. Institutions like DIAND and the band council system continue to be organized by Euro-Canadian principles of leadership, favouring hierarchical governance over consensus-based equality and exhibiting a residual patriarchalism over a potential Cree gyno-positive gender equality.

Unlike Alfred, however, Highway does not focus his critique solely on issues of Indigenous governance; he forcefully expresses the need for all institutions that deal with Indigenous people to reflect Indigenous values. For example, Highway superimposes the culturally informed pedagogical space of the Muskoosis Club over the memory of an oppressive residential school setting and later has his protagonists transform the government-financed hospital room in which Gabriel's death takes place into a sacred ceremonial site where a medicine woman can light her sacred herbs and "wail ... the death chant" (305) to ease the dancer's passing.

Dene leader George Erasmus states, "Our old people, when they talk about how the [traditional] ways should be kept by young people, they are not looking back, they are looking forward. They are looking as far ahead into the future as they possibly can."[86] By championing the relevance of traditional Cree orature and spirituality to the contemporary difficulties and future pursuits of Cree residential school survivors, Highway at once guards against the ongoing acculturation of those previously subject to the violence of institutionalized assimilation and exposes the inadequacies of Euro-Canadian ideology. *Kiss of the Fur Queen* strikes to the core of survivance: it not only argues for the relevance of tribal spirituality and orature to the political extremity of the contemporary moment, but also engages in the pedagogical project of unearthing a tribal-specific spiritual and oral archive on its Indigenous audience's behalf. Furthermore, and perhaps most crucially, it provides a blueprint in the substance of its narrative for the process of personal and cultural introspection it champions, illustrating how the Indigenous individual can perform such crucial psychological and spiritual work for her- or himself. Highway's focus on the spiritual is not in any way an avoidance of the political realities of post-residential school Native Canada. It is, rather, a reasoned response to the ideological problems underlying both Native and non-Native political realities and, more specifically, legacy discourse and the residential school claims process. *Kiss of the Fur Queen* is an extraordinarily political novel, and all the more so because of its seductive avoidance of well-worn paths of testimonial discourse and non-fictional political argumentation.

Cycle (of the black lizard)

It was a priest
who made him act that way
so shy he wouldn't say shit
if his mouth was full of it.
At least that's what his
old lady said
each time her face got smashed
with his drunk fist.
The last time
he just pushed her around
then passed out.
Later, her kôhkum said
a lizard crawled inside his mouth
and laid eggs.

It was a black lizard, she said
the kind who eat the insides
feasting slowly
until their young are hatched.
Already his tongue was gone
from so much confessing.
Other boys at the boarding school
never talked out loud
for fear the lizard would creep into their
beds.
At first it just moved around
inside his head
manoeuvring serpentine
like a bad dream.

Then one night
his brain caved in & oozed out
his ears, nose and mouth.

It was his mouth
that caused him so much trouble.
In there was rotten teeth
and stink breath
made by that gluttonous lizard.
Morning Mass
he swallowed hard to rid the slime
but nighttime it just returned
and slithered around.

Another boy, only older
had the same trouble.
Recess
they eyed each other's dirty holes
and spit, spit, spit.
Once they got caught
and had to scrub the stairs–
and neither said shit about it.

At school, the teacher
noticed his kids had dull eyes
and never spoke or laughed.
The girl was ten
and developed for her age.
When asked in class to tell an Indian story
she went crimson in her face
and cried.
Every few days
her brother got sent
to the principal's office.
They thought he was just naturally rough,
like all Indians.
What they didn't know
was in her pee-hole, his mouth
a lizard crawled around
leaving eggs
during the Lord's prayer.

from *Native Canadiana: Songs from the
Urban Rez* (1996)
by Gregory A. Scofield (Métis)

CONCLUSION

Creative Interventions in the Residential School Legacy

"Everything speaks. I have a friend, Flying Clouds, who one time said,
'Some people are such good listeners the trees lean towards them to tell their
secrets.' I think that's true.... [W]hite education ... want[s] us to believe we
don't exist. I realize now that the stories are eternal. They will go on as long
as there are people to speak them. And the people will always be there. The
people will listen to the world and translate it into a human tongue.
That is the job of the poet."
Linda Hogan,
in Laura Coltelli's *Winged Words*

"A new story will only be written by those who would
change the course of history."
Lee Maracle,
I Am Woman

The final story in Haisla/Heiltsuk author Eden Robinson's 1996 collection, *Traplines*, weaves a haunting tale of wounded adolescence in which a young Haisla woman's potential for love, health, maturity, and identity is imperilled by ongoing sexual abuse at the hands of her uncle. Near its close, the narrator of "Queen of the North" unearths a crucial piece of evidence through which she develops a more intricate understanding of the historical circumstances leading to her abuse, thereby arming herself with knowledge against the perpetuation of her victimization:

"Who's this?" I said to Mom. I'd been rummaging through the drawer, hunting for spare change.

"What?"

It was the first thing she'd said to me since I'd come back. I'd heard that she'd cried to practically everyone in the village, saying I'd gone to Vancouver to become a hooker.

I held up a picture of a priest with his hand on a little boy's shoulder. The boy looked happy.

"Oh, that," Mom said. "I forgot I had it. He was Uncle Josh's teacher."

I turned it over. *Dear Joshua*, it read. *How are you? I miss you terribly. Please write. Your friend in Christ, Archibald.*

"Looks like he taught him more than just prayers."

"What are you talking about? Your Uncle Josh was a bright student. They were fond of each other."

"I bet," I said, vaguely remembering that famous priest who got eleven years in jail. He'd molested twenty-three boys while they were in residential school.

Uncle Josh was home from fishing for only two more days. As he was opening my bedroom door, I said, "Father Archibald?"

He stopped. I couldn't see his face because of the way the light was shining through the door. He stayed there a long time.

"I've said my prayers," I said.

He backed away and closed the door.

In the kitchen the next morning he wouldn't look at me. I felt light and giddy, not believing it could end so easily. Before I ate breakfast I closed my eyes and said grace out loud. I had hardly begun when I heard Uncle Josh's chair scrape the floor as he pushed it back. (213)

The discovery and analysis of the forgotten (read repressed) photograph allows the narrator, Karaoke, to view her victimization as part of a broader historical narrative of colonial imposition, oppression, and violence, rather than as an isolated exchange of power between individuals. It allows her to deduce the likely seeds of her uncle's abusive behaviour in transgressions initiated at residential school, an interpretation she mobilizes by verbally associating Uncle Josh with his own perpetrator and making it impossible for him to segregate his actions entirely from those of his "teacher," Father Archibald—the man who presumably 'taught' Josh to abuse. Karaoke's verbal performance forces Uncle Josh to identify the abuse he has inflicted with the abuse he endured at residential school, which leads to his retreat from the role of victimizer. In this sense, Karaoke's awakened knowledge of the historical 'truth' of residential school violence empowers her to halt lateral violence and create positive change. In other words, through the serendipitous disclosure of residential school history, Karaoke is able to achieve the personal security in which healing might occur.

"Queen of the North," however, is far from a straightforward endorsement of historicization as the key to curing the corrosive social aftermath of residential school. After all, the truth of the young Josh's suspected abuse is never substantiated in the story beyond cryptic words on the back of a photograph in which, let us remember, "the boy looked happy." Through Uncle Josh's reaction to Karaoke's mimicry, Robinson implies the historical existence of some form of clandestine sexual encounter between the younger Josh and Father Archibald, but such evidence is circumstantial. Like Tomson Highway, who, as I argued in chapter 5, is skeptical of the capacity of standard historical methodologies and legal notions of 'fact' to adequately account for and understand childhood trauma (like institutionalized violence and abuse), and who champions in *Kiss of the Fur Queen* the exercise of art for dealing with the residential school legacy, Robinson refuses to bind the outcome of her narrative strictly to the characters' acknowledgement of historical 'truth.' For Karaoke, as for Highway's Jeremiah, the key to safety, healing, and empowerment is not merely gaining precise knowledge of the 'factual' past, but is, rather, invoking a personal understanding of that past in the creation of a potentially positive future through art. It is not a question of *what* exactly happened to Uncle Josh in residential school that will save Karaoke, but of *how* Karaoke can marshal her understanding of Uncle Josh's experiences in her seizure of power.

While conceding the need to interrogate standard historical accounts and to carefully analyze the implications of what I have called legacy discourse to discuss residential school survival literature intelligently, this book has been more concerned with the creative presentation of residential school history through art than with the solidification and verification of 'facts.' Recognizing legal proceedings, reconciliation programs, and historical treatises as themselves discourses relating to, rather than distinct from, literary discussions, I have attempted to analyze how literary survival narratives promote a rethinking of residential schooling that refuses to be bound to the deterministic victimhood predicted by oppressive history. The authorial agency demonstrated by the authors I've studied simply doesn't allow for their identification solely as victims. Their life-narratives are stories of "liberation and survivance,"[1] which overturn the tragic storylines of inevitable demise and extinction and create the imaginative conditions in which Indigenous empowerment might be individually and communally claimed.

In Robinson's story the libratory potential of Indigenous art is harnessed through what Homi K. Bhabha would call the "mocking spirit of mask and image."[2]

> I use a recent picture of Uncle Josh that I raided from Mom's album. I paste his face onto the body of Father Archibald and my face onto the boy. The montage looks real enough. Uncle Josh is smiling down at a younger version of me.
>
> My period is vicious this month. I've got clots the size and texture of liver. I put one of them in a Ziploc bag. I put the picture and the bag in a hatbox. I tie it up with a bright red ribbon. I place it on the kitchen table and go upstairs to get a jacket. I think nothing of leaving it there because there's no one else at home. The note inside the box reads, "It was yours so I killed it." (213)

Karaoke manipulates her own image and the image of her abuser to taunt, challenge, and change her intended audience.[3] Picking up on a recurring theme of dismemberment and re-membering throughout "Queen of the North," Karaoke fragments then reconfigures her image in the spirit of mimicry. She strategically reimagines and represents a younger version of herself within the context of an acculturative history—represented by Christian priest and Native child—to examine the negative influence of that history on the present and so create the potential for an altered future.

Karaoke's creation of the politically charged art object thus provides an appropriate metaphor for my use of Indigenous life-writing in this project. While I do not deny the connections between the life-writings I have examined and actual lived experience—note that Karaoke's "montage" is formed through the strategic editing of actual photographic records of the past—I break with disclosure-based reading strategies for these texts to discuss survival narratives as carefully crafted artistic creations, which exploit their chosen genre's perceived relationship to extra-literary reality in the service of communitism and survivance. The authors at the centre of this study use life-writing to move, inspire, heal, and empower the communities on behalf of whom they write. Residential school survival narratives are therefore forward-looking even as they interrogate the past. As Thomas King stated in his recent Massey Lectures Series, "Native writers ... [look] backward and forward with the same glance."[4] Significantly, Karaoke's 'gift' to her uncle is not the aborted foetus she claims it to be, but a specimen of congealed menstrual fluid. While the presentation of an aborted foetus might suggest in Karaoke a resolutely pessimist refusal to regenerate the Indigenous community she perceives to be locked in a cycle of lateral violence and perpetual victimhood by the tyranny of colonial history, the presentation of a menstrual clot bespeaks a latent optimism through its announcement of the narrator's ongoing capacity to reproduce. And as I quoted Métis writer Kim Anderson earlier, menstruation is "central" to Indigenous "understanding[s] of creative female energy."[5] The 'gift' is a petrified manifestation—as in the collapsed framing of time through literature—of the spiritually charged menstrual flow that acts as a harbinger to the perpetuation and indeed the healing of Indigenous community. Karaoke's present(ation) addresses the violence of an oppressive past through artistic posturing while portending the recreation and reclamation of Indigenous family and community, those integral cultural bodies so vociferously attacked by the residential school system.

Eden Robinson is not a residential school survivor and "Queen of the North" is not a life-narrative. Yet the story of Karaoke bears significantly on the present study because it illustrates that residential schooling cannot be confined to the category of history. The influence of residential school education endures throughout Native Canada in lateral violence, spiritual alienation, misogynist band politics, alcoholism and drug abuse, identity crises, and what Lee Maracle calls "languageless generations," all of which are as relevant to the younger generation of Native writers as they are to their forebears who suffered the pains of institutionalization. The long and debilitating shadow cast by residential schooling darkens the present and threatens to extend its serpentine fingers indefinitely into the future of Native Canada and Canada entire if there is not appropriately inspired reaction and redress. Only in the past decade have substantial efforts been made by the churches, the government, and First Nations leaders to address the appalling legacy of Canada's residential schools. These efforts, which include state-sponsored historical study, church-sponsored healing circles, and the jointly administered Alternative Dispute Resolution program, represent but a fraction of the work required to reverse the damage wrought by a century of residential schooling in Canada. And, as I argue above, following Taiaiake Alfred, if these reconciliation and healing strategies neither fundamentally challenge the power imbalance between Euro-Canadian political authorities and Indigenous communities, nor arrest the paternalistic position of non-Native Canada vis-à-vis the First Nations, the programs designed to address the residential school legacy will never facilitate meaningful Indigenous empowerment.

This is where the neglected resource of Native literature becomes so important. Through their writings, Native authors imagine alternative ideological and political horizons for Indigenous communities and individuals, loosening the neo-colonial bonds of non-Native authority and mapping out possible paths to empowerment and healing that reinvigorate traditional knowledges while refusing to rely solely on the structures of governmental power. This is not to say that monetary redress by the government and the churches, for instance, is an insignificant ingredient of progressive healing strategies, but such redress must occur in the context of reimagined relations within First Nations communities and between First Nations and non-Native Canada.

The purpose of *Magic Weapons* has been to analyze how the autonomous incarnations of residential school survival narratives, while intimately connected to individual understandings of historical reality, encourage new strategies for empowerment that seek to emancipate Indigenous peoples from the yoke of acculturative history. At the same time, I have been careful not to trivialize the very real benefits certain Indigenous students experienced by attending residential school, what Tomson Highway depicts in *Kiss of the Fur Queen* as "magic weapons" such as literacy and Euro-Canadian spiritual and political acumen. In chapter 4, for example, I argued that there are no ethical grounds from which to suggest that Rita Joe's advocacy of the positive aspects of residential school existence should be disbelieved, criticized, or condemned. My concern has been to locate individual residential school experiences within broader colonial narratives and tribal histories—both of which inevitably bear on individual survivors' interpretations of their institutionalization, although never programmatically—and to analyze how particular survivors utilize both their personal memories of residential school and their literary skills (often developed at least partially therein) to reimagine and recreate Indigenous identities, communities, and cultures. I have striven to examine and articulate the disparate ways in which individual residential school survivors invoke narrative to, in Gerald Vizenor's words, "touch" themselves and their communities "into being with words."[6] According to Vizenor, "You can't understand the world without telling a story," because "there isn't any center to the world but a story."[7] As Thomas King puts it, "The truth about stories is that that's all we are."[8] The goal of this project has been to discern how the stories survivors tell about their residential school experiences and the ways in which they tell them alter our understandings of "the world" and who "we are" within it.

In *Manifest Manners*, Vizenor defines survivance as "an active sense of presence, the continuance of native stories, not a mere reaction, or a survivable name. Native survivance stories are renunciations of dominance, tragedy, and victimry. Survivance means the right of succession or reversion of an estate, and in that sense, the estate of native survivancy" (vii). If we understand "estate" to refer to the sum of one's identifying features and properties, residential school survival narratives epitomize the exercise of what Vizenor describes as the "right of succession" by resisting the externally applied identities of victimhood—those identifying features imposed on Native individuals by non-Native forces within residential school and after—and creatively articulating the identifying features of an empowered estate that will supplant its dominated precursor. Such acts of narrative defiance are at once "succession" and "reversion" in that they reclaim features from the estate that preceded dominance (what I refer to in chapter 2 as the "communal/tribal identity" that precedes the "institutionalized identity") at the same time that they imagine and articulate those features that will identify a newly empowered estate (what I refer to in chapter 2 as the "imaginative literary identity").

The narratives studied in these pages are also stories of what Vizenor calls "continuance" in that they participate in the survival of their authors' communities and cultures. These stories refuse to be read as the tragic archives of Indigenous cultural extinction. Even Thrasher, who ultimately died a homeless alcoholic, imparts to future generations of Inuit their heritage of myth and legend (through stories like the Iliapaluk and Ananaa episode) and fights, in his literary work, the political, economic, and spiritual domination of the Inuit by southern forces. Thrasher's narrative serves what Jace Weaver calls a communitist function by "participat[ing] in the healing of the grief and sense of exile" felt by his Inuit community and "the pained individuals" in it,[9] despite the author's inability to conquer his own grief and soothe his own sense of exile. As Weaver astutely acknowledges throughout *That the People Might Live*, many Native people write and read literature from variously pervasive positions of cultural alienation induced by the genocidal policies of colonial and neocolonial governments; for the exiled, Native literature can become a catalyst for the resurrection and recreation of Native communities that have been muted and dispersed. Survival narratives hold mirrors to contemporary Native communities—urban, reserve, and otherwise—but, through the refractive lens of

181

autonomous imagination, they re-envision those communities and, in reciprocal engagement with readers, stimulate communal recreation.

These stories evidence the traumatic effects of Canada's most prolonged and legislatively codified attempted genocide, but, perhaps more importantly, they scream its failure. They declare and enact the survival of the Native cultures and identities the residential school system sought to suffocate, both proving and prompting radical Indigenous endurance. Basil Johnston recalls one of his colleagues exulting upon graduation from Garnier Indian Residential School: "'We toughed it out, didn't we? They couldn't break us down, could they?'"[10] The question elicits no response because its answer lies in its articulation. The defiant question announces both graduates' ongoing existence in the face of an oppressive history and a disparately empowered present, thereby proving what the colleague backhandedly declares: "They couldn't break us down." By committing the utterance to print in *Indian School Days*, Johnston extends its implications beyond the dialogue of two peers to a broader audience which, by this point in the narrative, is absolutely convinced of the boys' physical *and* cultural survival. Johnston's story, as Thrasher's story, Joe's story, and Highway's story, inspires change with its defiance of colonial narratives of assimilation and post-colonial narratives of obligatory victimhood crafted from without. Residential school survival narratives are written from *within*, redefining what it means to inhabit an Indigenous identity 'within' disparate contemporary Indigenous communities. They celebrate through stories the lives and cultures of those who have survived, of those who haven't, and of those whose words make the survival of others possible.

ENDNOTES

INTRODUCTION

[1] Robert Arthur Alexie, *Porcupines and China Dolls* (Toronto: Stoddart Publishing, 2002), 2.

[2] Phil Fontaine, qtd in Agnes Grant, *No End of Grief: Indian Residential Schools in Canada* (Winnipeg: Pemmican Publications Inc., 1996), 269.

[3] This, of course, is not meant to imply a one-to-one correlation between residential schooling and specific instances of suicide among Aboriginal people (although specific cases have been made for such causal connections), but rather to recognize how conditions caused by residential schooling have been integral to the fomentation of despair within Aboriginal communities. These conditions include not simply atmospheres of lateral violence provoked by experiences of residential school abuse, but economic powerlessness through inadequate education; disconnection from spiritual systems, Indigenous languages, and familial units; loss of parenting skills through removal from the home; and pervasive senses of alienation and exile that are often the by-product of assimilationist pedagogy.

[4] This pressure, from Aboriginal people at a grass-roots level through to the AFN, as well as from scholarly and activist outposts, helped bring about the apologies of the churches at various points during the 1990s for their role in residential schooling and the official apology of the federal government of Canada in 1998. More importantly, it was instrumental in forcing the negotiation of the historic Reconciliation and Compensation Agreement between the federal government and the AFN on November 23, 2005.

[5] John Milloy, *"A National Crime": The Canadian Government and the Residential School System, 1879 to 1986* (Winnipeg: University of Manitoba Press, 1999), 154.

[6] Gerald Vizenor, qtd in Laura Coltelli, *Winged Words: American Indian Writers Speak* (Lincoln: University of Nebraska Press, 1990), 159.

[7] Tomson Highway, *Kiss of the Fur Queen* (Toronto: Doubleday Canada, 1998).

CHAPTER 1: ACCULTURATION THROUGH EDUCATION

1   Eden Robinson, *Monkey Beach* (Toronto: Alfred A. Knopf Canada, 2000), 112.

2   I use the term "seemingly" because Robinson is careful not to provide easy historicization for the shadowy events of past trauma. Although clues abound that connect a series of violent events back to residential school abuse, that abuse is never substantiated unquestionably.

3   As I discuss in more detail in the conclusion, *Monkey Beach*, like Robinson's connected short story "Queen of the North," culminates in an act of violent artistry that illuminates the connections among residential school abuse, institutionalized violence, and lateral violence in Aboriginal communities. When Lisa-Marie happens upon a photograph of a young Native boy kneeling before a priest with the face of Karoake pasted over the young boy's and that of her Uncle Josh pasted over the priest's, accompanied by a note saying, "'Dear, dear Joshua. It was yours so I killed it'" (365), she is able to "piece" together a plausible storyline that involves Josh's sexual abuse at residential school, his subsequent abuse of Karoake, her pregnancy, abortion, and creation of the collage. This storyline, however, is never *proven* by Robinson's narrative, remaining elusive and cryptic and, therefore, all the more unnerving. As Jennifer Andrews posits, "the return of the repressed ... takes on a larger political significance in Robinson's novel, in which evil is primarily associated with Eurocentric interventions in the Haisla community rather than individual Native characters, a strategy that creates a[n] ... ambiguous and complicated vision of evil" ("Native Canadian Gothic Refigured: Reading Eden Robinson's *Monkey Beach*," *Essays on Canadian Writing* 73 [2001], 12).

4   Louise Halfe, *Bear Bones & Feathers* (Regina: Coteau Books, 1994).

5   Alice French, *The Restless Nomad* (Winnipeg: Pemmican Publishers, 1992).

6   Maria Campbell, *Halfbreed* (Lincoln: University of Nebraska Press, 1982).

7   See Jane Willis's *Geneish: An Indian Girlhood* (Toronto: New Press, 1973), 28–44.

8   See Alexie's *Porcupines and China Dolls*, 9–29.

9   See Basil Johnston's *Indian School Days* (Norman: University of Oklahoma Press, 1988), 28–47.

10   See Anthony Apakark Thrasher's *Thrasher ... Skid Row Eskimo*, eds. Gerard Deagle and Alan Mettrick (Toronto: Griffin House Publishers, 1976), 35–40.

11   See Isabella Knockwood's *Out of the Depths: The Experiences of Mi'kmaw Children at the Indian Residential School at Shubenacadie, Nova Scotia* (Lockeport, NS: Roseway Publishing, 1992), 3, 82, and 98.

¹² See Rita Joe's *Song of Rita Joe: Autobiography of a Mi'kmaq Poet* (Lincoln: University of Nebraska Press, 1996), in which the author celebrates her freedom from Shubenacadie Residential School with carnivalesque and triumphant laughter: "The confinement of my will had been going on for so long that I cried just until the school was out of sight. Then I began to giggle— and I sat there, giggling, to my heart's content" (56).

¹³ Alice French, *My Name Is Masak* (Winnipeg: Peguis Publishers, 1976).

¹⁴ The names of the titles, of course, anticipate the violence of residential school renaming and the stifling of Native names.

¹⁵ Rymhs illustrates Willis's unwillingness to identify easily with either side by suggesting that "her process of regaining a sense of place ... leaves her belonging neither to her traditional community nor to dominant white culture, whose ideology and institutions she appears to be unable to forgive" ("Autobiography and the Overdetermined Self: Jane Willis's *Geneish: An Indian Girlhood*," *Essays on Canadian Writing* 79 [2003]: 144).

¹⁶ Thrasher, *Skid Row Eskimo*, 1–48.

¹⁷ Terry Goldie and Daniel David Moses, eds., *An Anthology of Canadian Native Literature in English*, third edition (Don Mills: Oxford University Press, 2005).

¹⁸ Joe, *Song of Rita Joe*.

¹⁹ Earl Maquinna George, *Living on the Edge: Nuu-Chah-Nulth History from an Ahousaht Chief's Perspective* (Victoria: Sono Nis Press, 2003).

²⁰ Shirley Sterling, *My Name Is Seepeetza* (Toronto: House of Anansi Press, 2005).

²¹ Richard Van Camp, "Review of *Porcupines and China Dolls*," <http://www.richardvancamp.org/writing/Porcupines.html> (accessed 03 March 2007).

²² Beth Brant, "A Long Story," in *An Anthology of Canadian Native Literature in English*, third edition, eds. Terry Goldie and Daniel David Moses (Don Mills: Oxford University Press, 2005), 145–49.

²³ Maria Campbell, "Jacob," in *Stories of the Road Allowance People* (Penticton: Theytus Books Ltd., 1995).

²⁴ Gregory Scofield, "Cycle (of the Black Lizard)," in *Native Canadiana: Songs from the Urban Rez* (Vancouver: Polestar Book Publishers, 1996).

²⁵ Thomas King, *Truth & Bright Water* (Toronto: Perennial Canada, 1999).

²⁶ Residential schooling was more than an assimilationist attempt to 'civilize the savages' through cultural reinscription; it was an attempt to rid the country of Indigenous people by withholding from them what the government and the churches perceived as the distinguishing features of their cultures (an

endeavour designed at least partially to render Native people outside the fiscal
responsibilities of the Canadian government as articulated in treaties). Agnes
Grant (*No End of Grief*), Roland Chrisjohn (Haudenausaunee) and Sherrie
Young (*The Circle Game* [Penticton: Theytus Books, 1997]), and the Truth
Commission into Genocide in Canada (<http://canadiangenocide.nativeweb.
org/intro2.html> [accessed 11 January 2003]) have all argued that residential
schools were explicitly genocidal in their attempted destruction of "'all the
Indian there is in the race'" (qtd in Milloy, *A National Crime*, 42) and in their
forcible transfer of Native children to the care of non-Native guardians for
the purposes of undermining the strength and vitality of Indigenous cultures.
This, they argue, violates Article II of the United Nations' Convention on
Genocide, signed by Canada in 1949. I wish to express early on that the
rubric of genocide is not only critically appropriate, given the international
community's definition of the term (recognizing the international community
to be at least partially represented by the UN), but also rhetorically necessary
to express the severity of the effects of attempted cultural extermination on
generations of Native people. Unlike Chrisjohn and Young, however, I do not
perceive the retention of 'cultural' in 'cultural genocide' as an "unnecessary
ellipsis" (44), but rather assert that there are differences among manifestations
of genocide and that the perhaps politically effective generalization that
"*cultural genocide is genocide*" (44) might mask the complexities of individual
situations. In other words, I maintain that residential schooling sought a
genocidal effect on Native cultures without suggesting that this is precisely the
same thing as the physical murder en masse of a culturally specific population.

[27] J.R. Miller, *Shingwauk's Vision: A History of Native Residential Schools* (Toronto:
University of Toronto Press, 1996).

[28] Harold Cardinal, *The Unjust Society* (Toronto: Douglas and McIntyre, 1999), 2.

[29] Allan Greer, ed., *The Jesuit Relations: Natives and Missionaries in Seventeenth-
Century North America* (New York: Nedford/St. Martin's, 2000), 36.

[30] Milloy, *A National Crime*, 44.

[31] Celia Haig-Brown, *Resistance and Renewal: Surviving the Indian Residential
School* (Vancouver: Arsenal Pulp Press, 1998).16.

[32] Assembly of First Nations, *Breaking the Silence: An Interpretive Study of
Residential School Impact and Healing as Illustrated by the Stories of First
Nations Individuals* (Ottawa: Assembly of First Nations Press, 1994), 41.

[33] Chrisjohn and Young, *The Circle Game*, 84–88.

34 By this I do not mean to exonerate those who so horribly wounded the children in their care, but, rather, to recognize always how their transgressions were enabled by the functioning of the system itself.

35 Haig-Brown, *Resistance and Renewal*, 11.

36 Miller, *Shingwauk's Vision*, 413.

37 Milloy, *A National Crime*, xviii.

38 Miller, *Shingwauk's Vision*, 414.

39 Maureen Konkle, "Indian Literacy, U.S. Colonialism, and Literary Criticism," in *Postcolonial Theory and the United States: Race, Ethnicity, and Literature*, eds. Amritjit Singh and Peter Schmidt (Jackson: University Press of Mississippi, 2000).

40 John Richardson, *Wacousta*, New Canadian Library edition (Toronto: McClelland and Steward Inc., 1991).

41 Duncan Campbell Scott, "The Onondaga Madonna," in *An Anthology of Canadian Literature in English*, eds. Russell Brown, Donna Bennett, and Nathalie Cooke (Toronto: Oxford University Press, 1998), 165.

42 In "The Forsaken" (in *An Anthology of Canadian Literature in English*, eds. Russell Brown, Donna Bennett, and Nathalie Cooke, 167–68), Scott depicts another tragic Indigenous woman, stoically resigned to her own death and subject to the poem's overriding Christian imagery.

43 For example, at a time when the school at Spanish had instituted a half-day study/labour schedule for older children while the younger children received full-day schooling, at Kamloops Indian Residential School in British Columbia, "until the late 1940s, no child attended school for longer than two hours a day" (Haig-Brown, *Resistance and Renewal*, 66); also, given private donations to certain religious bodies collecting for individual schools, some schools had slightly better living conditions than others, although the most common complaints from students across the country and over divergent time-periods concerned hunger and cold.

44 I enlist the term "cultural genocide" not simply for provocative force, but as a reasoned response to the inadequacy of such possible alternatives as "assimilation" and "acculturation."

45 John A. Macdonald, qtd in Judith Ennamorato, *Sing the Brave Song* (Schomberg: Raven Press, 1998), 72.

46 Duncan Campbell Scott, qtd in Milloy, *A National Crime*, 46.

CHAPTER 2: READING RESIDENTIAL SCHOOL

1 Maggie Hodgson, "Rebuilding Community after the Residential School Experience," in *Nation to Nation: Aboriginal Sovereignty and the Future of Canada*, eds. Diane Engelstad and John Bird (Concord: Anansi Press, 1992), 105.

2 Jeannette Armstrong, "Invocation: The Real Power of Aboriginal Women," in *Women of the First Nations: Power, Wisdom, and Strength*, eds. Christine Miller and Patricia Chuchryk (Winnipeg: University of Manitoba Press, 1996), x.

3 Even a cursory glance at Celia Haig-Brown's *Resistance and Renewal*, the Assembly of First Nations' *Breaking the Silence*, or J.R. Miller's *Shingwauk's Vision* will amply support this claim. Invoked largely to force the Canadian government and the churches to acknowledge and address their roles in the strategic decimation of tribal nations, survivor testimonies have generally been framed within historical scholarship to suggest a causal relationship between acculturative practices and/or abuse within residential school and adverse conditions within contemporary Indigenous communities. As a result, such testimonies tend to evidence how invasive external control in the past has created an, in many ways, unpalatable present for Native Canadians. For example, one survivor declared to the Assembly of First Nations that his anger and madness was the result of all he had "lost by going to residential school: my childhood, my innocence, my family, my self respect" (Assembly of First Nations, *Breaking the Silence*, 128). Another survivor told the Royal Commission that even "'at 47,'" she or he could not "'consider [him- or herself] a whole person. One that can walk and associate and relate to people as a ... I don't know how to describe it... without shame, without any sense of embarrassment, because of what I experienced in residential school'" (qtd in Chrisjohn and Young, *The Circle Game*, 38). In both cases, as in countless others, the experience of residential school in youth is identified through testimony as the cause of suffering in adulthood.

4 Which is not to suggest that questions don't remain about the precise nature of that adverse impact or how it ought to be reacted against, but, rather, to acknowledge that there are simply no grounds from which to propose that residential schooling was a benign experiment whose effects were neither negative nor protracted.

5 Hodgson, "Rebuilding Community," 109.

6 Bev Sellars, qtd in Elizabeth Furniss, *Victims of Benevolence: The Dark Legacy of the Williams Lake Residential School* (Vancouver: Arsenal Pulp Press, 1995), 125.

7 Chrisjohn and Young, *The Circle Game*, 83.

8 My use of "we" to refer to scholars and commentators is not meant to suggest a binary between survivors and those discussing the residential school issue. Certainly this is not the case. Many of the most important and influential critics of residential schooling in the scholarly and public arenas are Aboriginal, many among them residential school survivors. The days of Aboriginal issues being lived by Aboriginals and discussed in print solely by non-Aboriginals are thankfully long behind us. However, I do wish to acknowledge my own status as a non-Aboriginal scholar, which I will discuss more fully later in this chapter.

9 These dangers underwrite some scholars' reluctance to discuss the residential school legacy in terms of what Alice Carroll and others have termed "Residential School Syndrome." According to Chrisjohn:

> RSS [Residential School Syndrome] sidetracks all interested parties in a variety of confusing ways, disabling those who are supposed to be suffering from RSS, and exonerating those who are responsible for the mess.... [S]uppose you are helping people address personal problems in their lives, and you find out they attended residential school. If you subscribe to reification of RSS, their supposed possession of RSS 'causes' them (in your view) to behave in the unproductive or destructive ways you are trying to remedy, much as the possession of a cold makes you sneeze, cough, and feel lousy. Just as you don't hold a person with a cold responsible for displaying cold symptoms, your tendency is to regard a 'person with RSS' as not responsible for displaying any of the supposed RSS symptoms.
>
> This enterprise soon gathers momentum. The people who went to residential school are told that they suffer from RSS, and indeed that 'their problems' arise from it ... [which] release[s] them from taking personal responsibility for their actions (e.g., 'I beat my wife because I am suffering from RSS) (Chrisjohn and Young, *The Circle Game*, 82).

10 I have included Highway's "novel" in my study of life-writings because it is built from the raw materials of the author's life and residential school experience. Also, it was originally conceived as an autobiography before Highway rewrote it as a novel. Like *Skid Row Eskimo* and *Song of Rita Joe*, Highway's narrative mobilizes personal history in creative ways to move audiences, to re-examine the discourse on the residential school legacy,

and to stimulate positive change. I include more on *Kiss of the Fur Queen*'s development in chapter 5.

11 Note that I am discussing "critical discourse" on Native texts specifically. In literary criticism, the critic *requires* the other two bodies in order to generate a valid reading. This, however, is not the case in the inverse. Readers from within Indigenous communities do not *require* critical discourse to make sense of text, although in some cases it may provide fertile ground for alternative reading possibilities.

12 Because I am setting up the critical framework for *Magic Weapons* and I happen to be a non-Native scholar, this section probes the positionality and limitations of the outsider critic. However, this is not meant to imply that the imagined critic is necessarily or even generally non-Native. Native scholars address these texts and issues in more and more encompassing ways. Nonetheless, to render my critical claims as useful as possible, I need to theorize my own critical position without diverting undue attention away from the main matters at hand.

13 Robert Allen Warrior, *Tribal Secrets: Recovering American Indian Intellectual Traditions* (Minneapolis: University of Minnesota Press, 1995).

14 Craig S. Womack, *Red on Red: Native American Literary Separatism* (Minneapolis: University of Minnesota Press, 1999).

15 For Womack, tribal heritage is neither static nor confined to the realms of spirituality and ceremony. He argues that "traditionalism has always been a complicated matrix of social, religious, political, and cultural aspects" (59) and, as *Red on Red* makes clear, that matrix is embroiled with contemporary issues as well as historical ones. "The attempt, then," Womack writes, "will be to break down oppositions between the world of literature and the very real struggles of American Indian communities, arguing for both an intrinsic and extrinsic relationship between the two. I will seek a literary criticism that emphasizes Native resistance movements against colonialism, confronts racism, discusses sovereignty and Native nationalism, seeks connections between literature and liberation struggles, and, finally, roots literature in land and culture. This criticism emphasizes unique Native worldviews and political realities, searches for differences as often as similarities, and attempts to find Native literature's place in Indian country, rather than Native literature's place in the canon" (11).

16 Womack does, however, make this argument specifically: "Native viewpoints are necessary because the 'mental means of production' in regards to analyzing Indian cultures have been owned, almost exclusively, by non-Indians" (5).

[17] Jace Weaver, Craig S. Womack, and Robert Warrior, *American Indian Literary Nationalism* (Albuquerque: University of New Mexico Press, 2006), 17.

[18] Helen Hoy, *How Should I Read These? Native Women Writers in Canada* (Toronto: University of Toronto Press, 2001), 11.

[19] Kim Anderson, *A Recognition of Being: Reconstructing Native Womanhood* (Toronto: Second Story Press, 2000), 27.

[20] Womack, *Red on Red*, 11.

[21] Jace Weaver, *That the People Might Live: Native American Literatures and Native American Community* (New York: Oxford University Press, 1997), 41. In both these examples, Womack and Weaver are referring to Native literature rather than criticism, but I believe their points hold equally well with what "Native American literary criticism" is intended to perform.

[22] The claim above plays on the title of Julie Cruikshank's *The Social Lives of Stories: Narrative and Knowledge in the Yukon Territory* (Lincoln: University of Nebraska Press, 1998).

[23] Arnold Krupat, *Ethnocriticism: Ethnography, History, Literature* (Berkeley: University of California Press, 1992), 30.

[24] Kathleen Mullen Sands, and Theodore Rios, *Telling a Good One: The Process of a Native American Collaborative Biography* (Lincoln: University of Nebraska Press, 2000).

[25] For a cogent argument about the ethical implications of Sands's critical position, see Deena Rymhs's review of *Telling a Good One* in *Studies in American Indian Literatures* 15, 2 (Summer 2003): 99–102.

[26] This awareness is most readily apparent in the intensely self-reflexive chapter with which Krupat concludes *The Turn to the Native* (Lincoln: University of Nebraska Press, 1996), entitled "A Nice Jewish Boy among the Indians."

[27] Krupat, *Ethnocriticism*, 30.

[28] Renate Eigenbrod, *Travelling Knowledges: Positioning the Im/Migrant Reader of Aboriginal Literatures in Canada* (Winnipeg: University of Manitoba Press, 2005), xv.

[29] Hoy, *How Should I Read These?*, 18.

[30] Although I would level the following critique at the work of neither Eigenbrod nor Hoy—both of whom I respect a great deal and have learned from extensively—I do worry that such qualifications might, at times, be disingenuous, presented as protocol rather than sincere reservation. I'm concerned that many non-Native critics believe their work to be valid, intelligent, and effective—after all, why else would they try to publish it?—and

yet they feel compelled to pay lip-service to their unworthiness in order to appease the current critical climate.

[31] Womack, *Red on Red*, 5.

[32] To clarify, this does not mean a power-laden dynamic in which non-Native paternalist scholars 'give Natives a chance' by *editing* their work, *organizing* their conferences, and *teaching* their grad courses. By contrast, it's a recognition that all of us, Native and non-Native, should be involved in expanding the field and the discipline so that there are multiple sites for engagement by the next generation of Native scholars who will increasingly guide the study of Native literatures in years to come. A recent example in which I've been involved, with scholars such as Kristina Fagan and Joanne Episkenew, has been the 2007 conference of the Canadian Association for Commonwealth Literature and Language Studies, focusing on Indigenous literatures and communities, in which the conference format was modified to encourage involvement from young scholars new to the conference circuit. Susan Gingell was instrumental in re-envisioning this format to make it more inclusive, culturally sensitive, and functional. Womack contends that "one measure" of a critic's commitment to Native community "is the degree to which he or she finds a way to turn over some of his or her work to the younger generation of critics who are coming up in the discipline." "This is, after all," he continues, "how nations are built, by training the next generation" (*American Indian Literary Nationalism*, 169).

[33] Krupat, *Ethnocriticism*, 30.

[34] Matt Herman, "The Krupat-Warrior Debate: A Preliminary Account," in *Culture & the State: Disability & Indigenous Studies*, eds. James Gifford and Gabrielle Zezulka-Mailloux (Edmonton: CRC Humanities Studio Publishers, 2003), 64.

[35] Weaver, Womack, and Warrior, *American Indian Literary Nationalism*, 169.

[36] Warrior, *Tribal Secrets*, xviii.

[37] Weaver, Womack, and Warrior, *American Indian Literary Nationalism*, 213.

[38] Ibid., 11.

[39] Jana Sequoya, "How (!) Is an Indian? A Contest of Stories," in *New Voices in Native American Literary Criticism*, ed. Arnold Krupat (Washington: Smithsonian Institution Press, 1993), 458.

[40] Kimberly Blaeser, "Native Literature: Seeking a Critical Center," in *Looking at the Words of Our People: First Nations Analysis of Literature*, ed. Jeannette Armstrong (Penticton: Theytus Books, 1993), 53.

41 In this way I consider my work nationalist, in the sense articulated in *American Indian Literary Nationalism*, although, given the emphasis on authorial voice in this project, I remain reticent to impose nationalist readings on the work of one, like Rita Joe, who clearly rejects nationalist postures.

42 Chrisjohn and Young, *The Circle Game*, 37.

43 Constance Deiter, *From Our Mothers' Arms: The Intergenerational Impact of Residential Schools in Saskatchewan* (Etobicoke: United Church Publishing House, 1999), 38.

44 Haig-Brown, *Resistance and Renewal*, 11.

45 Julia Watson and Sidonie Smith, "De/Colonization and the Politics of Discourse in Women's Autobiographical Practices," Introduction to *De/Colonizing the Subject: The Politics of Gender in Women's Autobiography* (Minneapolis: University of Minnesota Press, 1992), xiii.

46 I remain cautious of uncritical application of prefabricated analytical models—like those imported from postcolonial theory—to the interpretation of First Nations texts. In "Godzilla vs. Postcolonial," in *New Contexts of Canadian Criticism*, eds. Ajay Heble, Donna Palmateer Pennee, and J.R. (Tim) Struthers (Toronto: Broadview Press, 1997), Thomas King makes abundantly clear that the conditions of particular Native North American communities are not those that gave rise to post-colonial theory, rendering deployment of such theory suspect and dangerous in the Native context. More recently, Warrior, Womack, and Weaver have taken issue with the postcolonial championing of hybridity and its ubiquitous relation to resistance in Native American literary criticism. I wish to voice my awareness of these concerns and my intention to use Bhabha's work in a specific and critical manner in relation to work by Native theorists like Gerald Vizenor, King, and N. Scott Momaday.

47 Homi K. Bhabha, "Interrogating Identity: Frantz Fanon and the Postcolonial Prerogative," in *The Location of Culture* (New York: Routledge, 1994), 45.

48 N. Scott Momaday, "The Man Made of Words," in *The First Convocation of American Indian Scholars*, ed. Rupert Costo (San Francisco: Indian Historian Press, 1970), 43.

49 Thomas King, *The Truth About Stories: A Native Narrative* (Toronto: Anansi Press, 2003), 2, 32, 62, 92, 122.

50 Gerald Vizenor in Coltelli, *Winged Words*, 45.

51 Tomson Highway, qtd in Judy Stoffman, "Highway Confronts His Past in New Novel," *Toronto Star* (30 September 1998), p. E4.

52 Bhabha, "Interrogating Identity," 51.

53 Ibid., 62.

54 Watson and Smith, "De/Colonization and the Politics of Discourse," xx.

55 Lee Maracle, *I Am Woman: A Native Perspective on Sociology and Feminism* (Vancouver: Press Gang Publishers, 1999), 8.

56 For examples of such attempts at frustration, see Jennifer Andrews's interview with King in "Border Trickery and Dog Bones: A Conversation with Thomas King," in *Studies in Canadian Literatures* 24, 2 (1999), and Laura Coltelli's interview with Vizenor in *Winged Words*.

57 Weaver, *That the People Might Live.*

58 Womack, *Red on Red,* 11.

59 David L. Moore, "Decolonializing Criticism: Reading Dialectics and Dialogics in Native American Literatures," in *Studies in American Indian Literatures* 6, 4 (1994): 8.

60 Ibid.

61 Note that King's boarding school experience took place in an intercultural setting in the US rather than an Indian residential school in Canada.

62 Thomas King, qtd in Weaver, *That the People Might Live,* 151.

63 Thomas King, *Green Grass, Running Water* (Toronto: Perennial Canada, 1999).

64 Thomas King, *Truth & Bright Water* (Toronto: Perennial Canada, 1999). King states in an interview that Neugin "is a real historical character who was a young girl of eight when the Trail of Tears took place and she was ripped out of her house so quickly by the soldiers that the only thing she could take with her was a duck, and on the first couple of days on the trip she was holding onto the duck so tightly she killed it. And when they interviewed her in Oklahoma, when she was in her eighties or nineties, the thing she remembered most vividly was that duck and that march. It still haunted her" (Andrews, "Border Trickery and Dog Bones," 180).

65 Weaver, *That the People Might Live,* 151–52.

66 The forces that have 'problematized' some contemporary Native communities are not simply relocation, amalgamation, and diasporic flight to urban centres, but also the poverty, alienation, and despair that have accompanied colonial interventions like residential school. Also, the use of "modern" and "traditional" above is not meant to suggest mutual exclusivity. The traditional persists into the modern, a point emphasized by Vine Deloria, Jr., for whom constant evolution and adaptation are the primary characteristics of

"traditional" Native cultures. See Deloria, qtd in Warrior, *Tribal Secrets*, 84, and also Warrior's discussion of Deloria throughout his book.

67 Kristina Fagan, "Tewatatha:wi: Aboriginal Nationalism in Taiaiake Alfred's *Peace, Power, Righteousness: An Indigenous Manifesto*," *The American Indian Quarterly* 28, 1 & 2 (2004): 14.

68 Devon A. Mihesuah, "Finding Empowerment through Writing and Reading, or Why Am I Doing This? An Unpopular Writer's Comments about the State of American Indian Literary Criticism," *American Indian Quarterly* 28, 1 & 2 (2004): 98.

CHAPTER 3: "WE HAVE BEEN SILENT TOO LONG"

1 Highway himself has spoken about his novel in these terms, suggesting it reveals that "'if you dream hard enough you can do anything'" (Joel Yanofsky, "Highway of Dreams," *Montreal Gazette*, [4 February 1995], p. J1). Similarly, A. Lavonne Brown Ruoff describes Rita Joe's autobiography as "'an inspiring story of survival, endurance, love, and achievement'" (*Song of Rita Joe*, quoted on the book's back cover).

2 This is the reason, I would argue, Johnston takes such care in *Indian School Days* (1988) to identify the whole community of students at St. Peter Clavers Residential School at the time of his tenure—even cataloguing names, nicknames, and current whereabouts (where possible)—and Highway makes the death of the younger sibling from an AIDS-related illness such a crucial aspect of *Kiss of the Fur Queen*. Each author desires to write those silenced by their residential school experiences back into the literary and historical discussion of these institutions.

3 Greg Young-Ing, "Aboriginal Peoples' Estrangement: Marginalization in the Publishing Industry," in *Looking at the Words of Our People: First Nations Analysis of Literature*, ed. Jeannette Armstrong (Penticton: Theytus Books, 1993), 180.

4 Maracle, qtd in Young-Ing, "Aboriginal Peoples' Estrangement," 180.

5 To evaluate adequately how this historical context is addressed and embodied in the ultimate published document, I bring a materialist critical perspective to *Skid Row Eskimo* that is somewhat indebted to Krupat's *Ethnocriticism*, viewing the published text in relation to the original manuscript Thrasher produced in prison (unless marked "*ms.*," all references will be to the published work). However, recognizing that any understanding of political effect outside the

possible psychological 'recovery' of the individual author must deal with the text to which audiences have access, I will use the manuscript predominantly to provide context for, and to elucidate, my analysis of the eventual published narrative. I would here like to reiterate my gratitude to Thrasher's lawyer, William Stilwell, who graciously provided me with the manuscript for study. Also, I must qualify my use of the term "manuscript." Thrasher's original prison writings were conducted in pencil on "literally thousands of scraps of paper" ("Editors' Foreword," viii). Stilwell had these typed by his secretary to produce what I call the "manuscript." And although no effort was made during this transcription process to correct spelling and grammar or to alter the writings in any way, the typed manuscript is nonetheless a step removed from the no longer extant writings from Thrasher's own hand. I will similarly avoid correcting spelling and grammar in my use of the manuscript throughout this chapter in an effort both to recognize Thrasher's original narrative autonomy and to acknowledge the difficulty of the eventual editing process for Gerard Deagle and Alan Mettrick.

[6] Alootook Ipellie, "Walking Both Sides of an Invisible Border," in *An Anthology of Canadian Native Literature in English*, third edition, eds. Terry Goldie and Daniel David Moses (Don Mills: Oxford University Press, 2005).

[7] Gerard Deagle and Alan Mettrick, "Foreword" to *Skid Row Eskimo*, eds. Gerard Deagle and Alan Mettrick, viii.

[8] Pat McMahon, "What Ever Happened to Anthony Apakark Thrasher?" *Calgary Herald* (8 October 1982), p. B1.

[9] Here I will attempt to remain cognizant of Métis critic Kristina Fagan's astute acknowledgement that "'Politics' as they are typically conceived in literary studies could more accurately be called 'textual politics.' A work is considered subversive if it subverts the structures of thought and language. Much less attention is generally given to whether the work exerts a force for change outside the text itself" ("Tewatatha:wi," 14).

[10] Dylan Rodriquez, "Against the Discipline of 'Prison Writing': Toward a Theoretical Conception of Contemporary Radical Prison Praxis," *Genre* 35, 3–4 (2002): 409.

[11] A note on terminology: "Inuk" is the singular form of "Inuit." Also, "Eskimo," although technically improper and a colonial imposition, is considered synonymous with "Inuit" and is the term Thrasher uses throughout his narrative. I've generally opted to use the term "Inuit" wherever possible.

12 Olive Patricia Dickason, *Canada's First Nations: A History of Founding Peoples from Earliest Times* (Toronto: Oxford University Press, 1997), 358.

13 The Inuit were added to the *Indian Act* in 1924, but this decision was reversed through legislation passed in 1951. In other words, unlike other First Nations, the Inuit "were brought under Canadian jurisdiction as ordinary citizens," a status that has effectively "never been altered" (Dickason, *Canada's First Nations*, 359).

14 Milloy, *A National Crime*, 240.

15 Robin McGrath, *Canadian Inuit Literature: The Development of a Tradition*, Canadian Ethnology Service Paper No. 94 (Ottawa: National Museums of Canada, 1984), 7.

16 Deagle and Mettrick, "Foreword," x.

17 Perry Shearwood, "The Writing of the Inuit of Canada's Eastern Arctic," in *New Voices in Native American Literary Criticism*, ed. Arnold Krupat (Washington: Smithsonian Institution Press, 1993), 175.

18 Inuit literacy was not solely the product of missionary influence in the North, although this was certainly its primary impetus; whalers, anthropologists, and fur traders all to varying degrees encouraged literacy among their guides, sources, and business associates, often in the service of rendering navigation easier through the composition and circulation of maps and written descriptions by those who knew the land and sea most closely. As Perry Shearwood argues, "the spread of literacy [often] preceded the arrival of the missionaries, for syllabics was imparted informally by travelling Inuit" ("The Writing of the Inuit," 175). Here, "syllabics" refers to the system of orthography adapted to Inuktitut by Anglican missionaries John Horden and E. A. Watkins in the latter half of the nineteenth century and used among eastern Inuit peoples ever since. Thrasher uses the Roman orthography more common to western Inuit writing, even when writing in Inuktitut.

19 Although Christianity was often invoked to kill Native traditions, as the 'kill the Indian and save the man' mentality of residential schooling clearly attests, I am at pains to suggest that this was not everywhere and always the case, and that some Indigenous people have adapted Christianity to their tribal traditions in a fertile rather than strictly corrosive way. This is particularly true of the Mi'kmaq, who adapted Roman Catholicism to their traditional worldview as far back as the seventeenth century. Thrasher writes from a Christian perspective, but one that views Inuit tradition, spirituality, and

orature as far more appropriate to true Christian living than, say, modern capitalist economics or aggressive evangelization. Furthermore, he recognizes the wielding of Christianity in the destruction of Indigenous traditions as wrong-headed and opposed to proper biblical understanding. So while Christianity can, to a certain degree, be viewed as the antithesis of tribal spirituality, and has been so viewed by such Indigenous writers as Tomson Highway and Thomas King, the concept of impossible or inauthentic integration must itself be seen as a construct.

20 Thrasher, *Skid Row Eskimo*, 68.

21 Anthony Apakark Thrasher, Unpublished Manuscript (Calgary: Spy Hill Penitentiary, 1973), 480–81.

22 Milloy notes that some Inuit children during this period were placed in less northern residential schools at Fort Providence, Fort Resolution, and Moose Factory, and that "a small number were even sent far to the south to Edmonton, Sturgeon Lake, Portage, Shingwauk, Fort Frances, Birtle, and Joussard" (*A National Crime*, 240).

23 Milloy, *A National Crime*, 247.

24 According to the autobiography, "Before the course, I was making as much as twelve hundred dollars a month in some jobs. Now I was only able to make two hundred dollars a month, plus room and board, working sixteen hours a day in the jobs the government found me" (80).

25 Dale S. Blake, "Inuit Autobiography: Challenging the Stereotypes," Doctoral dissertation, Department of English, University of Alberta, p. 103.

26 Thrasher, *Skid Row Eskimo*, 110.

27 Thrasher details his conviction and sentencing as follows: "Six months after arriving at Spy Hill, I was found guilty of a reduced charge of manslaughter. Jeepers—that's a long word, like Tuktoyaktuk. I was sentenced to be locked up for fifteen years. Two months later, an appeal court reduced it to seven" (114).

28 Blake, "Inuit Autobiography," 104.

29 Chris Cunneen, *Conflict, Politics and Crime: Aboriginal Communities and the Police* (Sydney: Allen and Unwin, 2001), 4.

30 The Gladue court in Toronto has recently been set up to attend to just this sort of deficiency in the criminal court's dealings with Aboriginal offenders. The Gladue initiative provides both extensive personal histories of the Indigenous accused and extensive colonial background to the judges, lawyers, and clients involved in Indigenous cases.

31 Rodriquez, "Against the Discipline," 410.

32 Elsewhere in his manuscript Thrasher states: "Things that I have written can get me killed by criminals and also I can be taken into a small room and be given a working over by the R.C.M.P. and city police or detectives for things I have written. I have also written things the north west territories the Alberta and Ottawa government won't like but I don't mind as long as I get some thing across to some one who may understand some problems which many officials close their ears on" (185).

33 Thrasher, Unpublished Manuscript, 426.

34 While Thrasher is writing during the reign of Queen Elizabeth II, this story is said to take place shortly after the turn of the century.

35 Blake, "Inuit Autobiography," 104.

36 The final chapter of part four, entitled "Silent Too Long," however, does include a good deal of didactic material from the earlier manuscript, arranged and presented to illustrate the relevance of Thrasher's life-story to larger colonial concerns and contemporary Inuit issues.

37 David H. Brumble, III, *American Indian Autobiography* (Berkeley: University of California Press, 1998), 138.

38 Of course, there were a handful of Native publishing houses in existence when Krupat made these statements, which are flourishing. In the Canadian context, Pemmican Publications in Winnipeg and Theytus Books in Penticton were both founded in 1980.

39 Arnold Krupat, *For Those Who Come After: A Study of Native American Autobiography* (Berkeley: University of California Press, 1985), 27.

40 Kathleen M. Sands, "Narrative Resistance: Native American Collaborative Autobiography," in *Studies in American Indian Literatures* 10, 1 (Spring 1998): 6.

41 Krupat, *Ethnocriticism*, 30.

42 Sands, "Narrative Resistance," 12.

43 Ibid.

44 I assume missionary and editor Maurice Metayer's recognition that Nuligak's autobiography fit extremely well with anthropological interests influenced his careful editing of the text according to contemporary anthropological procedures. Metayer's translated edition of Nuligak's autobiography (first published in 1965), which, like Thrasher's, was presented to its editor in manuscript form, offers what critic Robin McGrath refers to as an "erudite approach to editing" (*Canadian Inuit Literature*, 86). In McGrath's words,

Metayer "went to considerable trouble to preserve the authenticity of Nuligak's work; he deleted repetitious accounts of fishing and hunting expeditions but he rarely altered the order of the sentences and used footnotes rather than additions to the text to clarify obscurities in the manuscript. The four appendices to the book include additional information from the author not initially included in the manuscript, a glossary of Inuit terms, and a word for word translation of the final page of the Eskimo text which illustrates the changes that occur in the process of translation" (86).

[45] Charis Wahl, e-mail to the author (14 November 2003).

[46] Womack, *Red on Red*, 11.

[47] Weaver, *That the People Might Live*, ix.

[48] Moore, "Decolonializing Criticism," 8.

[49] "Inuvialuit" is an Inuktitut term meaning "the real people," with which the Inuit refer to their own cultural grouping.

[50] As I argued earlier in this chapter, Thrasher imagined many audiences for his narrative. Because my interests in this book rest primarily on how residential school survival narratives participate in the cultural revitalization and political mobilization of Indigenous communities, I am particularly concerned with the effects of *Skid Row Eskimo* on an Inuit readership. However, much could be said about how Thrasher directs his indictment of hegemonic colonial policies toward a non-Native audience, or how Thrasher *does* seek to archive some Inuit cultural material for a younger Inuit readership. Although it is beyond the scope of this chapter, a fertile ground for future research would be Thrasher's use of ethnographic tropes in his recording of Inuit traditional culture in comparison to his use of ethnographic tropes in relation to his time in the non-Native South.

[51] Renée Hulan, "Literary Field Notes: The Influence of Ethnography on Representations of the North," *Essays on Canadian Writing* 59 (1996): 49–50.

[52] Two examples of Thrasher's self-identifying as virile masculine hero occur while he is in prison. In the first instance, he becomes a protector of the vulnerable during a prison riot at Prince Albert Penitentiary. Hearing "screaming and shouting and thumping" coming from the gymnasium, Thrasher "figured I'd better get in there and help somebody." So he "ripped off a table leg and went in swinging. When I saw more than two guys ganging up on a friend, I just put my stick in between them and broke it up" (124). In the second instance, Thrasher describes coming to the aid of a female nurse,

of whom he was fond, who had been threatened by prison drug traffickers. Confronting the "two ring leaders," Thrasher "punched the one guy hard in the face" and then "walloped" the other guy in the gut. When the second guy fell down, Thrasher "just kept kicking him. Blood was coming out of his mouth and his ears." Thrasher "kicked and kicked and kicked until the guards came running and somehow they pulled me out of that room and hauled me away" (145). Significantly, the physical agency and violent power Thrasher claims in the second of these episodes are ultimately neutralized by the carceral space in which it occurs. The consequence of his 'rescue' of the female 'victim' is his transfer to a maximum security prison in British Columbia.

53   Blake, "Inuit Autobiography," 102.

54   Ibid.

55   James (Sakéj) Youngblood Henderson, "Postcolonial Ghost Dancing: Diagnosing European Colonialism," in *Reclaiming Indigenous Voices and Vision*, ed. Marie Battiste (Vancouver: University of British Columbia Press, 2000), 61.

56   Bhabha, "Interrogating Identity," 62.

57   That is just the position Youngblood Henderson takes, however, in his critique of Eurocentric diffusionist policies. He argues for the completeness and wholeness of Indigenous systems of thought, thereby rejecting the assumption that they are violable. Henderson "reject[s] the concept of 'culture' for worldview" in the Indigenous context: "To use 'culture' is to fragment Aboriginal worldviews into artificial concepts. The worldview is a unified vision rather than an individual idea" ("*Ayukpachi*: Empowering Aboriginal Thought," in *Reclaiming Indigenous Voices and Vision*, ed. Marie Battiste, 261).

58   Duncan Campbell Scott, qtd in Milloy, *A National Crime*, 46.

59   According to their 'divine purpose' of bringing 'the Lord's Truth' to those in the 'darkness of paganism,' the missionaries tended to construct the power of conversion, adaptation, progress, and development as unidirectional: the Inuit would change according to their absorption of biblical teachings, but the church and its laws and truths would remain intact, untouched, unwavering. Some missionaries did adapt their Christian teachings to the Inuit audience they hoped to reach—as Thrasher notes, "Father Biname used to preach to us in Eskimo" (7)—but such cultural sensitivity was infrequent and seldom engendered what might be called Inuit agency. Thrasher continues, "But along came a new priest, big and tough, and he preached of fire and brimstone like a Holy Roller. His name was Father Griffimle and he used to scare the daylights

out of us, shaking his finger and hollering. I hid under a bench most of the time. I would pity the poor devils from Hell if Father Griffimle ever got hold of them. I don't think there was an evil spirit within fifty miles of Paulatuk" (7). By the time Thrasher got to residential school in Aklivik, this latter model of proselytization, represented by Father Griffimle, was firmly instituted and systemically established, and it is clearly to this type of dominating assimilationist Christian action that Thrasher objects.

[60] Note the similarity here to Rita Joe's speaker's strategic adoption of a position of apparent powerlessness in "I Lost My Talk."

[61] One example of this personal editorial technique, of which there are many, occurs in Thrasher's introduction of Bob Cackney (a.k.a. Nuligak) and his family. He writes, "Mr. and Mrs. Bob cackney and their children—walter, stan, Bill, Andy, Agnes was the only girl. No there was lilly. I thought she was really cute her mother Bessie is also a member of the family. I got mixed up. Bessie is Bob cackney's daughter and her children are Andy and lilly" (31).

[62] Sands, "Narrative Resistance," 5.

[63] Womack, *Red on Red*, 61.

[64] Constance Deiter, *From Our Mothers' Arms: The Intrgenerational Impact of Residential Schools in Saskatchewan* (Etobicoke: United Church Publishing House, 1999), 81.

[65] David Neels, qtd in Deiter, *From Our Mothers' Arms*, 84.

[66] Campbell, *Halfbreed*, 144.

CHAPTER 4: "ANALYZE, IF YOU WISH, BUT LISTEN"

[1] Johnston, *Indian School Days*, 12.

[2] Chrisjohn and Young, *The Circle Game*, 41.

[3] Basil Johnston, qtd in Hartmut Lutz, *Contemporary Challenges: Conversations with Canadian Native Authors* (Saskatoon: Fifth House Publishers, 1991), 239.

[4] Deena Rymhs, "A Residential School Memoir," *Canadian Literature* 178 (2003): 59.

[5] This may represent an adherence to traditional Ojibway teaching methodology, as Johnston describes it in *Ojibway Heritage*: "To foster individuality and self-growth children and youth were encouraged to draw their own inferences from the stories. No attempt was made to impose upon them views. The learner learned according to his capacity, intellectually and physically. Some learned quickly and broadly; others more slowly and with narrower scope. Each

according to his gifts" (*Ojibway Heritage* [Toronto: McClelland and Stewart, 1998], 70).

6   Lisa Emmerich, "*Indian School Days* [Review]," *Western Historical Quarterly* 22 (1991): 219.

7   Johnston, *Indian School Days*, 11. Although, like Deena Rymhs, I consider Johnston's choice of phrasing—"'tried to instruct us,' rather than 'instructed us'" ("Memoir," 66)—significant, I would not go so far as to suggest along with Rymhs that "the dubious effectiveness of the residential school" implies that Johnston's dedication should be read "as somewhat ironic" (66). During the period of Johnston's tenure, St. Peter Claver's Indian Industrial School was renamed Garnier Residential School to mark an important change in function from preparing students for laborious careers in "obsolete ... trades" (Johnston, *Indian School Days*, 164) toward educational training "more in keeping with the modern world's changes" (165). The extremity of this shift, instituted by Father Superior R.J. Oliver, is difficult to overemphasize (although it would be a mistake to consider the changes absolute), given that Garnier's inaugural high school program, attended by Johnston and his colleagues, was voluntary, staffed by trained teachers, and conducted in a full- rather than half-day format. Johnston writes that under the new program he and his colleagues "were no longer preoccupied with leaving 'the place' [because] they [now] had some control over their lives and their destinies" (184). And while in spite of its two primary functions—"to train Indian youth for some vocation.... [and] to foster religious vocations by frequent prayer and adoration"—St. Peter Claver's "produced neither tradesmen nor priests" (26–27), as Johnston's life attests, Garnier did provide some students with the tools to attend post-secondary educational institutions or gain employment in a non-manual labour capacity. This is not meant to imply that because of these changes Garnier was beyond reproach on moral or ethical grounds or that all students were able to navigate their post-Garnier lives successfully because of its more 'progressive' approach, but rather to suggest that there seems little cause to doubt the sincerity of Johnston's appreciation for the spirited instruction of some members of school staff. Johnston's explicit admiration for certain teachers—discussed in the paragraph above—seems less ironic than it is circumscribed by systemic barriers that prevented some teachers from achieving the ends they desired. As I quote Gerald Vizenor elsewhere in this chapter, "No one has the right to erase ... the ardent manners of certain [boarding school] teachers" ("Native American Indian

Literatures: Narratives of Survivance," in *Native North America: Critical and Cultural Perspectives*, ed. Renée Hulan [Toronto: ECW Press, 1999], 60).

8   Again, this may signal a reliance on Ojibway worldview. In "Is that all there is? Tribal Literature," Johnston argues that the Anishinabek "knew that men and women were often deflected from fulfilling their good intentions and prevented from living up to their dreams and visions, not out of any inherent evil, but rather from something outside of themselves. Nanabush also represented this aspect of human nature. Many times Nanabush or the Anishinaubaeg fail to carry out a noble purpose. Despite this, he is not rendered evil or wicked but remains fundamentally and essentially good" (*Canadian Literature* 128 [1991]: 58–59).

9   Milloy, *A National Crime*, xv.

10   Johnston, qtd in Lutz, *Contemporary Challenges*, 237.

11   Rymhs, "Memoir," 61.

12   Menno Boldt, "*Indian School Days* [Review]," *Canadian Literature* 124–25 (1990): 311.

13   Rymhs, "Memoir," 62.

14   Tsianina K. Lomawaima, *They Called it Prairie Light* (Lincoln: University of Nebraska Press, 1994), xii.

15   Jamie S. Scott, "Colonial, Neo-Colonial, Post-Colonial: Images of Christian Missions in Hiram A. Cody's *The Frontiersman*, Rudy Wiebe's *First and Vital Candle* and Basil Johnston's *Indian School Days*," *Journal of Canadian Studies* 32, 3 (1997): 151.

16   Rymhs, "Memoir," 67, 59.

17   Ibid., 67.

18   Scott considers the "delicate balance" Johnston achieves "between justified indignation and considered appreciation for the mixed blessings the school conferred upon its students" crucial to "a more fully rounded portrayal of Indigenous peoples in their encounters with the colonial and neo-colonial establishment" ("Images of Christian Missions," 151).

19   Scott, "Images of Christian Missions," 151.

20   Joe, *Song of Rita Joe*, 48.

21   Rita Joe, qtd in Hartmut Lutz, *Contemporary Challenges: Conversations with Canadian Native Authors* (Saskatoon: Fifth House Publishers, 1991), 256.

22   Scott, "Images of Christian Missions," 153.

23   I would stress here that Scott's critical agenda, insofar as it seeks to foreground Indigenous voice against hegemonic neo-colonial discourse, is itself politically

appropriate and that even with the aforementioned misquote, Scott's article is on the whole well-argued and convincing.

24 Furniss, *Victims of Benevolence,* 35.

25 Vizenor, "Native American Indian Literatures," 60.

26 Warrior, *Tribal Secrets,* xviii.

27 In *Out of the Depths,* Knockwood briefly introduces the Mi'kmaq concept of "*Mukk petteskuaw,*" which illustrates helpfully the level of respect and reverence for the words of others I consider essential to the critical discourse on survival narratives. Knockwood defines the "underlying meaning" as, "'Don't walk in front of people who are talking.'" She goes on to explain, "This custom stems back to the old belief that everyone is a spirit and a conversation between people is a spiritual experience because they are also exchanging their most valuable possession, their word" (14).

28 Bonita Lawrence, e-mail to the author (28 August 2004).

29 Olive Patricia Dickason, "Amerindians between French and English in Nova Scotia, 1713–1763," in *Sweet Promises: A Reader in Indian-White Relations in Canada,* ed. J.R. Miller (Toronto: University of Toronto Press, 1991), 46.

30 James (Sakéj) Youngblood Henderson, *The Mikmaw Concordat* (Halifax: Fernwood Publishing, 1997), 32. Dickason, *Canada's First Nations,* 87.

31 Harald E.L. Prins, *The Mi'kmaq: Resistance, Accommodation, and Cultural Survival* (New York: Harbourt Brace College Publishers, 1996), 49.

32 Prins, *The Mi'kmaq,* 27. The post-epidemic estimate of 2000 surviving Mi'kmaq in Prins's book is taken from the writings of the early Jesuits.

33 Prins, *The Mi'kmaq,* 65. The political and military alliance among the Mi'kmaq, Maliseet, Passamaquoddy, Penobscot, and other Wabenaki (or Abenaki) peoples of New England and the Eastern Seaboard, which predated European settlement, was strengthened and modified in response to the complexities of the colonial situation. Known as the Wabenaki Confederacy, this geopolitical alliance—which shifted and evolved throughout the colonial period due to the differing needs and circumstances of its member nations and was complicated by individual and confederate agreements with the French— was responsible for the longest armed resistance to British expansionism in North American history. Dickason has declared this "war" "a unique episode in Canada's history, since it was the only one in which Amerindians fought on their lands for their lands" ("Amerindians," 60).

34 Prins, *The Mi'kmaq,* 69. Mi'kmaq historian Daniel N. Paul agrees, arguing in *We Were Not the Savages* (Halifax: Nimbus Publishing, 1993) that "in contrast

[to the English], the Micmac were willing partners of the French. The French treated the Micmac with respect as human beings. They ate their food and were quite willing to learn about their culture and to adapt to their ways while enjoying their hospitality" (46). For Paul, the "prime reason" for the good relations between the two nations "was that the French did not display an overwhelming desire to convert the Aboriginal communities completely to their cultural values" (46). This lack of desire on the part of the French had perhaps more to do with historical context than ideology or altruism. Clearly, having a migratory, warrior-based Mi'kmaq population in its corner was of far more use to the small and vulnerable French settlements in terms of protection and economics than having a settled farming population that emulated French culture.

[35] Cornelius J. Jaenen, "French Sovereignty and Native Nationhood during the French Régime," in *Sweet Promises*, ed. J.R. Miller, 30. Marc Lescarbot, the first historian of New France, wrote in 1618: "The earth then, by divine right to the children of God, there is here no question of applying the law and policy of nations, by which it would not be permissible to claim the territory of another. This being so, we must possess [Acadia] and preserve its natural inhabitants, and plant therein with determination the name of Jesus Christ and of New France" (qtd in Jaenen, "French Sovereignty," 25).

[36] Brian Slattery, qtd in Jaenen, "French Sovereignty," 34.

[37] Paul, *We Were Not the Savages*, 46.

[38] Rita Joe, "Mouipeltu' (Membertou)," in *Song of Eskasoni: More Poems of Rita Joe* (Charlottetown: Ragweed Press, 1988), 42.

[39] Henderson, *The Mikmaw Concordat*, 85.

[40] Ibid.

[41] For more in-depth discussions of Mi'kmaq Catholicism and spiritual history, see Henderson's *The Mikmaw Concordat* as well as Prins's *The Mi'kmaq* (chapters 3 and 6) and Paul's *We Were Not the Savages* (chapters 1 to 4). Also, in response to one aspect of Henderson's argument, it is important to remember that some contemporary Mi'kmaq have begun fighting against Catholic supremacy in the tribe, labelling the religion a colonial relic intimately tied to Mi'kmaq dispossession, subordination, and oppression. As a result, we cannot universalize the practice of Mi'kmaq Catholicism or disregard variations among Mi'kmaq spiritual practices.

[42] Dickason, "Amerindians," 47.

43 Prins, *The Mi'kmaq*, 151.

44 Ibid., 165.

45 Dickason, "Amerindians," 60.

46 Prins, *The Mi'kmaq*, 183.

47 J. Ralph Kirk, qtd in Paul, *We Were Not the Savages*, 286.

48 R.A. Hoey, qtd in Paul, *We Were Not the Savages*, 286–87.

49 See the discussion of Duncan Campbell Scott's work in chapter 1, which deals with the confused state of residential school policy in greater detail.

50 Joe, *Song of Rita Joe*, 17.

51 Death during childbirth was all too common during this period of Mi'kmaq history in which the inadequate conditions and arduous lifestyles compelled by poverty conspired with the Catholic Church's attacks on traditional birth control practices to endanger Mi'kmaq women. The patriarchal character of Catholicism functioned to identify Indigenous women more closely and more completely with their reproductive capacities than they had hitherto been within their traditional societies, leading to situations in which women might be consistently pregnant from marriage to death, at which point their male partners would move on to other women with whom to procreate. Josie clearly falls into this category of serial impregnator, searching out new and much younger women upon the deaths of prior brides.

52 Joe's refusal to ascribe the term 'father' to her abuser evidences a reverence for and strategic protection of the word itself and the caring individual it is supposed to reference. Knockwood relates a similar crisis of terminology from her residential school experience: "I felt betrayed when I was older and began to understand English and discovered that the people whom I feared the most in the whole world as a child were being called 'father' and 'sister' and even, 'mother superior'—the very words used for those dearest to me" (*Out of the Depths*, 32).

53 Johnston, *Indian School Days*, 7.

54 Joe, *Song of Rita Joe*, 48.

55 F.B. McKinnon, qtd in Milloy, *A National Crime*, 215.

56 Ibid.

57 "The nuns and the school principal provided us with their own version of sex education, which was that all bodily functions were dirty—dirty actions, dirty noises, dirty thoughts, dirty mouth, dirty, dirty, dirty girls. [One nun] took [a] girl who had just started her first period into the cloakroom and asked her if

she did dirty actions. The little girl said, 'I don't know what dirty actions are Sister. Do you mean playing in the mud?' [The nun] took the girl's hand and placed it between her legs and began moving it up and down and told her, 'Now, you are doing dirty actions. Make sure you tell the priest when you go to confession'" (Knockwood, *Out of the Depths*, 52).

58 Knockwood quotes survivor Peter Julian, stating: "'Sister Paul of the Cross put a strapping across [the] bum [of a runaway] and after the first blow he rolled right over on his back with his front showing. But Sister didn't stop at that. She laced it right across his privates and the poor boy let out a scream that could be heard all over the dormitory and Sister hollered, 'The longer you lay that way, the longer I'm going to keep whacking.' So he rolled back again. She was a sadist'" (*Out of the Depths*, 87). Knockwood also quotes a different male student with reference to the sexual interference he suffered and his coping strategies: "'Some of the other kids told me the secret of how to deal with that was to run away to the pipes. When we finished showering—they'd powder you—and sometimes they'd powder your genitals a little too long…. One of the kids that was with me used to tell me, 'Run away to the pipes.' In the shower room there used to be pipes and he told me to pretend that I'm up there in that pipe. Really think about it. You're crawling down to the end—and then there's dust—and then you meet the joint—the elbow—one pipe would be too hot—so you don't go down there—you go down the other one. By the time you're finished travelling the pipes—usually the act is over. That's how I learned to cope with it—by running away to the pipes'" (*Out of the Depths*, 93).

59 Isabelle Knockwood, qtd in Joe, *Song of Rita Joe*, 48.

60 Phil Fontaine, qtd in Grant, *No End of Grief*, 269.

61 James Grainger, "Review of *Porcupines and China Dolls*," *Quill & Quire* (May 2002): 25.

62 Alexie, *Porcupines and China Dolls*, 185.

63 Ibid.

64 Weaver, *That the People Might Live*, xiii.

65 Rita Joe, qtd. in Knockwood, *Out of the Depths*, 38.

66 David Newhouse, "*Song of Rita Joe: Autobiography of a Mi'kmaq Poet* [Review]," *Quill & Quire* 62, 7 (1996): 51.

67 Joe's refusal to invoke the tropes of documentary reportage in dealing with past trauma is similar to, although not precisely the same as, narrative techniques employed by Tomson Highway in *Kiss of the Fur Queen*. As I

discuss in chapter 5, Highway complicates his protagonists' memories of residential school abuse through the obscuring mechanisms of psychological repression and dreaming, but, like Joe, he never compromises the audience's understanding that abuse has occurred.

[68] Examples of Joe's recognition of mistreatment in residential school include: "It is true that bad things happened while I was there. You can't help having a chip on your shoulder if you are told, military style, when to go to the bathroom, when to eat, when to do this and that, when to pray. We were even told when to yawn and cough" (*Song*, 50); and elsewhere: "Over the years, so much trauma had happened in the residential school—so many people were hurt" (*Song*, 57).

[69] I wish to make clear that I do not intend to use the terms "victim" and "survivor" in a value-laden manner. Both Knockwood and Joe write in effective, although disparate, ways and I do not want to champion one over the other. I do, however, want to articulate as precisely as I am able the differences between their literary strategies.

[70] Agnes Grant, *Finding My Talk: How Fourteen Native Women Reclaimed Their Lives after Residential School* (Calgary: Fifth House Publishers, 2004), 37.

[71] Rita Joe, *AMMSA Archive*, <http://www.ammsa.com/achieve/AA97-R.Joe.html> (accessed 23 June 2004).

[72] Knockwood, *Out of the Depths*, 142.

[73] Also, it should be noted, by the time she was writing *Song of Rita Joe*, an abundance of information regarding the negative aspects of residential schooling had been made publicly available, through such texts as *Out of the Depths*, and as such was not in danger of being entirely lost without her focusing on it in the autobiography.

[74] Gerald Vizenor, *Manifest Manners: Narratives of Postindian Survivance* (Lincoln: University of Nebraska Press, 1999), 68.

[75] Ruth Holmes Whitehead, "Introduction to *Song of Rita Joe*, 9.

[76] Wendy Rose, "Neon Scars," in *I Tell You Now: Autobiographical Essays by Native American Writers*, eds. Brian Swann and Arnold Krupat (Lincoln: University of Nebraska Press, 1987), 253.

[77] Rita Joe, *Lnu and Indians We're Called* (Charlottetown: Ragweed Press, 1991).

[78] Joe, *Song of Eskasoni*.

[79] While it is always dangerous to collapse poet and speaker, I believe Joe's inclusion of these first-person poems within the narrative of her autobiography (neither sectioned off with markers nor highlighted as unique

by title) gestures toward vindicating such a move in this case. As mentioned above, Joe's poetry is overtly autobiographical and the poem in question, "Indian Residential Schools," deals specifically with the unenviable position of being a residential school survivor and being forced through economic necessity to place one's own child within one, conditions relevant to Joe's life. In 1956 Joe placed her five-year-old daughter, Phyllis, in Shubenacadie when the family was "barely surviving" (78) after she had been requested to do so by her husband and the child's stepfather, Frank. Although this was extremely difficult for both mother and daughter, Joe writes in the poem, "My daughter says she didn't have it hard / ... [She] knew the forgiving song" (49).

[80] Joe, *Song of Rita Joe*, 49. In *Out of the Depths*, Knockwood quotes Joe's memory of the episode as follows: "'I was there for four years and at Christmas, I used to hide in the bathroom and cry silently because I never received any presents. I used to envy all the children who received parcels from home. In my last year, a particular Sister who worked in the laundry gave me a present. Remember we used to peek in the key hole of the reading room where the presents were kept? And the ones who cleaned used to tell us the names of those who had parcels from home. Every year, I would ask, 'Is there a parcel there for me?' No, no, never, until that last year I was told, 'Your parcel is there!' I was jumping all over the place; I was so happy. It was from that nun from the laundry. It read: 'To Rita from your friend.' I was the happiest fifteen-year-old in the world'" (40).

[81] Joe, qtd in Knockwood, *Out of the Depths*, 40.

[82] Joe, *Song of Rita Joe*, 53.

[83] Joe, *We Are the Dreamers*, 57.

[84] Joe's methodology here resonates with Anthony Thrasher's manipulation of the 'passive Inuit' stereotype to mask latent authorial power in *Skid Row Eskimo*. Thrasher similarly presents his call for Indigenous empowerment as a plea to white authority but immediately checks himself to say the Inuk "has to gain back his old faith in himself" (*ms.* 404).

[85] Joe, qtd in Lutz, *Contemporary Challenges*, 257.

[86] Joe, *Song of Rita Joe*, 25.

[87] Warrior, *Tribal Secrets*, 48.

[88] Marilyn Dumont, "Popular Images of Nativeness," in *Looking at the Words of Our People: First Nations Analysis of Literature*, ed. Jeannette Armstrong (Penticton: Theytus Books, 1993), 48.

[89] Joe, *Song of Rita Joe*, 49.

[90] Dumont, "Popular Images of Nativeness," 49.

CHAPTER 5: FROM TRICKSTER POETICS TO TRANSGRESSIVE POLITICS

[1] Recent scholarly works that incorporate Indigenous testimony in their critiques of governmental and church transgressions include the Secwepemc Cultural Education Society's *Behind Closed Doors* (2000), Constance Deiter's *From Our Mother's Arms* (1999), Judith Ennamorato's *Sing the Brave Song* (1998), J.R. Miller's *Shingwauk's Vision* (1996), the Royal Commission on Aboriginal People's *Report* (1996), Elizabeth Furniss's *Victims of Benevolence* (1995), the Assembly of First Nations' *Breaking the Silence* (1994), and Celia Haig-Brown's seminal *Resistance and Renewal* (1988).

[2] Suzanne Methot, "The Universe of Tomson Highway," *Quill & Quire* 64, 11 (November 1998): 12.

[3] Judy Stoffman, "Highway Confronts His Past in New Novel," *Toronto Star* (30 September 1998), p. E4.

[4] Vizenor, *Manifest Manners*, 72.

[5] Vizenor illustrates the precariousness of this semiotic situation through the example of the word "Indian," which is itself a non-Native imposition. The word bears no connection to tribal cultures, but, rather, to the imaginative constructions by non-Native society of Native-as-other and Native-as-image. "The simulation of the *indian* is the absence of real natives—the contrivance of the other in the course of dominance," writes Vizenor. "*[I]ndians* are immovable simulations, the tragic archives of dominance and victimry" (*Manifest*, vii, x). The pervasiveness of white semiotic control in this regard, and the need politically to engage in this field, has meant that, in the words of Sioux scholar Vine Deloria, Jr., "the more we try to be ourselves, the more we are forced to defend what we have never been" (*Custer Died for Your Sins* [Norman: University of Oklahoma Press, 1988], 2). In other words, non-Native control over the documentation of tribal traditions has created conditions in which Natives endeavouring to safeguard their cultural history have occasionally had to emulate the simulations of dominance because they constitute broader society's understandings of traditional culture; under the oppressive weight of non-Native simulations of indigeneity, Natives have at times been cornered into becoming what Vizenor calls "kitschymen of resistance" (42). Jean Baudrillard's work on simulation provides a

helpful critical bridge for understanding this development. For Baudrillard, "Simulation ... is the generation by models of a real without origin in reality: a hyperreal. The territory no longer precedes the map, nor survives it. Henceforth, it is the map that precedes the territory—Precession of Simulacra" (*Simulations*, trans. Paul Foss, Paul Patton, and Philip Beitchmar [New York: Foreign Agents Series, Semiotext(e), 1983], 2). The images of Natives within the semiotic field are not simply illusory as both art and artifice, but, according to Baudrillard, should bear tangibly on what might be termed "Native reality." The crises of identity inflicted upon Native youth by the assimilative technologies of the residential school are thus complicated not only by forced separation from family and community, but also by the semiotic simulation of a cultural heritage from without, which obscures issues of Native autonomy and cultural integrity. The power of the creative wielder of words and images is thus paramount.

6   Vizenor, qtd in Coltelli, *Winged Words*, 160.

7   Ibid., 156.

8   Here Baudrillard discusses "the successive phases of the image:
   - it is the reflection of a basic reality
   - it masks and perverts a basic reality
   - it masks the *absence* of a basic reality
   - it bears no relation to any reality whatever: it is its own pure simulacrum"
   (*Simulations*, 11)

9   Barry E. Laga, "[Review] *Manifest Manners*," *American Indian Quarterly* 20, 1 (1996): 119.

10   Colin Samson, "Overturning the Burdens of the *Real*: Nationalism and Social Science in Gerald Vizenor's Recent Works," *Third Text* 48 (Autumn 1999): 55.

11   Krupat, *Ethnocriticism*, 77.

12   Gerald Vizenor, "Trickster Discourse: Comic and Tragic Themes in Native American Literature," in *Buried Roots and Indestructible Seeds: The Survival of American Indian Life in Story, History, and Spirit*, eds. Mark Allan Lindquist and Martin Zanger (Madison: University of Wisconsin Press, 1994), 68.

13   Tomson Highway, "Nine Visions of Where We're Going," *Toronto Star* (1 January 1995), p. F4.

14   Tomson Highway, "My Canada," *Imperial Oil Review*, < http://www. imperialoil.com> (accessed 20 January 2003).

15   Highway, "Nine Visions," F4.

16   Alfred, *Peace, Power, Righteousness*, 76.

[17] Albert Braz, "Nanabush's Return: Cultural Messianism in Tomson Highway's Plays," in *Changing Representations of Minorities East and West*, eds. Larry E. Smith and John Rieder (Honolulu: College of Languages, Linguistics, and Literature, University of Hawaii, 1996).

[18] Alan Filewod, "Averting the Colonizing Gaze: Notes on Watching Native Theatre," in *Aboriginal Voice: Amerindian, Inuit and Sami Theatre*, eds. Per Brask and William Morgan (Baltimore: Johns Hopkins University Press, 1992), 22.

[19] Filewod, "Averting the Colonizing Gaze," 21.

[20] Ibid., 22.

[21] Ibid., 23.

[22] I would like briefly to state, however, that Braz's claim regarding Highway's "falsification" of Indigenous tradition through his depiction of Nanabush rests almost entirely on the information provided in a single textual source from 1976 (Basil Johnston's *Ojibway Heritage*). Braz states, "The *fact* is that Nanabush is a rather problematic symbol for any matriarchy. After all, he was a male spirit, with a wife and children (Johnston 154). While he has the power to transform himself into a woman—or a seagull or a hawk—he is clearly not female in the sense that the historical Jesus was male" (Braz, "Nanabush's Return," 155, my emphasis). Not only does Braz ignore the anti-master-narrative force of Highway's trickster poetics by attributing undeniable truth-status to a single discussion of Ojibway spirituality, but he also conveniently neglects the importance of non-gendered grammar in Cree and Ojibway to the plays' understandings of the spiritual realm as free of anatomical constraints. Furthermore, he fails to note Highway's intentional conflation of Cree and Ojibway history, language, and spirituality in the Rez plays, resulting from Wasaychigan reserve's "mixture of both Cree and Ojibway residents" (*Rez Sisters*, xi), which requires the reader to understand Nanabush in relation to the Cree trickster figure Weesageeshak. For a sophisticated discussion of Filewod's articles, see Randy Lundy's 2001 article, "Erasing the Invisible: Gender Violence and Representations of Whiteness in *Dry Lips Oughta Move to Kapuskasing*," in *(Ad)ressing Our Words: Aboriginal Perspectives on Aboriginal Literatures*, ed. Armand Garnet Ruffo (Penticton: Theytus Books, 2001).

[23] Womack, *Red on Red*.

[24] Alfred, *Peace, Power, Righteousness*, 83, 70.

[25] Such articles as Frad Favel's "Born of the Sky" (Ottawa: Indian and Northern Affairs Canada, 1998) represent Highway's own life within just this form of liberal narrative. Favel's article begins: "From a Disneyesque childhood in the

northernmost part of Manitoba, through the nightmare of residential school, with his sheer determination and drive ...[Highway] is a shining beacon of hope to the Aboriginal community" (1). Highway himself has spoken about the novel in these terms, suggesting the novel is about "'how if you dream hard enough you can do anything'" (Joel Yanofsky, "Highway of Dreams," *Montreal Gazette* [4 February 1995], J1).

26 Heather Hodgson, "Survival Cree, or Weesageechak Dances down Yonge Street: Heather Hodgson Speaks with Tomson Highway," *Books in Canada* (February 1999): 5.

27 Marlene Brant Castellano, "Education and Renewal in Aboriginal Nations: Highlights of the Report of the Royal Commission on Aboriginal Peoples," in *Voice of the Drum: Indigenous Education and Culture*, ed. Roger Neil (Brandon: Kingfisher Publications, 2000), 264.

28 Michael Posner, "Highway Is Back with a Vengeance," *Globe & Mail* (17 October 1998), p. C12.

29 Alfred, *Peace, Power, Righteousness*, xviii.

30 Eva Tihanyi, "First Novels," *Books in Canada* (Novermber/December 1998): 47.

31 Furniss, *Victims of Benevolence*, 35.

32 Qtd in Milloy, *A National Crime*, 301.

33 Ibid.

34 Bernard Schissel and Terry Wotherspoon, *The Legacy of School for Aboriginal People: Education, Oppression, and Emancipation* (Toronto: Oxford University Press, 2003), 62.

35 Milloy, *A National Crime*, 302.

36 According to Milloy, money was "put into such solutions as psychological counselling and healing circles. To facilitate these programs, the government, in 1991, supplemented its Family Violence and Child Abuse Initiative with provisions and funds directed specifically to Aboriginal concerns" (*A National Crime*, 301); however, the Aboriginal Rights Coalition has declared the amounts "'relatively modest'" (qtd in Milloy, *A National Crime*, 302). Also, funding for some small-scale healing efforts was made available through the band councils, but it was only granted on an individual basis at the behest of DIAND.

37 Roland Chrisjohn, qtd in Chrisjohn and Young, *The Circle Game*, 83.

38 As recently as 2005, NDP MP Pat Martin condemned the federal government's emphasis on proof, arguing that although there is "a national consensus to

close this shameful chapter of our history by compensating survivors, ... we continue to victimize the victims by making them meet impossible tests for eligibility. Enough is enough" (New Democratic Party, "Residential Schools Compensation Plan a Catastrophic Failure Says NDP MP Pat Martin," 2 February 2005, <http://www.ndp.ca/page/1129> (accessed 8 February 2006).

[39] Chrisjohn and Young, *The Circle Game*, 41.

[40] This is not in any way to undermine ongoing historical work relating to individual institutions, nor is it meant to suggest that the final historical word on residential schooling has already been spoken. Clearly, individual experiences of various institutions have yet to be accounted for in the existing scholarship, leaving much of the story untold, and, inevitably, important historical debate will continue, particularly in light of new information emerging from such heavily guarded sources as the DIAND archives. I merely mean to suggest that the initial functions of the historical research, to reveal the connection between residential schooling and adverse conditions among Indigenous people and to indicate the culpability of various governmental and church bodies in the development and administration of this system, have been largely accomplished and the time has come to embolden this historical knowledge with the task of addressing the future of Native Canada.

[41] *Reconciliation and Healing: Alternative Resolution Strategies for Dealing with Residential School Claims* (Ottawa: Minister of Indian Affairs and Northern Development, March 2000), 107.

[42] Fagan, "Tewatatha:wi," 21, 22.

[43] I attempted to contact Highway to arrange an interview in which I could verify my understanding of *Kiss of the Fur Queen*'s generic development, but Highway was in northern Manitoba in the summer of 2003 and unavailable.

[44] Stoffman, "Highway Confronts His Past," E4.

[45] Favel, "Born of the Sky," 2.

[46] Judy Steed, "Tomson Highway: My Way," *Toronto Star* (24 March 1991), p. D1.

[47] Kevin Prokosh, "Highway of Hope: Native Playwright Uses Theatre as the Road to Soulfulness," *Winnipeg Free Press* (20 October 1990), p. C28.

[48] Posner, "Highway Is Back," C1.

[49] Kathleen Kenna, "Tomson Highway Coaxed out to Read," *Toronto Star* (21 October 1993), p. E6.

[50] Paul Gessell, "Playwright Eyes Big Shows," *Toronto Star* (20 April 1994), p. A19.

[51] Ibid.

52 Yanofsky, "Highway of Dreams," J1.

53 In this way, the movement of *Kiss of the Fur Queen* is similar to the movement found in Rita Joe's "I Lost My Talk" and "Hated Structure." As I argued in the preceding chapter, Joe's poems, like Highway's novel, exhibit the process of empowerment they explicitly call for. Both authors use their artistry to argue for the need to create change and claim personal and communal empowerment, and to illustrate potential paths toward those ends.

54 Jennifer Preston, "Tomson Highway: Dancing to the Tune of the Trickster," Master's thesis, University of Guelph, p. 50.

55 Suzanne Methot, "The Universe of Tomson Highway," *Quill & Quire*, 64, 11 (November 1998): 12.

56 Tomson Highway, *The Rez Sisters* (Calgary: Fifth House Publishers, 1988), vi–vii.

57 Preston, "Tomson Highway," 7.

58 Ibid., 46.

59 Ibid.

60 Alfred, *Peace, Power, Righteousness*, 81.

61 Ibid., xviii.

62 Isabelle Knockwood states that "Traditionally ... [o]lder brothers and sisters were absolutely required to look after their younger siblings. When they went to the residential school, being unable to protect their younger brothers and sisters became a source of life-long pain" (*Out of the Depths*, 60). Robert Arthur Alexie writes near the beginning of his novel *Porcupines and China Dolls* about unnamed siblings taken to residential school in the "1920s or 1930s" (9): "Sometime during the first month, [the boy will] watch his sister speak the language and she will be hit, slapped or tweaked. He'll remember that moment for the rest of his life and will never forgive himself for not going to her rescue. It will haunt him, and each time he remembers it, he will silently promise to kill anyone who has ever laid a hand on him or his sister. It will be a silent promise and no one will ever know it" (12).

63 Which the novel translates from the Latin to: "Through my fault, through my fault, through my most grievous fault" (81).

64 Vine Deloria, Jr., "Religion and Revolution among American Indians," *Worldview* 17 (January 1974): 15.

65 Given René Highway's crucial role not only in providing the biographical background for one of the novel's central characters, but also in acting as a

source of inspiration for the author—Tomson Highway has stated that the "novel is like a grand piano that Jeremiah the pianist receives from his brother, Gabriel, at the end of his life" (H. Hodgson, "Survival Cree," 46)—the author's choice of the Son of Ayash myth seems appropriate. In the year of his death, René Highway was slated to direct and choreograph Native Earth's production of *Son of Ayash*, adapted to the stage by Jim Morris, which was ultimately produced in his honour between 14 February and 10 March 1991. Jennifer Preston glosses the performance: "Taken from a traditional hero myth, *Son of Ayash* is the story of a young man who falls into disfavour with his father and is sent out into the wilderness. He enters the spirit world and encounters various monsters and anti-heroes, all of whom he defeats with physical strength and magical power. He emerges into the real world and decides to destroy it, allowing the Great Spirit to create it once again. In the play, this traditional legend is told to a young dying man by his mother to comfort him. As she begins the story, the young man leaves his dying body and enters the spirit realm. When the son of Ayash returns from the spirit world, the young man returns to his death bed and is able to face his death" ("Weesageechak Begins to Dance: Native Earth Performing Arts Inc.," *TDR—The Drama Review* 36, 1 [1992]: 153–54).

[66] Robert Brightman, *âcaôôhkîwina and âcimôwina: Traditional Narratives of the Rock Cree Indians* (Quebec: Canadian Museum of Civilization, Canadian Ethnology Service Series Paper 113, 1989). Given Highway's northern Manitoba Rock Cree heritage and the fact that Brightman's text is the most recently published collection of Rock Cree narratives, it is quite possible that Highway has actually read this very version. One piece of evidence that points to this possibility is Jennifer Preston's inclusion of Brightman's work as the only source for Cree orature in her 1990 thesis on Highway's theatre. Given that Preston worked closely with Highway at Native Earth Performing Arts and interviewed him on several occasions regarding Cree myth, it seems probable that they may have shared sources.

[67] "Sooni-eye-gimow" is the Cree term for Indian Agent.

[68] A. Martin, "Finding Joy Behind the Rage," *Globe & Mail* (3 October 2001), p. R1.

[69] Alfred, *Peace, Power, Righteousness*, 70.

[70] Jay Scott, "*Dry Lips*' Lack of Intimacy Transforms Visceral Images into Picturesque Tableaux," *Globe & Mail* (22 April 1991), p. C1; Marian Botsford Fraser, "Contempt for Women Overshadows Powerful Play," *Globe & Mail* (17 April 1991), p. C1.

71 While not explicitly a survivor of residential school, Big Joey, identified in the play's liner notes as thirty-nine years old in 1990, would have experienced adolescence during the late '50s and early '60s when residential schooling was still in full swing.

72 Maracle, *I Am Woman*, 99. Randy Lundy uses this very quote as support for a similar line of argument in his 2001 article, "Erasing the Invisible," the most important article on the play since Sheila Rabillard's 1993 "Absorption, Elimination, and the Hybrid: Some Impure Questions of Gender and Culture in the Trickster Drama of Tomson Highway," *Essays in Theatre* 12, 1 (1993).

73 Maracle, *I Am Woman*, 100.

74 Gitta Honegger, "Native Playwright: Tomson Highway," *Theater* 23 (1992): 91.

75 Tomson Highway, *Dry Lips Oughta Move to Kapuskasing* (Calgary: Fifth House Publishers, 1989), 119–20.

76 Brightman, *Traditional Narratives*, 7. It should be noted that Big Joey is identified as Ojibway in the play.

77 Steed, "My Way," D2.

78 Anderson, *A Recognition of Being*, 74, 75.

79 There are interesting parallels to be made between Big Joey's characterization and Anthony Thrasher's misogyny and unwillingness to parent. See chapter 3.

80 Preston, "Tomson Highway," 74.

81 Qtd. in Anne McGillivray and Brenda Comaskey, *Black Eyes All of the Time: Intimate Violence, Aboriginal Women, and the Justice System* (Toronto: University of Toronto Press, 1999), 44.

82 Milloy, *A National Crime*, 298. Haisla writer Eden Robinson, in her short story "Queen of the North," in *Traplines* (Toronto: Vintage Canada, 1998), provides one of the most brutal and engaging depictions of second-generation sexual violence emanating from residential schooling available in print.

83 Tomson Highway, *Caribou Song* (Toronto: HarperCollins, 2001); Tomson Highway, *Dragonfly Kites* (Toronto: HarperCollins, 2002); Tomson Highway, *Fox on the Ice* (Toronto: HarperCollins, 2003). While I hesitate to make definitive claims about the precise effect of *Kiss of the Fur Queen* on its author (for reasons I dealt with earlier in this chapter and more fully in chapter 2), I will posit that the recognition within the novel of Jeremiah's need to teach Native children in culturally sensitive ways in order to deal with his own childhood trauma resonates with Highway's decision to turn to children's literature. Furthermore, the connection between the plot material of the children's books and the novel, which all borrow extensively from the author's

own experiences, suggests a symbiotic relationship between literature and life for Highway that is extremely intriguing, although beyond the scope of the present study.

[84] Eduardo Galeano, "In Defense of the Word," in *Days & Nights of Love & War*, trans. Judith Brister (New York: Monthly Review, 1983), 191.

[85] Stoffman, "Highway Confronts His Past," E4.

[86] George Erasmus, qtd in Dene Nation, *Denedeh: A Dene Celebration* (Toronto: McClelland and Stewart, 1984), 65.

CONCLUSION

[1] Vizenor, *Manifest Manners*, 21.

[2] Bhabha, "Interrogating Identity," 62.

[3] In Robinson's novel, *Monkey Beach*, which develops from the seeds of "Queen of the North," Uncle Josh ultimately dies (or so it would seem) after being confronted with his transgressions through the 'gift,' suggesting that Karaoke's defiant creation might itself be edged with a vengeful violent impulse.

[4] King, *The Truth About Stories*, 112.

[5] Anderson, *A Recognition of Being*, 74.

[6] Vizenor, qtd in Coltelli, *Winged Words*, 159.

[7] Ibid., 156.

[8] Thomas King, *The Truth About Stories*, 2, 32, 62, 92, 122.

[9] Weaver, *That the People Might Live*, xiii.

[10] Johnston, *Indian School Days*, 243.

BIBLIOGRAPHY

Adams, David Wallace. *Education for Extinction: American Indians and the Boarding School Experience, 1875–1928*. Lawrence: University of Kansas Press, 1995.

Alexie, Robert Arthur. *Porcupines and China Dolls*. Toronto: Stoddart Publishing, 2002.

Alfred, Taiaiake. *Peace, Power, Righteousness: An Indigenous Manifesto*. Toronto: Oxford University Press, 1999.

_____. *Wasáse: Indigenous Pathways of Action and Freedom*. Peterborough: Broadview Press, 2005.

Anderson, Kim. *A Recognition of Being: Reconstructing Native Womanhood*. Toronto: Second Story Press, 2000.

Andrews, Jennifer. "Border Trickery and Dog Bones: A Conversation with Thomas King." *Studies in Canadian Literatures* 24, 2 (1999): 161–185.

_____. "Native Canadian Gothic Refigured: Reading Eden Robinson's *Monkey Beach*." *Essays on Canadian Writing* 73 (Spring 2001): 1–24.

Armstrong, Jeannette. "For Tony." In *An Anthology of Canadian Native Literature in English*. Second Edition. Eds. Daniel David Moses and Terry Goldie. Toronto: Oxford University Press, 1998.

_____. "Invocation: The Real Power of Aboriginal Women." In *Women of the First Nations: Power, Wisdom, and Strength*. Eds. Christine Miller and Patricia Chuchryk. Winnipeg: University of Manitoba Press, 1996.

Assembly of First Nations. *Breaking the Silence: An Interpretive Study of Residential School Impact and Healing as Illustrated by the Stories of First Nation Individuals*. Ottawa: Assembly of First Nations Press, 1994.

Baker, Marie Annharte. "Angry Enough to Spit But With *Dry Lips* it Hurts More Than You Know." *Canadian Theatre Review* 68 (1991): 88–89.

Baudrillard, Jean. *Simulations*. Trans. Paul Foss, Paul Patton, and Philip Beitchmar. New York: Foreign Agents Series, Semiotext(e), 1983.

Bauman, Zygmunt. *Modernity and the Holocaust*. Ithaca, NY: Cornell University Press, 1989.

Bhabha, Homi K. "Interrogating Identity: Frantz Fanon and the Post-colonial Prerogative." In *The Location of Culture*. New York: Routledge, 1994.

Billy, Cherlyn. *Behind Closed Doors: Stories from the Kamloops Indian Residential School.* Kamloops: Secwepemc Cultural Education Society, 2000.

Blaeser, Kimberly. "Native Literature: Seeking a Critical Center." In *Looking at the Words of Our People: First Nations Analysis of Literature.* Ed. Jeannette Armstrong. Penticton: Theytus Books, 1993.

Blake, Dale S. "Inuit Autobiography: Challenging the Stereotypes." Doctoral Dissertation. Department of English. Edmonton: University of Alberta, 2000. Boldt, Menno. "*Indian School Days* [Review]." *Canadian Literature* 124/125 (1990): 311–312.

Brant, Beth. "A Long Story." In *An Anthology of Canadian Native Literature in English.* Second Edition. Eds. Daniel David Moses and Terry Goldie. Toronto: Oxford University Press, 1998.

Braz, Albert. "Nanabush's Return: Cultural Messianism in Tomson Highway's Plays." In *Changing Representations of Minorities East and West.* Eds. Larry E. Smith and John Rieder. Honolulu: College of Languages, Linguistics, and Literature, University of Hawaii, 1996.

Brightman, Robert. *âcaôôhkîwina and âcimôwina: Traditional Narratives of the Rock Cree Indians.* Quebec: Canadian Museum of Civilization (Canadian Ethnology Service Series Paper 113), 1989.

Brumble, H. David III. *American Indian Autobiography.* Berkeley: University of California Press, 1988.

_____. *An Annotated Bibliography of American Indian and Eskimo Autobiographies.* Lincoln: University of Nebraska Press, 1981.

Campbell, Maria. *Halfbreed.* 1973. Reprint, Lincoln: University of Nebraska Press, 1982.

_____. "Jacob." In *Stories of the Road Allowance People.* Penticton: Theytus Books Ltd., 1995.

Canton, Jeffrey. "Coyote Lives: Thomas King by Jeffrey Canton." In *The Power to Bend Spoons: Interviews with Canadian Novelists.* Ed. Beverley Daurio. Toronto: Mercury Press, 1998.

Cardinal, Harold. *The Unjust Society.* 1969. Reprint, Toronto: Douglas and McIntyre, 1999.

Castellano, Marlene Brant. "Education and Renewal in Aboriginal Nations: Highlights of the Report of the Royal Commission on Aboriginal Peoples." In *Voice of the Drum: Indigenous Education and Culture.* Ed. Roger Neil. Brandon: Kingfisher Publications, 2000.

Chrisjohn, Roland, and Sherri Young, with Michael Maraun. *The Circle Game: Shadows and Substance in the Indian Residential School Experience in Canada*. Penticton: Theytus Books, 1997.

Churchill, Ward. "A Little Matter of Genocide: Colonialism and the Expropriation of Indigenous Spiritual Tradition in Academia." In *From a Native Son: Selected Essays in Indigenism, 1985–1995*. Boston: South End Press, 1996.

Coltelli, Laura. *Winged Words: American Indian Writers Speak*. Lincoln: University of Nebraska Press, 1990.

Cook-Lynn, Elizabeth. "American Indian Intellectualism and the New Indian Story." In *Natives and Academics*. Ed. Devon A. Mihesuah. Lincoln: University of Nebraska Press, 1998.

_____. "Some Thoughts About Biography." *Wicazo Sa Review* 10, 1 (Spring 1994).

Crew, Robert. "Highway Leads Back to True Culture of North America." *Toronto Star*. 15 April 1989, pp. J1, J4.

Cruikshank, Julie. *The Social Lives of Stories: Narrative and Knowledge in the Yukon Territory*. Lincoln: University of Nebraska Press, 1998.

Cunneen, Chris. *Conflict, Politics and Crime: Aboriginal Communities and the Police*. Sydney: Allen and Unwin, 2001.

Deagle, Gerard, and Alan Mettrick. "Foreword." In *Thrasher ... Skid Row Eskimo*. Eds. Gerard Deagle and Alan Mettrick. Toronto: Griffin House Publishers, 1976.

Deiter, Constance. *From Our Mothers' Arms: The Intergenerational Impact of Residential Schools in Saskatchewan*. Etobicoke: United Church Publishing House, 1999.

Deloria, Vine, Jr. *Custer Died for Your Sins: An Indian Manifesto*. 1969. Reprint, Norman: University of Oklahoma Press, 1988.

_____. "Foreword." In *New and Old Voices of Wah'Kon-Tah*. Eds. Robert K. Dodge and Joseph B. McCullough. New York: International, 1985.

_____. "Religion and Revolution among American Indians." *Worldview* 17 (January 1974): 12–15.

Dene Nation. *Denedeh: A Dene Celebration*. Toronto: McClelland and Stewart, 1984.

Dickason, Olive Patricia. "Amerindians between French and English in Nova Scotia, 1713–1763." In *Sweet Promises: A Reader in Indian-White*

Relations in Canada. Ed. J.R. Miller. Toronto: University of Toronto Press, 1991.

_____. *Canada's First Nations: A History of Founding Peoples from Earliest Times*. Toronto: Oxford University Press, 1997.

Dumont, Marilyn. "Popular Images of Nativeness." In *Looking at the Words of Our People: First Nations Analysis of Literature*. Ed. Jeannette Armstrong. Penticton: Theytus Books, 1993.

Eigenbrod, Renate. *Travelling Knowledges: Positioning the Im/Migrant Reader of Aboriginal Literatures in Canada*. Winnipeg: University of Manitoba Press, 2005.

Emmerich, Lisa. "*Indian School Days* [Review]." *Western Historical Quarterly* 22 (1991): 219–220.

Ennamorato, Judith. *Sing the Brave Song*. Schomberg: Raven Press, 1998.

Fagan, Kristina. "Tewatatha:wi: Aboriginal Nationalism in Taiaiake Alfred's *Peace, Power, Righteousness: An Indigenous Manifesto*." *The American Indian Quarterly* 28, 1 & 2 (2004): 12–29.

Fanon, Frantz. *Black Skin, White Masks*. Trans. Charles Lam Markmann. New York: Grove Press, 1969.

_____. *The Wretched of the Earth*. Trans. Constance Farrington. New York: Grove Press, 1963.

Favel, Fred. *Born of the Sky: Tomson Highway Cree Playwright, Novelist, Pianist*. Ottawa: Indian and Northern Affairs Canada, 1998.

Fee, Margery. "Aboriginal Writing in Canada and the Anthology as Commodity." In *Native North America: Critical and Cultural Perspectives*. Ed. Renée Hulan. Toronto: ECW Press, 1999.

Filewod, Alan. "Averting the Colonizing Gaze: Notes on Watching Native Theatre." In *Aboriginal Voices: Amerindian, Inuit, and Sami Theatre*. Eds. Per Brask and William Morgan. Baltimore: Johns Hopkins University Press, 1992.

_____. "Receiving Aboriginality: Tomson Highway and the Crisis of Cultural Authenticity." *Theatre Journal* 46, 3 (1994): 363–373.

Foucault, Michel. *Discipline and Punish: The Birth of the Prison*. Trans. Alan Sheridan. New York: Vintage Books, 1995.

Fraser, Marian Botsford. "Contempt for Women Overshadows Powerful Play." *Globe & Mail*. 17 April 1991, p. C1.

French, Alice. *My Name Is Masak*. Winnipeg: Peguis Publishers, 1976.

_____. *The Restless Nomad*. Winnipeg: Pemmican Publications, 1992.

Furniss, Elizabeth. *Victims of Benevolence: The Dark Legacy of the Williams Lake Residential School.* Vancouver: Arsenal Pulp Press, 1995.

Galeano, Eduardo. "In Defense of the Word." In *Days & Nights of Love & War.* Trans. Judith Brister. New York: Monthly Review, 1983.

George, Earl Maquinna. *Living on the Edge: Nuu-Chah-Nulth History from an Ahousaht Chief's Perspective.* Victoria: Sono Nis Press, 2003.

Gessell, Paul. "Playwright Eyes Big Shows." *Toronto Star.* 20 April 1994, p. A19.

Grace, Sherrill E. "Gendering Northern Narrative." In *Echoing Silence: Essays on Arctic Narrative.* Ed. John Moss. Ottawa: University of Ottawa Press, 1997.

Grainger, James. "Review of *Porcupine and China Dolls*." *Quill & Quire* (May 2002): 25.

Grant, Agnes. *Finding My Talk: How Fourteen Native Women Reclaimed Their Lives after Residential School.* Calgary: Fifth House Publishers, 2004.

_____. *No End of Grief: Indian Residential Schools in Canada.* Winnipeg: Pemmican Publications, 1996.

Greer, Allan. *The Jesuit Relations: Natives and Missionaries in Seventeenth-Century North America.* New York: Nedford/St. Martin's, 2000.

Haig-Brown, Celia. *Resistance and Renewal: Surviving the Indian Residential School.* 1988. Reprint, Vancouver: Arsenal Pulp Press, 1998.

Halfe, Louise. *Bear Bones & Feathers.* Regina: Coteau Books, 1994.

Harjo, Joy. "Anchorage." In *She Had Some Horses.* New York: Thunder's Mouth, 1983.

Henderson, James (Sakéj) Youngblood. "*Ayukpachi:* Empowering Aboriginal Thought." In *Reclaiming Indigenous Voices and Vision.* Ed. Marie Battiste. Vancouver: University of British Columbia Press, 2000.

_____. *The Mikmaw Concordat.* Halifax: Fernwood Publishing, 1997.

_____. "Post-colonial Ghost Dancing: Diagnosing European Colonialism." In *Reclaiming Indigenous Voices and Vision.* Ed. Marie Battiste. Vancouver: University of British Columbia Press, 2000.

Herman, Matt. "The Krupat-Warrior Debate: A Preliminary Account." In *Culture & The State: Disability Studies & Indigenous Studies.* Eds. James Gifford and Gabrielle Zezulka-Mailloux. Edmonton: CRC Humanities Studio, Publishers, 2003.

Highway, Tomson. *Caribou Song.* Toronto: HarperCollins, 2001.

_____. *Dragonfly Kites.* Toronto: HarperCollins, 2002.

_____. *Dry Lips Oughta Move to Kapuskasing.* Calgary: Fifth House Publishers, 1989.

_____. *Fox on the Ice.* Toronto: HarperCollins, 2003.

_____. *Kiss of the Fur Queen.* Toronto: Doubleday Canada, 1998.

_____. "My Canada." *Imperial Oil Review.* <http://www.imperialoil.com>. Accessed 20 January 2003.

_____. *The Rez Sisters.* Calgary: Fifth House Publishers, 1988.

_____. "Nine Visions of Where We're Going." *Toronto Star.* 1 January 1995, p. F4.

_____. "We Love Canada Because (10 Prominent Canadians Talk from the Heart)." *Chatelaine* 65, 7 (July 1992): 29–33.

Hodgson, Heather. "Survival Cree, or Weesakeechak Dances Down Yonge Street: Heather Hodgson Speaks with Tomson Highway." *Books in Canada* (February 1999): 2–5.

Hodgson, Maggie. "Rebuilding Community after the Residential School Experience." In *Nation to Nation: Aboriginal Sovereignty and the Future of Canada.* Eds. Diane Engelstad and John Bird. Concord: Anansi Press, 1992.

Honegger, Gitta. "Native Playwright: Tomson Highway." *Theater* 23 (1992): 88–92.

Howells, Coral Ann. "Towards a Recognition of Being: Tomson Highway's *Kiss of the Fur Queen* and Eden Robinson's *Monkey Beach*." *Revista Canaria de Estudios Ingleses* 43 (2001): 145–159.

Hoy, Helen. *How Should I Read These? Native Women Writers in Canada.* Toronto: University of Toronto Press, 2001.

Hulan, Renée. "Literary Field Notes: The Influence of Ethnography on Representations of the North." *Essays on Canadian Writing* 59 (1996): 147–163.

Ipellie, Alootook. "Walking Both Sides of an Invisible Border." In *An Anthology of Canadian Native Literature in English.* Second Edition. Eds. Daniel David Moses and Terry Goldie. Toronto: Oxford University Press, 1998.

Jaenen, Cornelius J. "French Sovereignty and Native Nationhood during the French Régime." In *Sweet Promises: A Reader in Indian-White Relations in Canada.* Ed. J.R. Miller. Toronto: University of Toronto Press, 1991.

Joe, Rita. *AMMSA Archive.* <http://www.ammsa.com/achieve/AA97-R.Joe.html>. Accessed 23 June 2004.

_____. *Lnu and Indians We're Called.* Charlottetown: Ragweed Press, 1991.

_____. *Song of Eskasoni: More Poems of Rita Joe.* Charlottetown: Ragweed Press, 1988.

_____. *Song of Rita Joe: Autobiography of a Mi'kmaq Poet.* Lincoln: University of Nebraska Press, 1996.

_____. *We Are the Dreamers: Recent and Early Poetry.* Cape Breton: Breton Books, 1999.

Johnston, Basil. *Indian School Days.* Norman: University of Oklahoma Press, 1988.

_____. "Is That All There Is? Tribal Literature." *Canadian Literature* 128 (1991): 54–64.

_____. *Ojibway Heritage.* 1976. Reprint, Toronto: McClelland and Stewart, 1998.

Johnston, Denis W. "Lines and Circles: The 'Rez' Plays of Tomson Highway." *Canadian Literature* 124–125 (1990): 254–265.

Justice, Daniel Heath. "Conjuring Marks: Furthering Indigenous Empowerment through Literature." *American Indian Quarterly* 28, 1 & 2 (2004): 2–11.

Kenna, Kathleen. "Tomson Highway Coaxed Out to Read." *Toronto Star.* 21 October 1993, p. E6.

King, Thomas. *All My Relations: An Anthology of Contemporary Canadian Native Fiction.* Toronto: McClelland and Stewart Inc., 1990.

_____. "Godzilla vs. Post-colonial." In *New Contexts of Canadian Criticism.* Eds. Ajay Heble, Donna Palmateer Pennee, and J.R. (Tim) Struthers. Toronto: Broadview Press, 1997.

_____. *Green Grass, Running Water.* Toronto: Perennial Canada, 1999.

_____. *The Truth About Stories: A Native Narrative.* Toronto: Anansi Press, 2003.

_____. *Truth & Bright Water.* Toronto: Perennial Canada, 1999.

Knockwood, Isabelle. *Out of the Depths: The Experiences of Mi'kmaw Children at the Indian Residential School at Shubenacadie, Nova Scotia.* Lockeport: Roseway Publishing, 1992.

Knowles, Richard Paul. "Reading Material: Transfers, Remounts, and the Production of Meaning in Contemporary Toronto Drama and Theatre." *Essays on Canadian Writing* 51–52 (1993–1994): 258–295.

Konkle, Maureen. "Indian Literacy, U.S. Colonialism, and Literary Criticism." In *Post-colonial Theory and the United States: Race, Ethnicity, and Literature.* Eds. Amritjit Singh and Peter Schmidt. Jackson: University Press of Mississippi, 2000.

Krupat, Arnold. *Ethnocriticism: Ethnography, History, Literature.* Berkeley: University of California Press, 1992.

_____. *For Those Who Come After: A Study of Native American Autobiography*. Berkeley: University of California Press, 1985.

_____. "The Indian Autobiography: Origins, Type, and Function." *American Literature: A Journal of Literary History, Criticism, and Bibliography* 53, 1 (1981): 22–47.

_____. *The Turn to the Native: Studies in Criticism and Culture*. Lincoln: University of Nebraska Press, 1996.

Laga, Barry E. "[Review] *Manifest Manners*." *American Indian Quarterly* 20, 1 (1996): 119–121.

Lawrence, Bonita. E-mail to the author. 28 August 2004.

Lomawaima, Tsianina K. *They Called it Prairie Light*. Lincoln: University of Nebraska Press, 1994.

Lundy, Randy. "Erasing the Invisible: Gender Violence and Representations of Whiteness in *Dry Lips Oughta Move to Kapuskasing*." In *(Ad)dressing Our Words: Aboriginal Perspectives on Aboriginal Literatures*. Ed. Armand Garnet Ruffo. Penticton: Theytus Books, 2001.

Lutz, Harmut. *Contemporary Challenges: Conversations with Canadian Native Authors*. Saskatoon: Fifth House Publishers, 1991.

Maracle, Lee. *I Am Woman: A Native Perspective on Sociology and Feminism*. 1996. Reprint, Vancouver: Press Gang Publishers, 1999.

Martin, A. "Finding Joy behind the Rage." *Globe & Mail*. 3 October 2001, pp. R1, R7.

Maufort, Marc. "Recognizing Difference in Canadian Drama: Tomson Highway's Poetic Realism." *British Journal of Canadian Studies* 8, 2 (1993): 230–240.

McGillivray, Anne, and Brenda Comaskey. *Black Eyes All of the Time: Intimate Violence, Aboriginal Women, and the Justice System*. Toronto: University of Toronto Press, 1999.

McGrath, Robin. *Canadian Inuit Literature: The Development of a Tradition*. Canadian Ethnology Service Paper No. 94. Ottawa: National Museums of Canada, 1984.

_____. "Inuit Literature in the South." *Canadian Review of Comparative Literature* (September/December 1989): 700–706.

McMahon, Pat. "What Ever Happened to Anthony Apakark Thrasher?" *Calgary Herald*. 8 October 1982, p. B1.

Methot, Suzanne. "The Universe of Tomson Highway." *Quill & Quire* 64, 11 (November 1998): 1, 12.

Mihesuah, Devon A. "Finding Empowerment through Writing and Reading, or Why Am I Doing This? An Unpopular Writer's Comments about the State of American Indian Literary Criticism." *American Indian Quarterly* 28, 1 & 2 (2004): 97–102.

Miller, J.R. *Shingwauk's Vision: A History of Native Residential Schools.* Toronto: University of Toronto Press, 1996.

Milloy, John S. *"A National Crime": The Canadian Government and the Residential School System, 1879 to 1986.* Winnipeg: University of Manitoba Press, 1999.

Momaday, N. Scott. "The Man Made of Words." In *The First Convocation of American Indian Scholars.* Ed. Rupert Costo. San Francisco: Indian Historian Press, 1970.

Moore, David L. "Decolonializing Criticism: Reading Dialectics and Dialogics in Native American Literatures." *Studies in American Indian Literatures* 6, 4 (1994): 7–35.

Morrow, Martin. "Cree Author Explores Dark Territory with Highway Humour." *Calgary Herald.* 15 October 1998, p. B12.

Moses, Daniel David, and Terry Goldie, eds. *An Anthology of Canadian Native Literature in English.* Second Edition. Toronto: Oxford University Press, 1998.

Murray, David. *Forked Tongues: Speech, Writing and Representation in North American Indian Texts.* London: Pinter Publishers, 1991.

New Democratic Party. "Residential Schools Compensation Plan a Catastrophic Failure Says NDP MP Pat Martin." 2 February 2005. <http://www.ndp.ca/page/1129>. Accessed 8 February 2006.

Newhouse, David. "*Song of Rita Joe: Autobiography of a Mi'kmaq Poet* [Review]." *Quill & Quire* 62, 7 (1996): 51.

Nothof, Anne. "Cultural Collision and Magical Transformation: The Plays of Tomson Highway." *Studies in Canadian Literature* 20, 2 (1995): 34–43.

Paul, Daniel N. *We Were Not the Savages: A Micmac Perspective on the Collision of European and Aboriginal Civilizations.* Halifax: Nimbus Publishing Ltd., 1993.

Posner, Michael. "Highway Is Back with a Vengeance." *Globe & Mail.* 17 October 1998, pp. C1, C12.

Preston, Jennifer. "Tomson Highway: Dancing to the Tune of the Trickster." Master's Thesis. University of Guelph, 1990.

———. "Weesageechak Begins to Dance: Native Earth Performing Arts Inc." *TDR—The Drama Review* 36, 1 (1992): 135–159.

Prins, Harald E.L. *The Mi'kmaq: Resistance, Accommodation, and Cultural Survival.* New York: Harcourt Brace College Publishers, 1996.

Prokosh, Kevin. "Highway of Hope: Native Playwright Uses Theatre as the Road to Soulfulness." *Winnipeg Free Press.* 20 October 1990, p. 25.

———. "Highway Runs into Creative Traffic Jam." *Winnipeg Free Press.* 25 June 1992, p. C28.

Rabillard, Sheila. "Absorption, Elimination, and the Hybrid: Some Impure Questions of Gender and Culture in the Trickster Drama of Tomson Highway." *Essays in Theatre* 12, 1 (1993): 3–27.

Reconciliation and Healing: Alternative Resolution Strategies for Dealing with Residential School Claims. Ottawa: Minister of Indian Affairs and Northern Development, March 2000.

Richardson, John. *Wacousta.* New Canadian Library edition. Toronto: McClelland and Stewart Inc., 1991.

Robinson, Eden. *Monkey Beach.* Toronto: Alfred A. Knopf Canada, 2000.

———. "Queen of the North." In *Traplines.* 1996. Reprint, Toronto: Vintage Canada, A Division of Random House of Canada, 1998.

Rodriquez, Dylan. "Against the Discipline of 'Prison Writing': Toward a Theoretical Conception of Contemporary Radical Prison Praxis." *Genre* 35, 3–4 (2002): 407–428.

Rose, Wendy. "Neon Scars." In *I Tell You Now: Autobiographical Essays by Native American Writers.* Eds. Brian Swann and Arnold Krupat. Lincoln: University of Nebraska Press, 1987.

Rymhs, Deena. "A Residential School Memoir." *Canadian Literature* 178 (2003): 58–70.

———. "Autobiography and an Overdetermined Self: Jane Willis's *Geneish: An Indian Girlhood." Essays on Canadian Writing* 79 (Spring 2003): 132–154.

———. "Review of *Telling a Good One: The Process of a Native American Collaborative Biography." Studies in American Indian Literatures* 15, 2 (Summer 2003): 99–102.

Samson, Colin. "Overturning the Burdens of the *Real*: Nationalism and Social Science in Gerald Vizenor's Recent Works." *Third Text* 48 (Autumn 1999): 55–64.

Sands, Kathleen M. "Narrative Resistance: Native American Collaborative Autobiography." *Studies in American Indian Literatures* 10, 1 (Spring 1998): 1–18.

Sands, Kathleen Mullen, and Theodore Rios. *Telling a Good One: The Process of a Native American Collaborative Biography.* Lincoln: University of Nebraska Press, 2000.

Sartre, Jean-Paul. "Preface." In *The Wretched of the Earth.* Frantz Fanon. Trans. Constance Farrington. New York: Grove Press, 1963.

Schissel, Bernard, and Terry Wotherspoon. *The Legacy of School for Aboriginal People: Education, Oppression, and Emancipation.* Toronto: Oxford University Press, 2003.

Scofield, Gregory. "Cycle (of the black lizard)." In *Native Canadiana: Songs from the Urban Rez.* Vancouver: Polestar Book Publishers, 1996.

Scott, Duncan Campbell. "The Onondaga Madonna." In *An Anthology of Canadian Literature in English.* Eds. Russell Brown, Donna Bennett, and Nathalie Cooke. Toronto: Oxford University Press, 1998.

Scott, Jamie S. "Colonial, Neo-Colonial, Post-Colonial: Images of Christian Missions in Hiram A. Cody's *The Frontiersman*, Rudy Wiebe's *First and Vital Candle* and Basil Johnston's *Indian School Days*." *Journal of Canadian Studies* 32, 3 (1997): 140–161.

Scott, Jay. "*Dry Lips'* Lack of Intimacy Transforms Visceral Images into Picturesque Tableaux." *Globe & Mail.* 22 April 1991, p. C1.

Sequoya, Jana. "How (!) Is an Indian? A Contest of Stories." In *New Voices in Native American Literary Criticism.* Ed. Arnold Krupat. Washington: Smithsonian Institution Press, 1993.

Shackleton, Mark. "Language and Resistance in the Plays of Tomson Highway." In *Post-colonialism and Cultural Resistance.* Eds. Jopi Nyman and John A. Statesbury. Joensuu, Finland: Joensuun yliopiston humanistinen tiedekuuta, 1999.

Shearwood, Perry. "The Writing of the Inuit of Canada's Eastern Arctic." In *New Voices in Native American Literary Criticism.* Ed. Arnold Krupat. Washington: Smithsonian Institution Press, 1993.

Steed, Judy. "Tomson Highway: My Way." *Toronto Star.* 24 March 1991, pp. D1, 2.

Sterling, Shirley. *My Name Is Seepeetza.* Toronto: House of Anansi Press, 2005.

Stoffman, Judy. "Highway Confronts His Past in New Novel." *Toronto Star.* 30 September 1998, p. E4.

Swann, Brian, and Arnold Krupat. "Introduction." In *I Tell You Now: Autobiographical Essays by Native American Writers.* Lincoln: University of Nebraska Press, 1987.

Tappage, Mary Augusta. "Christmas at the Mission." In *An Anthology of Canadian Native Literature in English.* Second Edition. Eds. Daniel David Moses and Terry Goldie. Toronto: Oxford University Press, 1998.

Thiong'o, Ngugi wa. *Decolonizing the Mind: The Politics of Literature in African Literature.* London: James Currey, 1986.

Thrasher, Anthony Apakark. *Thrasher ... Skid Row Eskimo.* Eds. Gerard Deagle and Alan Mettrick. Toronto: Griffin House Publishers, 1976.

_____. Unpublished Manuscript. Calgary: Spy Hill Penitentiary, 1973.

Tihanyi, Eva. "First Novels." *Books in Canada* (November/December 1998): 46–47.

Todorov, Tzvetan. *The Conquest of America: The Question of the Other.* Trans. Richard Howard. New York: Harper & Row, 1984.

Truth Commission on Genocide, The. "Chronology of Events." <http://canadiangenocide.nativeweb.org/intro2.html>. Accessed 11 January 2003.

Van Camp, Richard. "Review of *Porcupines and China Dolls.*" <http://www.richardvancamp.org/writing/Porcupines.html>. Accessed 03 March 2007.

Vizenor, Gerald. *Manifest Manners: Narratives on Postindian Survivance.* Lincoln: University of Nebraska Press, 1999.

_____. "Native American Indian Literatures: Narratives of Survivance." In *Native North America: Critical and Cultural Perspectives.* Ed. Renée Hulan. Toronto: ECW Press, 1999.

_____. "Trickster Discourse: Comic and Tragic Themes in Native American Literature." In *Buried Roots and Indestructible Seeds: The Survival of American Indian Life in Story, History, and Spirit.* Eds. Mark Allan Lindquist and Martin Zanger. Madison: University of Wisconsin Press, 1994.

Wahl, Charis. E-mail to the author. 14 November 2003.

Warrior, Robert Allen. *Tribal Secrets: Recovering American Indian Intellectual Traditions.* Minneapolis: University of Minnesota Press, 1995.

Watson, Julia, and Sidonie Smith. "De/Colonization and the Politics of Discourse in Women's Autobiographical Practices." Introduction to *De/Colonizing the Subject: The Politics of Gender in Women's Autobiography.* Minneapolis: University of Minnesota Press, 1992.

Weaver, Jace. *That the People Might Live: Native American Literatures and Native American Community.* New York: Oxford University Press, 1997.

_____, Craig S. Womack, and Robert Warrior. *American Indian Literary Nationalism.* Albuquerque: University of New Mexico Press, 2006.

Whitehead, Ruth Holmes. "Introduction." In *Song of Rita Joe: Autobiography of a Mi'kmaq Poet.* Lincoln: University of Nebraska Press, 1996.

Willis, Jane. *Geneish: An Indian Girlhood.* Toronto: New Press, 1973.

Womack, Craig S. *Red on Red: Native American Literary Separatism.* Minneapolis: University of Minnesota Press, 1999.

Yanofsky, Joel. "Highway of Dreams." *Montreal Gazette.* 4 February 1995, p. J1.

Young-Ing, Greg. "Aboriginal Peoples' Estrangement: Marginalization in the Publishing Industry." In *Looking at the Words of Our People: First Nations Analysis of Literature* Ed. Jeannette Armstrong. Penticton: Theytus Books, 1993.

INDEX